THERAPY
CONFIDENTIAL

Gregg E. Bernstein, PhD

Introduction

It seems to me that, at least to the public, psychotherapy has always been a dark, forbidding haunted house glimpsed far off in the gloom, down a creepy, winding path guarded by a clanging iron gate of arcane knowledge.

Or, as a young patient of mine once said at his first session, "So, like, what do you guys even *do*?"

Maybe all that secrecy and mumbo jumbo had its origins in a young and often-questioned art form trying to wrap itself in a validating blanket of science and intellectuality. Certainly the field has always had more than its share of fierce infighting and dueling orthodoxies, as various practitioners and academics vied for primacy.

However, all of this rarefied-air tumult and debate has left the general public— people who are suffering from depression, anxiety or a host of other psychological maladies—with very little idea about what kind of therapy to seek, or whom in the vast spectrum of practitioners to trust for real help.

In this book, as in my previous book, *The Heart Is My Beat*, I don't present any definitive answers to these questions, but rather seek to provide a window into the art and practice of therapy, and the road to becoming a therapist, so that the reader will come away with a clearer understanding that therapy is practiced by ordinary people, not ivory tower savants, shamanic demigods or infallible "certified" experts in any one particular approach.

Yes of course therapists are, or at least should be, highly trained and experienced individuals who have fulfilled the basic requirements for whatever academic degrees they possess, as well as any professional licensing that may follow.

These things at least allow the public to have some baseline information to rely on in choosing a practitioner. But what the public may not know is that ultimately the relative success or failure of the therapy, no matter what the therapeutic modality, is going to depend upon the character, self-honesty and dedication of the therapist, and his or her openness to utilizing whatever works for that particular patient.

Frequently, it is not a mystery what "happened" to a patient to create the problem; even an intelligent layperson could listen for an hour or two to the person's background story and begin to identify some of the circumstances that created a gap, or an unproductive detour, in that patient's developmental arc. But what to do about the problem is a far more challenging conundrum, one that requires a therapist with patience, perseverance, experience and a mind that is open to fresh ways of seeing things, even when that requires sitting with "not knowing" for uncomfortable periods of time.

My hope is that this book will help the reader respect the skills that go into doing psychotherapy, and understand some of the challenges of being, and becoming, a therapist—not because these things are secrets locked in a haunted house or cloaked in impressive scientific terminology, but because in basic human terms, being an effective therapist requires sustained, disciplined work and a continuing commitment not only to the healing of the patient, but to one's own personal growth as well. You can hardly expect your patients to commit to the most difficult journey of their lives when you have not walked your own path with humility and even humor.

In these pages I will present some of the way stations of my own life and show you what therapy can look like from the therapist's point of view, in words and concepts that I hope are easily understandable, human and free of jargon.

You may notice that I often use the term "patient" instead of "client," and as I explained in my previous book, that is because to me patient is more associated with a healing relationship, rather than a mercantile transaction. Yes, I understand that the word patient carries unfortunate medical connotations from past years, having to do with sickness, but I still feel that although client may seem more egalitarian, it is also carries businesslike and monetary connotations that don't feel right to me in the context of therapy.

Though the stories that I tell inside are closely based on real people's therapy with me, I, of course, have altered the details to preserve my patients' anonymity and confidentiality and to make the stories more cogent and impactful for the reader.

But enough talk—please join me on a guided tour of my own development, my life as a therapist and my practice. I'll try to shine some light into that old haunted house, maybe sweep a few cobwebs away too, and if it helps demystify and humanize the world of therapy and therapists, the world I love, then I will have accomplished my purpose.

This book is dedicated to William Saroyan, Henry Miller, Jack Kerouac, Harper Lee, Fats Waller, Laura Nyro, Maria Tallchief, Donald Winnicott, Carl Rogers, Ram Dass and all the others who showed me that life and even truth can survive adulthood.

TABLE OF CONTENTS

The Sleeping Cinderella of Boyle Heights 1

My Small World 25

Precious 33

The Mystery of All Beginnings 39

The Memphis Moment 46

Just Passing Through 55

The Diary of Anne Candid 60

Ready to Fly 68

The Lady is a Bum...................................... 77

Red Sky 89

Not Knowing 99

Grow Up, But Stay Small 109

The Professor Earns Tenure............................. 117

Do You Believe in Magic? 127

Grist for the Mill 138

Is Rain an Inanimate Object? 147

The Steamer 171

Doin' What Comes Natur'lly 175

I'll Be There 183

A House Full of Girls 194

Apache Ways... 217

Emmaline 220

Little Things... 227

What We Came Here For 234

Note to Self... 241

The Goner 258

Alone.. 284

Down By the L&N 288

Fighting with the Air 295

The Sleeping Cinderella
of Boyle Heights

"Can you give me a life that's worth getting out of bed for?"

That was the first thing Darla Escovido ever said to me.

And for a long time after she said it—too long a time—I just sat there in silence, blinking my eyes stupidly like a fighter being counted out by the referee. Finally, I rallied enough to say, "Well, that's a hard question."

She shot back, "Because of me, or just because it's a hard question?"

I was a little quicker on the uptake this time. "It could hardly be because of you, Ms. Escovido, since I know next to nothing about you—at least yet."

She hugged her purse to her chest and slumped like someone had let the air out of her body. Then she said, "Well, you're the last stop on this train line, so if even you don't have anything to offer me . . ."

"I didn't say I had nothing to offer you. Just that I don't even have any way to assess the situation yet."

She slumped down even further in her chair. "Is that what I've become, a situation?" She gave a sardonic laugh. "Well, I suppose you're right at that."

I held out my hands. "I didn't mean it that way, Ms. . . ."

"Darla." She paused. "You know, like the Little Rascals."

I smiled. "You're pretty young to know about the Little Rascals, aren't you?"

"Believe me, when your name's Darla, you know about the Little

Rascals." Her full lips turned up the teensiest bit. It was a pretty smile, what little there was of it.

I nodded. "Yeah, I see what you mean."

She fixed me for a long moment with her dark eyes, then the lids fluttered down and she murmured, "I'm so tired. I'm tired, and I'm tired of being tired." She looked at me again for a second and said, "Wake me when it's over, will you? I don't want to see the rest of this movie."

Then she shut her eyes again and actually went to sleep. I couldn't believe it. I was left sitting there with a store full of therapy and no customer.

We were only fifteen minutes into the session. We had plenty of time left, but I don't normally sit and watch somebody sleep during the first session. I looked at her carefully and listened to her deep, regular breathing. Yes, she was definitely asleep, and even on the verge of snoring. Well, I could wake her up and "make something happen" or sit there and see what I could make out of what was already happening. Since I had been lecturing supervisees for decades that if you pay close attention, "there's always something happening," I decided to take my own advice and see what a little observation could do.

She had already said more than once that she was "so tired." Okay, point taken, point demonstrated. She'd also asked about "a life worth getting out of bed for," another indication that sleep and bed were going to be major players in this drama. Her body had also collapsed like a flat tire after she'd gotten her first few sentences out. All of which added up to depression, unless she had a sleep disorder, a substance abuse problem, or some kind of medical condition. She had also said I was the "last stop," which indicated that she'd been trying to find a solution to whatever was ailing her for a long time. Had she already been to doctors? Was she on some kind of psychiatric medication? Was she dying of some mysterious illness? She seemed awfully young to have some deep, dark progressive disease—maybe thirty, thirty-five at most, with an attractive face, healthy looking skin and a slim, athletic body. Of course, looks can be deceiving, but then looks were about all I had to go by at the moment.

"Why are you looking at me like that?"

Her eyes were wide open again, though her body hadn't changed position.

"Sorry, but you kind of left me in the lurch there, Darla. I didn't want to wake you up, so I was trying to use the time to figure out what kind of help you needed from me."

"By staring at me?"

"I wasn't staring. You were asleep; what was I supposed to do, read a book?"

"That would be better than reading me, when I'm helpless."

I sighed. "Okay then, I'm sorry if I made you feel uncomfortable. I just didn't know what else to do."

She sat up a little straighter. "Okay then I'm sorry, too. It just comes on me sometimes."

"You mean you just conk out like that, involuntarily? What about driving?"

"I don't drive, never did."

"Have you seen a doctor?"

She laughed out loud. "Tons. They say there's nothing wrong with me, medically speaking."

"What about medication?"

"What about it?"

"Have you been evaluated for antidepressants?"

"The last doctor I talked to said I don't meet criteria for depression."

I tilted my head. "And what kind of a doctor was that?"

She shrugged. "Ear, nose and throat—but he's very smart."

"I'm sure he is, but . . ."

"Besides, I'm not interested in drugs. I'm positive that biochemistry is not my problem."

"Well then, what is?"

"That's what I'm hiring you to find out."

I sighed. "And I'm willing to explore that with you, but in the meantime you're exhausted, you're falling asleep in the middle of therapy sessions, and you're telling me you'd rather lie in bed than get up and live your life. That's a pretty bad meantime, wouldn't you agree?"

"So you won't work with me, then?" She looked like a whipped puppy.

"I didn't say that. I'm just trying to be responsible and sensitive to what you're going through right now."

She shook her head, then waved her hand at me like a magician's wand. "Poof, I hereby absolve you of all responsibility for everything I'm going through. All I need from you is therapy."

"So if you go to sleep during a session, or say you don't want to live, I'm just supposed to ignore it and go on with the therapy?"

She threw her arms out comically. "I'm entirely in your hands." Then I could see tears of desperation in her eyes. "Please."

I was moved, but moved is not convinced. "But if I feel we need to bring in a psychiatrist, a medical specialist or some other kind of consultant, you have to agree to at least meet with that person."

She nodded her head reluctantly. "Okay then."

"For that matter, what if you go to sleep again?"

"Then cover me with a blanket and sing me a lullaby. At least I'll be resting in your care."

Whew. Maybe it wasn't the weirdest beginning to someone's therapy I'd ever been a party to, but it was pretty high on the leaderboard. I wanted to say yes, but something told me to leave myself, and maybe her, an out. I said, "Okay, here's what I'm willing to do: we'll agree to meet for five sessions, then we'll take stock and reevaluate how it's going. If it's still a go at that point, we'll continue to meet. Okay?"

She grimaced. "That's kind of a wimpy commitment, but if it's the best you can do, then okay, I suppose I'm in."

I turned to the little nightstand that sits next to my chair to pick up my writing pad and trusty green pen and start to ask my usual intake questions. Then I turned back, ready to begin.

Darla was asleep again.

Okay, either she was tremendously hung over from a spree the night before, or a barking dog had kept her up all night, or we were in trouble. I went over and covered her up gently with the blue quilt. Unfortunately, I hadn't sung "Hobo's Lullaby" to anybody since the twins were little and I couldn't remember the words anymore, so I just sat there and waited for Darla to come up for air.

As the minutes ticked by, I found myself thinking the same thing patients often ask when things turn unusual: "Is this still therapy?" Because at this rate, the answer to "Can you give me a life worth getting out of bed for?" was going to be, "No, but if we make lying in bed your whole life, we won't have to deal with the question." And that, for sure, ain't no kind of therapy.

My eyes drifted to a group of crows perched on the roof of the school next door, grooming each other like they didn't have a worry in the world.

"Okay, I'm back."

Darla was sitting up again, rubbing the sleep out of her eyes. "Ooh, thanks for putting the blanket on me."

"You're welcome."

Hmm, what came next: breakfast?

I tried to make noises like a therapist. "So, while you're still with us, I'd like to get a little background information on you."

She smiled agreeably. "Sure, like what?"

"Like, where do you come from? Who do you come from? And what do you remember about your childhood, for starters."

She stretched extravagantly, still waking up, then sighed. "I come from a place in East LA."

"Boyle Heights?"

"How'd you know that?"

"That's where I'm from, too."

She frowned suspiciously. "You don't look like Boyle Heights."

I chuckled. "We moved to a tract house in the Valley when I was a month old."

She gave a knowing smirk. "That, you look like."

"But back to you. Who were your family members? Who are your people?"

"My maiden name is Mendez. I was the last of four girls, and also the ugly duckling."

My eyes narrowed. "Not to be inappropriate, but I find that hard to believe."

She smiled. "You wouldn't if you saw a family photo. But also, I didn't come into my looks till I was in my twenties. I was always a loner, the girl with her nose buried in a book. I never even had a date until I was twenty." Suddenly, she got a tortured, faraway look in her eyes.

I said, "Let me guess: and then you married one of the first guys you dated because he pressured you and you figured you were lucky just to find somebody who liked you?"

She sat up straighter. "What are you, some kind of a mind-reader?"

"If you could have seen the expression on your face when you mentioned that first date, you would have known, too."

"I . . . I'm getting tired again." She hugged the purse to her chest like she had done before. I was learning her: it often preceded her getting tired and going to sleep.

I checked the clock. "Darla, we have about ten minutes left, so if you do go to sleep again, I'll have to wake you up when the session's over. Is that okay?"

She was fading away quickly. "Sure, do whatever you have to do." Her eyelids drooped for a moment, then opened again. "It's funny, this doesn't really happen anywhere else. I mean, I spend a lot of time in bed, but once I'm up, I'm usually up." And with that, she dropped off to sleep.

My new theory, and what I hoped was more than a theory, was that something about coming to therapy was triggering alarm bells in her subconscious, and that the sleeping was the body's way of tuning out the perceived danger. If I was right, or even in the ballpark, I felt I could eventually reach her and treat the underlying problem. But I couldn't just rely on a therapist's wishful thinking; I felt responsible now for getting to the bottom of this whole thing, and if there was some alternate explanation, either medical, substance-related or "other," I still had to keep my head in the game and use whatever ancillary help was needed.

Darla could afford to sleep, but I couldn't.

Ten minutes later I shook her awake gently. "Can I call you a cab?"

She licked her lips and rubbed her sleepy eyes. "No, I already set it up before the session." Then she stood up, unsteadily listing a bit to starboard.

I waited till she could stand up straight, then walked over and opened the door for her. "Are you sure you'll be okay?"

"Sure," she smiled, "I'm a big girl now."

I wasn't so sure of that.

*　　*　　*

We had agreed to meet again the following Monday at noon. By then I had spent considerable time looking up involuntary daytime sleeping as a symptom, and found the usual suspects: hypersomnia, narcolepsy and a lot of impressive terminology and abbreviations, all of which didn't help me much with Darla. Depression seemed like the best bet, or at least a partial explanation, but even that didn't explain her sleeping during the session. As for sleepiness during therapy as a symptom, I drew a big fat blank. So I made up my own provisional diagnosis: *Idiopathic Situational Hypersomnia As A Defense Against Unidentified Implied Psychological Threat, With Features Of Exhaustion.* I'd love to see the diagnostic poohbahs come up with an acronym for that one! As outlandish as it might be, at least it gave me something to hang on to for the moment.

"I got a good night's sleep last night, so fire away."

Darla sat across from me looking as shiny as an A student on the first day of school. I said, "Okay, you said you used to read all the time as a kid. What are you reading now?"

Her face fell. "Nothing. I don't read much anymore. All that stuff seems like it was from another lifetime."

I said, "What happened?" It was a dumb question, but sometimes dumb questions are as good a place as any to start.

She shrugged. "That, my friend is a long, sad story, one that would

8

probably bore you—I know it bores me."

I shook my head. "I don't bore easy. Start anywhere you want."

Now I could see tears rimming her big, sad brown eyes. "Anywhere I want? I don't want any of it. It all just . . . happened to me." Her eyes flicked up at me. "Is that even possible, that a life just happens to a person, without their permission? Do other people give their permission for the things that happen to them, or do we all just get steamrollered by events, flattened like roadkill on a highway?" She paused. "Is it normal to feel like you didn't have any say in your own life, and other people just fake being okay with it better than I do?" She looked at me and said, "That's a real question, by the way."

"If it helps, I've heard that question many times before, and asked it myself at times, too. But no, I don't think it's normal to experience your life like it just happened to you. I think most people feel they had some say in it." I thought a moment, then continued. "But if you never know what you feel inside or what to say on your own behalf, life will roll over you, like you just told me. But we can do something about that in here." I could feel tears starting in my own eyes now, always a good sign. "I don't want you to feel like roadkill for the rest of your life."

Darla clutched her purse and looked woozy. "I . . . I think I need to rest for just a minute." She turned to look at my couch. "Would it be okay if I just lie down . . . ?"

I nodded. "Sure, that's what couches do best."

Why did the thought of "recess" in elementary school suddenly come to my mind as I sat there watching Darla sleep? Is that what this was for her—a break from her lessons? The more I thought about it, it did makes sense in a way; all along, I felt she gave off the energy of a five-year-old girl, maybe one who might still need Mommy to put her down for her nap.

"I did it again, didn't I?" Darla sat up and rubbed her eyes, looking refreshed and ready for more.

I nodded. "Yes, but it's okay, I'm kind of getting used to it."

She grinned as she took her usual seat in the patient's chair. "Guess you never knew you'd be running a motel for transients, did you?"

I did another mental check inside, and thought to myself that most patients, if they were falling asleep like this in sessions, would be at the least disturbed, frightened, maybe even embarrassed and mortified. But Darla seemed to thrive on it—maybe some more "clinical evidence" to back up my nascent guess about there being a five-year-old inside her.

She asked, "So, what do we do now?"

I smiled. "Between catnaps? I guess we get back to the so-called boring details of your life. Such as, what was it like growing up in your family? Who was your mom? Your dad? Your sisters?"

She held up her hands. "Whoa there, one at a time."

"I'm trying to make hay while the sun shines. Can you blame me?"

She said, "No, I suppose not." Then the sunny expression on her face suddenly turned dark. "Do you hate me?"

I angled my head at her. "Why would I hate you?" I grinned, hopefully. "I don't even know you well enough to hate you."

"It's just a matter of time. They all end up hating me."

"Oh? Like who?"

"Let's start with my family."

I nodded. "All right then, let's start with your family. I want to hear it, the whole story."

She shook her head. "You say that now, but when you hear how ordinary and boring I am, and what a loser, you'll sing a different tune."

"You tell me the lyrics, then I'll see what kind of tune comes to mind."

She shrugged listlessly. "Okay, but remember, you asked for it."

"I take full responsibility. Now let's go, before it's naptime again."

Her eyes searched the ceiling and she gave an audible sigh. "Well, like I said, I'm the youngest of four girls—and the ugliest. Or maybe I should say, the only non-beautiful one."

"The jury's still out on that one, but please proceed with your testimony."

"My sisters all seemed to be smart—you know, about life and stuff. They seemed to know what to do with people, how to use people, how to get their way. They pushed me around every day of my life and made me do their jobs around the house, but I never seemed to be able to stand up and say no."

I grimaced. "Uh, they sound just lovely."

"Lovely or not, they always knew where they were going. As my mom always used to say, they knew how to use what they had."

"Was she saying that as a compliment?"

She looked surprised. "Of course. As opposed to me, who was so shy I couldn't even raise my hand in class when I knew the right answer, because it might make someone else feel bad, and because people might think I was a know-it-all."

"Shy is not the same as boring."

She shook her head. "What planet are you from? In my family, and most everywhere I've ever been, shy is a social death sentence. If you can't stick up for yourself, and if you don't even know what you'd say if you could, shy is a deal-killer. If you have nothing to say, most people just label you as a zero, a blob and a loser. And after you've been knocked down enough times, you get used to it and stop expecting anything different."

"Just because most people don't have the patience or the imagination to look a little deeper beneath the surface, doesn't mean there's nothing there."

"Well, it might as well, because if you can't put it out there, it's the same as not having it." Her eyes went inward for a moment. "I can't tell you how many interviews I've been on where I didn't even get to the second round, because when they even asked me basic questions, I just sat there and froze, like a dummy."

"That's funny, because you seem to be very articulate in here."

She smiled. "Yeah, that is kind of weird. I seem to be able to talk to you."

"Maybe it has something to do with the other person believing in you."

"Ha ha, maybe if you could just go door-to-door around the whole world and tell everyone to believe in me, even when I act boring, my problems would be over."

"I may just do that. But I'd start in Boyle Heights, where we need to go right now."

"For example?"

"For example, what is your mother like?"

"Was."

"Okay then, what was your mother like?"

"A very determined woman. She ruled the roost—there was no question about that. She was pretty when she was young, and I think my dad thought she was above him, that he was . . ."

"Lucky to have her?" I couldn't help making the mental connection to what I'd said about Darla and her husband.

She nodded. "Yeah, that's what it always felt like."

"And your father?"

"He was a dreamer, or at least that's what Mom always said about him. He started drinking when I was about five, and eventually it got the best of him."

"And what were his dreams?"

"Funny you should ask that. Mom told me after he died that he always wanted to be an artist. But he didn't even graduate high school, so she helped him see that it was ridiculous for him to think he could paint for a living, so he became an apprentice electrician, and eventually a journeyman. She always told us that it was thanks to her that he didn't become a bum." She yawned twice, and I thought she was going to go to sleep again, but she said, "Mom once told me that I reminded her of him—a dreamer, quiet and shy—and that's why she was always afraid I was going to end up a bum, too. She always said I needed to find a man to take care of me and run my life." She looked down. "I don't know, maybe she was right."

Then her eyes opened wide and she glanced up at me. "Oh my God, is that what I'm looking for here?"

I shook my head. "Maybe, but that's not what you're going to find here. Because I'm a lot more interested in helping you find you, than running your life for you. Besides, I think you can do that just fine for yourself, with a little encouragement."

I noticed that our time was up and passed the news on to Darla. I also thought to myself, "Wow, we got through a whole session with only one nap!" but of course I didn't say that to her, lest she think that was her new "goal" and that she was a failure and a loser if she needed to sleep during the sessions. At the moment I was more interested in helping her feel the therapy space was hers, to utilize freely as needed, rather than one more performance demand.

As I often do, I sat for a while after she left and just let my thoughts and feelings wander at will. I kept coming up with the image of Cinderella, being bullied by her sisters and seen as an "inferior" drudge by the women of the family. I was determined not to let life crush Darla, like her mother had done to her father's dreams.

*   *   *

As the weeks went by, I learned more and more about Darla's world. Her marriage had failed not because they were incompatible, but because her husband was never there, a fact that, in Darla's mind, only attested to how boring she was. Also, far from "taking care of her," he was constantly getting fired from jobs and she ended up supporting him by going back to school and getting some training in business. The marriage finally broke up when she found out he was having an affair with a neighbor who was a "friend" of hers, and she started a business doing accounting and bookkeeping for small companies, working mostly out of her home. She had married at seventeen, divorced at twenty-five and was now thirty-five. As for relationships, she had steered clear since her husband. In her own words, "First of all, I don't trust myself not to choose the wrong man; second, what really good man would want me anyway; and third, if a man wanted children, I'm terrified of being a horrible mother. Like Mom always told me after the divorce, 'Girl, if you can't cook, stay out of the kitchen.'"

Gee, Mom, thanks a heap. Clearly, we had a steep mountain to climb in her therapy to reach the heights of decent self-esteem. But an old patient of mine once called me a Sherpa, so I grabbed my ice axe, pitons and carabiners, determined to summit or bust.

It was about a year into Darla's therapy. We had long forgotten about the agreement to evaluate things after five sessions and Darla was starting to feel a little better about herself. She still took "naps" every so often, but it was feeling more and more like a legitimate developmental need rather than a problem. She hadn't talked about being a loser or a failure in quite some time, and I certainly knew better than to bring it to her attention and start a whole new round of self-consciousness, so I just filed it under "progress" and kept swinging my climbing axe. She even started dressing like a mid-thirties single woman, instead of the "before" version of Cinderella. There was even a man interested in her—a guy who worked at one of the companies she did the books for. She came in to work there several days a month, and he had started flirting with her, much to her surprise.

"Do you think I'm ready?

It was nice to see a genuine smile on her face again. "Ready for what?"
"You know, to go back into the kitchen."
"Well, is anyone ever really fully ready for dating? We all have our issues."
"I only wonder about one thing."
"What's that?"
"Why would he like me? What does he want?"
I smiled. "Taking them in order: because you're beautiful, smart, fun and nice; and he probably wants what any man wants."
She smiled knowingly. "You mean sex?"
I shook my head. "Well sure, of course he probably wants sex, but that's not all a man wants from a woman."
"What else then?"
"All right, let's turn it around: what would you want from a man?"
She looked confused. "I don't know—to leave me alone?"
I laughed. "Come on, you can do better than that."
"Okay then, to be nice to me. To not put me down. To put up with me?"
Oh my God, I could see she wasn't being sarcastic! "How about companionship? Emotional support? Caring?"
"I thought I was getting that here."
"Well you are, I hope, but people can get those things in a relationship too."
She shook her head definitively. "Nope, not me. No man is going to do that for me without being paid."
"You think I only care about you because I'm being paid?"
"Well you have to admit, it helps."

Then, before I could respond, she started looking woozy again, and glanced longingly at the couch.

"Go ahead, if you need to lie down."

She stood up and reached over for the blue quilt, then lay down and draped it over herself. "I won't be long, promise."

"You just take all the time you need." I couldn't resist adding, "After all, I'm being paid."

She permitted herself a tiny smile before she conked out.

We had about fifteen minutes left in the session. It was becoming increasingly clear now, at least in my opinion, that the sleeping was actually not a defense against harmful or hurtful things happening in the therapy, but against being cared about. She tended to get tired whenever things felt more intimate or close, or she had felt accepted by me in some way. In that sense, it functioned like "tilt" does in an arcade game, or a breaker in an electrical system, to ward off the "unprocessable" fact of her being lovable or accepted by another person. She herself had once said she thought it was because she felt comfortable enough with me to let down her defenses and finally rest in the company of a trusted person, and that may be true—the dynamics of a therapy relationship can have more than one cause—but to my way of looking at it, it had more to do with the rejection of acceptance, to coin a bizarre phrase.

"Where did you drift off to?"

I reeled myself back in from la la land. "You caught me. I was off in the wild blue yonder."

"What were you thinking?"

"Hey, I'm supposed to be asking the questions."

"Who says? Didn't you tell me I make the rules in here, too?"

I laughed. "Damn, hoist on my own petard. Okay then, I was thinking about your sleeping."

She looked alarmed. "What about it? Are you mad that I'm still going to sleep after all this time? Are you mad that I said you only care about me because you're being paid? Are you . . ."

"Darla, now don't go off to the races on me. I'm not mad about anything. I was just thinking."

"About what?"

"About how a lot of times when you go to sleep, it seems like it's when you feel I care about you."

She turned red as a beet. "See? I knew you felt insulted about my saying you were being paid! Why don't you just admit it? Oh my God, why did I ever have to say that?" She looked panicky, and was starting to feel around for her purse, getting ready to go.

"Darla, please! Don't just assume all your feelings are accurate!"

"But you were the one who told me to believe in myself!"

"Believing in yourself is not the same as believing every last feeling that comes down the pike."

She bolted to her feet and headed for the door. "I knew it was a mistake to . . ."

"What, to trust me?"

'You said it, not me!" She was out the door.

For the first time in my professional life, I actually went out into the hall and yelled after her, "You're wrong!"

Just then, my officemate came into the hallway from the waiting room, leading a patient to her office. I could see her eyes widen, the whites rolling at me like a panicky horse.

I wanted to say, "Well, she *was* wrong," but thank goodness restraint prevailed.

*   *   *

Well, Darla and I had reached "the moment of truth," as my old supervisor used to call it. He said it comes with every therapy patient sooner or later, if you've been skillful enough to even get to "later." At least in this case the "neurotic misunderstanding" (ibid: my old supervisor) was that Darla thought I was mad, as opposed to her being mad at me for anything I had actually done. Ironically, the whole contretemps just convinced me that my take on her sleeping was absolutely right on; once we lit the powder keg of her being genuinely cared about, things were bound to blow up, one way or another. Yes, maybe I had made a mistake by bringing it out in the open too soon, but I had waited a long time, and it was she who had pushed me into it, so some part of her must have been ready to hear it, or at least fight about it.

I've been around this caring/not caring maypole countless times with patients, so I was pretty sure of my interpretation, but that doesn't cut any ice with a patient who's going through it for the first time, in the midst of an internal battle royale of denial vs. emotional reality. For Darla to accept that she was lovable, that she was really worth something, that she was good enough, would mean taking a wrecking ball to a skyscraper of defensive beliefs, constructed story by story over many years, that justified and excused her mother's behavior, her sisters' treatment of her, her husband's absences and philandering, and her own isolation and aloneness. And that's asking an awful lot of somebody, to dismantle the whole structure of their life, even if it is a seriously flawed structure that has held them prisoner forever.

But fortunately, I wasn't just a helpless bystander. I needed to reach out to her, even if my gestures were rejected. This was no time for me to be licking my wounds and expecting the mountain to come to Mohammad. Even if she was going to slam the phone down on me, I knew she wanted me to at least try to reach out and reassure her. As they say in the writing game, this was a chance to show, not tell, that I cared about her and her feelings. And to a patient's unconscious defenses, especially if they're so primitive and deeply embedded that they can only be expressed in bodily terms such as sleeping, words only whisper, while actions yell.

I looked up her number and called. I heard, "Hello, this is 510-111-1111, please leave a message at the beep."

It was a man's voice: this was very common at that time, for a vulnerable woman living alone to ask a man friend or even hire a service that would leave a man's voice on their outgoing message, telling the caller, "Beware, I am not alone; there's a man here."

I was at bat. I wished that I'd thought a bit more about what I was going to say, but the truth is usually a good idea, and I didn't want it to sound canned. "Darla, I'm so sorry that you thought I was mad at you. I'm not. I don't want to start trying to discuss the whole thing on a phone answering machine, but try and believe me, that you misinterpreted what I was trying to say. Well, like I said, I hope we can discuss it in person soon. If you're willing, please call me and we can set something up as soon as possible, whenever it's convenient for you. Once again, I'm not mad or upset about anything you said or did. Please believe me. I hope we can talk soon. Goodbye."

As I hung up the phone it suddenly occurred to me that the whole outburst might have been triggered by her telling me about the man flirting with her at work, and the possibility of her going out with him. On some unconscious level, could she have been mad at me, and hurt too, that I wasn't angry, jealous or threatened by the prospect of a "new man" in her life? That I was enthusiastic about it? Of course I would never say any of this to her—as a therapist you don't say everything that crosses your mind, as I had been painfully reminded of in the previous session—but I would certainly make a mental note of it for future reference whenever we talked about this or any other man, and stay aware that it could be an active dynamic in our relationship going forward. If I was right, it also told me that some part of her now had enough confidence and self-esteem to at least entertain the concept of my being possessive of her. We were getting somewhere!

I sweated it out that Monday night and all the next day. Then, around seven Tuesday evening, just as I was considering leaving her another message, I checked my machine and heard this:

I don't know what happened. It felt like a big explosion went off inside of me, for no reason. I knew I would eventually ruin things and push you away, and now I've done it. Thanks for the nice message, but I know you don't really mean it. Like everyone else, you're sick of me and probably just want out. I had no business treating you like that, so I guess this is goodbye. I only hope that that last horror show isn't your only memory of me.

Of course I was glad and relieved to hear from her. Her defenses had seen to it that she swung all the way back from terrifying (to her) rage to safe self-loathing. From the therapist's side of the room, it's always amazing that someone can actually think that I could be "through with them" after all this time just because of an outburst that's actually a core part of psychotherapy. The intensity of the anger, and the patient's right to feel it and express it, is never in question for the therapist; the task of the therapist is to help the person stop spraying the anger around willy nilly (at self, others or the world as a whole) and finally pin the tail on the donkey, i.e. the ones who were initially responsible for the damage. No, that doesn't mean she needed to indulge herself in rage fests at her parents or other family members, just that she needed to see the past for what it was: in her case, parents who were emotionally flawed and limit-ed, trying to raise a child who was "different," and siblings who were allowed to take their own frustrations out on a sweet, self-doubting child who might as well have had a "kick me" sign on her back. And sadly, this kind of family dynamic becomes the gift that keeps on giving, because the bullying and the low self-image set the tone for the rest of the child's interactions in life. Sometimes the drama is so deeply ingrained in them that I've sat with someone in therapy and literally felt a strong pull to be mean to them, which is entirely foreign territory for me normally.

I called Darla's machine and got to the beep. "Hi, this is Gregg." Then, just as I was about to enter my plea for a continuance, she picked up. "Hello, this is Darla Mendez."

I smiled to myself. "Hmm, Mendez, eh?"

"Well, I figured as long as I'm starting over, I might as well go home with the name that brung me."

"I'm glad to hear you say you're starting over. I'd like to pitch in on that project."

She was silent for a long time. "Why aren't you mad? I treated you pretty badly."

"You treated me like you never got the chance to treat anyone else. You felt like I didn't really care about you, and you let me know it. What's so bad about that?"

She was quiet again for several long moments. Then she said, "Well, for one thing, I don't really believe it."

"You mean that I don't care?"

"Yeah."

"But right or wrong, you still have the right to say it. I mean, it's not like someone was taking dictation for the Declaration of Indepen-dence or anything."

"But you're not mad or hurt about it?"

"No, but even if I was, it still wouldn't mean we couldn't resolve it together."

"That's definitely a new concept for me."

I laughed. "Well, yelling like a fishwife at a patient who's going down the hallway was a new concept for me, too."

I could hear her smile. "Yeah, that was pretty freaky all right. But at least it showed me you cared."

I needed to get things back on track. "So, can we meet at our usual time Monday? We have a lot to talk about."

There was a long pause. "Okay. That is, if you really want to see me again."

"Darla, that was never in question. Only in your mind."

"What do you do when you can't even trust your own mind?" She sounded like a lost puppy again.

"I understand the question, but let's continue this in person, okay?"

"Good, that'll give me time to think of more reasons why you hate me."

I laughed. "Good luck with that. But at least make 'em creative—I'd hate to look like a complete idiot."

It seems my old supervisor was right about the moment of truth. Our sessions for the next few months were what they call "productive." Darla still slept occasionally, but it felt more like the safe sleeping than the scared sleeping. And she reported that at home she didn't spend nearly as much time in bed; real life was starting to make a comeback. Then one day she said something I had been secretly hoping to hear for a long time.

"I've started reading again."

Once again, I didn't say, "Yay!" because that would sound too much like a pat on the head for being a good patient. So I said, "Wow, interesting. What are you starting with?"

"*The Secret History*, by Donna Tartt."

Before I could stop myself I asked, "Is it literary fiction?" Damn me, I had managed to sneak in another way of defining "good patient"! She nodded. "Yes, I guess you could call it that. But honestly it doesn't matter if I read this or *Green Eggs and Ham*; the point is that I'm reading again."

If I'd had any decency I would have been the one blushing now. To have to be lectured by a patient about what progress looks like is a therapist's ultimate shame. But I still managed to say, "I agree. It seems you're picking up the strands of your life again."

She nodded. "Yes, my life, not someone else's idea of what a life should look like."

I hoped that didn't mean me and my big mouth.

Darla went on. "Mother always told me I'd never make it on my own. And by the time she and my sisters had put me down for sixteen years, she was right. Now I can see that I was just different, and they didn't know what to do with me. And when stupid people don't know what to do with you, they put you down."

I was pleasantly surprised that she had the nerve now to call her sisters "stupid." And even more pleased that she didn't immediately have to soften it with, "Well that's not completely fair; they did their best." I think she knew by now that I knew she was just expressing her feelings, and that she had the right to a few negative emotions without feeling like she'd just shot somebody. There was enough room in her world now for her to take up the space that a human being takes up.

In the remaining months that I saw Darla, she not only continued reading, but started writing. She placed several articles and stories in newspapers and magazines, and had an idea for a novel. It was a coming-of-age story about a Mexican-American girl who feels like a freak in her own family. She laughed when she told me about it. "Well, they say write what you know. And now, I know a lot about coming of age." In terms of man-woman relationships, she still felt she wasn't ready, especially when the flirtatious guy at work turned out to be married. I said that he didn't represent all mankind, and she told me it wasn't the guys she didn't trust, but herself.

Besides, she said she was having too much fun building the structure of her own life, from the ground floor up. In fact, she told me that's what she was going to call her new book: *Story by Story*.

Not every Cinderella tale ends with a prince. Some of them end with a book project, a life worth staying awake for, and a smiling therapist.

My Small World

I don't understand the world—I never did understand the world, and I don't understand it now. But baseball is a little universe that is simple enough that you kind of understand some of it, and everything that is true in baseball is true in the world at large, only it's small enough that you can understand it.

— Bill James, pioneer of modern baseball analysis

Smart guy, that Bill James.

Well, to me, the same thing is true of psychotherapy. In fact, isn't that why anybody becomes a specialist? The world in toto is too big to take in, but if you whittle it down, you have a chance to come to terms with it in microcosm; then you can scale up some of the understanding you gained in that small world and voila, you have somewhere to stand.

That's what psychotherapy has been for me: a way to look at a small part of the world—one of life's "minor leagues"—and then extrapolate what I saw there to life at large.

But that doesn't mean things in that small world are simple, or easy.

A therapist was recently talking to me about sitting with a particularly challenging patient of hers. In dismay, she finally said, "I don't even know what I'm doing!"

What I told her was, think of it this way: when you really look at psychotherapy, we have a lot of nerve to think we can "fix" a human being. I mean, sure, if you bring your car in to a reputable car repair shop, you can reasonably expect the mechanic to figure out what's wrong with it. And if your shoes need to be re-soled, any competent cobbler should be able to do the job for you.

But human behavior, human emotions, the human brain? What we really know can be put in a thimble, with lots of room to spare. That's why theories of psychology, psychotherapy and the etiology of emotional disorders are just that: theories. If you're in the business, you hear therapists all the time saying, "I don't believe in psychodynamic therapy," or, "Cognitive Behavior Therapy seems like it was devised for robots."

Why?

Because, in large part, they're belief systems, not car repair manuals. And the fact that their adherents are so sure that they're right is a tipoff to that fact: just try asking a true believer in any hard-core religion about their "product" and you'll find out all about the desire for certainty.

These systems admit no contradictions, no questioning.

But just around the next corner is a member of a different sect who is just as sure of their "ism."

That's one of the reasons I quoted Bill James above: when he first started writing about baseball from a measured, objective, out-of-the-box point of view, the hue and cry went up for his scalp in traditional baseball circles, when he was noticed at all. He was a fool, an idiot, a numbers-cruncher and a stat-head who had no love for the game, no appreciation of history and, worst of all, he hadn't played the game! He dared to challenge baseball's time-honored wisdom about what numbers were important and how to value players.

Hell, he was just a night watchman at a Van Camp's pork and beans cannery. What did he know? And yet, as an outsider, not needing to be an expert, he was able to say, "Look, I don't know anything, but I'm going to try to look at this game from a commonsense point of view, and see if I can answer some basic questions."

He could afford to be nimble and innovative, because he had no reputation to protect, no axe to grind, no tradition to uphold.

He could just shut up and listen.

None of us in the therapy game really knows exactly what we're doing. Oh sure, you can believe in one approach or another, even have a lot of success with it. But how do you really know that your approach was the best way to get those results? That another approach couldn't have gotten the same results, or better? That the results you were getting weren't actually because you were inadvertently putting your patients in a hypnotic trance state? Or that your subliminal reactions to your patients weren't differentially reinforcing their "getting well" behaviors? Or that no matter what you thought you were doing, it was the force of your personality, or the fact that you were able to convey caring, that were really doing the job?

You don't.

One last baseball story. A beginning baseball scout once asked an old, grizzled veteran scout for any sophisticated tips or expertise that he could pass on.

The old guy said, "Find a ballpark. Get in it."

I'll take the guy who doesn't know what he's doing over the expert any day of the year. I don't mean a bumbler, or someone who doesn't care, but someone who has humility, doesn't play the expert and isn't too proud to be quiet, listen and learn.

Maybe I had an advantage in a way, because I always felt that I didn't know what I was doing. Well, let me amend that a bit: I knew I was fascinated by people, by the mystery of their behavior and that I felt privileged that they were willing to share their innermost secrets with me.

But as far as having a system? Nope, I was more empirical than that, I guess. For me, I couldn't see going into it with a fixed system when I had no first-hand evidence that using one system was any better than any other system, or for that matter, better than just winging it. Also, with a system, you might miss a lot of useful information, because your attention is narrowed so much by the selectivity imposed by the system that your take on things becomes skewed by your need to fit it into the system.

So, for all the possible disadvantages I might have had because I didn't have a system, I see now that I may have had a compensatory advantage—the courage, and the confidence to not know. At the time, I think I saw it as low self-esteem (*Who the hell am I to say I know how to help this guy?*), but in retrospect, I see that going into battle without armor meant that I could be more agile and spontaneous in my responses, lighter on my feet, without the need to mentally run things by any pre-existing theory or school of thought. I had an underlying confidence in my ability to ride the wave of the patient's story without committing myself to any particular answer.

Without any pre-commitment to a system, you are always in "beginner's mind."

And by not having a system, instead of saying to the patient, "Listen to me," you are saying, "C'mon, we're going to solve this thing together, as we go along."

But here's one drawback about conscious "not knowing" as an approach to anything: you can't teach it as a curriculum, you can't take credit for it, you can't say you discovered it, you can't name it after yourself and you can't market it.

Try creating your "brand" by saying, "I don't really know what I'm doing, but I can teach you my methods, so buy my book!" How many patients would stay if you said to them, "I don't have the answers, but I can help you find *your* answers"?

Maybe some, but most people come to therapy desperate. Their way hasn't worked, and they're finally ready to surrender to an expert who'll tell them what's wrong with them, and how to fix it.

"Help me!"

At least that's what they're saying consciously. In truth, their desperate request to be told what to do is just a slick cover story. Underneath, they're as stubborn as ever, as ornery, as sassy and as rebellious. If they were truly capable of following good advice, they wouldn't even need you. After all, the overweight person has already been told, "Eat less, exercise more," a thousand times, and the alcoholic, "Stop drinking."

So nope, my experience in the small world of therapy has taught me this: you don't tell, and you don't know—you create a safe space, and then you listen and let things emerge. And if you keep listening, with an open mind (and yep, that means not leaning on any one system or approach), you'll eventually hear things. But it's hard to not know, for both you and the patient, when you're being paid to know and the patient is desperate to know. So maybe the real skill in therapy is conveying enough sincerity and connection, in that first meeting or two, that the patient is willing to sit with not knowing long enough to let things bubble up organically.

A patient once said, "Why should I trust you?"

I said, "Because I trust *you*."

He gave me a funny look, and said, "That's more than I can do."

I said, "I know, but we're going to work on that, together."

Not knowing—it's not for wimps. And strangely enough, trust goes hand in hand with not knowing. Because if you trust that something will happen, it does, and it happens without anybody *knowing* anything.

If we could take that lesson from the small world of psychotherapy and extrapolate it to the world at large, we'd have fewer experts and a lot more trust in each other.

Voltaire once said, "Uncertainty is an uncomfortable position, but certainty is an absurd one."

Smart guy, that Voltaire.

So, in psychotherapy, I found a small world where not knowing was not only acceptable, but in my opinion, required. And it allowed me to pull the curtain back and see what was really going on for people—the things that, in the world at large, I could always sense but never really get at. A small world where people could be as open, as desperate, as wacky, as funny, as crazy, as sad, as confused and as magnificent as they really are.

And having had a chance to see behind the scenes in my little universe, then I was ready to scale things up and enter the big world knowing that the subtle things that I'd only suspected were going on, really were going on, that the many things that didn't make sense on the face of them did make sense when you knew the personal and quirky motivations that were beneath the surface.

A huge corporation sells a profit-making subsidiary for much less than market value. Why? Well, I had sat with a CEO who said, with his face purple with rage, "I don't care how many millions we lose—that son of a bitch (the head of the subsidiary) will never take my job!"

I had sat with a famous baseball player, a star, before a big game. He went 0-for-4 with two errors in the big game, but only I knew that the night before, he had found out that a player on the opposing team had been having an affair with his wife for years.

Having had an opportunity to see behind the scenes, the big world made a lot more sense to me now—I had a way to understand that the "human element" is always at play, that no matter how they act, or try to fool themselves, nobody is beyond being influenced by the personal, and often irrational, elements that are at work in all of us.

So, like baseball was for Bill James, psychotherapy became for me a small world that I could study, and then scale up, making the big world more understandable, more meaningful and yes, more bearable.

To see the world in a grain of sand
And heaven in a wildflower,
Hold infinity in the palm of your hand
And eternity in an hour.
—William Blake

Smart guy, that Bill Blake.

Precious

Years ago, when I was in my early thirties, I was the divorced solo father of two young children, living in half of a small duplex in Berkeley. I was trying to juggle work, parenting and a mostly faltering re-entry into a "singles" scene that I hadn't really had to deal with since I was eighteen. And, uh, it showed. Sample internal reminder: *Okay, try to keep in mind that these women have actually been with men before!*

I worked long hours in my practice Monday through Friday. I was trying to meet the needs of my kids, pay alimony and child support and maybe, who knows, eventually have some kind of a future. My limited cooking skills and time constraints meant that most weeks our family's culinary highlights ran along the lines of frozen fish sticks with macaroni and cheese. Thank God, the kids loved those. My other specialty was mulligan stew, made in Daddy's little helper, the magic crock pot, so I could dump everything into the pot in the morning, slam the lid down, set it to low and ladle it out, hot and hearty, twelve hours later. Unless, of course, I had forgotten to plug it in, or had set it too low or too high, in which case there was always—wait for it ... frozen fish sticks (which the two-year-old Hillary called "pit-tick") and macaroni and cheese. All hail, Messrs. Gorton and Stouffer!

Mornings worked perfectly, as I just had to drop the kids off at the Claremont Day Nursery, or later, Emerson Elementary School. But what about after school? I don't think I'm spilling any professional secrets by saying that, when you're a therapist, most of the full-pay and higher-functioning patients work during the day, which means you can only see them in the late afternoon or evening hours. So, I needed to find somebody with a car, to pick the kids up after school, bring them home and ride herd on them until I got home at seven or eight. And if we were lucky, the person would actually care about them.

Hmm, perhaps a woman, maybe even a nice woman, possibly even—praise God—a non-crazy, functional, nice woman, because my kids are special. But I guess that goes without saying.

Enter Maryanne. I can't really remember where I found her anymore—maybe a newspaper ad, maybe through a friend—but we sure struck gold. When, decades later, I first watched the TV series *Friday Night Lights* and heard its football team's mantra, "Clear eyes, full hearts, can't lose!" I thought immediately of Maryanne.

A tall, young, African-American single mother, she was one of those people who seem like they were just born on the right side of the moral compass: intuitive, kind, patient, wise, funny and sometimes maybe a bit sad, because the truth is, life isn't always kind to those who are born innocent, and stay that way. She was the kind who might be described as "leading with her chin," emotionally speaking, something I have been accused of, too. I never asked her about her relationship history, but I seem to remember that there had been a married man in her past, one who had lied to her and strung her along for years. I'm not sure though, that may be my imagining. The point is, for all she had been through, Maryanne hadn't allowed it to curdle her sweetness or cause her kind heart to skip even a single beat.

She was wide open and filled with love, something my kids and I both benefited from immensely, especially on one particular night that I will never forget.

I was in the kitchen, cleaning up after a late dinner. I had already put the kids down in their bunk beds next door to the kitchen. But Maryanne, as she often did, had gone in after me to do her own special bedtime ritual. I think maybe I had the record player going, volume set low, to one of my "regulars" like the Moody Blues' *Days of Future Passed* and was caught up in the music, not really paying much attention to what was going on in the bedroom.

The record ended, and in the fresh silence I could hear Maryanne's low, throaty voice murmuring something to the kids.

It was quiet a moment and then, clear as a bell, Maryanne said to them, "I love you, precious."

It pierced me like a sudden crack of thunder. My breath caught for a moment, and I had to leave the room or I might have burst out crying. I'm sorry if this sounds politically insensitive by today's standards, but it's the kind of thing only an African-American woman can really say *right*.

I got myself together and acted normal as Maryanne gathered her things and drove off into the night. But those words stayed in my mind all the rest of the night. I realized that, for all the courage it had taken me to leave a relationship I had been in since I was a teenager, and set out in life alone with two young children, I still had a need for someone to say, "I love you, precious," to me. In fact, I don't think anyone had ever said that to me, not with the sincerity and kindness that were in Maryanne's voice that night.

And then a funny thing happened. It occurred to me for the first time ever: what was stopping me from saying it to myself? Not only that, but come to think of it, I had a potential *good parent* with me at all times: me! But wait—was it weird to talk to yourself, or weird to love yourself? And did it "count" if you said these things to yourself?

And then, oh my God, I realized that I even had my own "therapist" on board at all times, too: me! Why couldn't I talk to myself like I did to my patients, or my friends?

Of course, I was only too familiar with the mean voices inside me, those regular visitors that told me that I was a loser, a failure, not good enough. But heck, why limit my repertoire to the mean voices? Couldn't I intentionally create *good voices* who loved me, who supported me, who actually gave a damn about me?

Okay, it was time to put up or shut up. I turned out the light and lay down on my bed, feeling like Frankenstein's monster, before the lightning bolts. I arranged my pillow, took a deep breath, and said out loud, "I love you, precious."

Nothing.

Maybe it was still too unfamiliar for me to take in—after all, I had never done anything like this. I took another breath and tried to "get out of my head" a bit more, breathing deeply for a moment. Then, trying to muster all of Maryanne's depth and sincerity, I kind of stroked my head and said, "Gregg, I love you, precious. I really mean it."

Tears began to rise. Not sobbing, mind you, but it had definitely reached *someone* inside of me. I decided to try ad-libbing a bit: "Are you really such a bad person that you don't deserve someone to love you?"

"You're doing the best job you can in your life, and considering your background (years of therapy could attest to that), it's kind of heroic how far you've come. Give yourself some credit."

While I was saying these things, I continued to kind of stroke my hair and my arm. It definitely felt weird, but again, this whole thing was new and different, and anything new takes practice. And yes, my mean voices tried to pipe up and ruin things, saying, "Okay, now you've really gone off the edge: talking to yourself? You know who talks to themselves, right?" And on and on they continued, their Greek chorus hurling insults and rotten fruit.

But now I had something to counter those mean voices. I had some friendly voices, so that in the future, when the mean voices did their thing, I could say, "Okay, thanks for sharing. Have a seat. Now, can I hear from someone else?" And then I could bring in the good voices to provide some loving balance to the issue.

And the cool thing is, after that night, I never felt really alone again, because I always had my own rooting section, my own good parent and even my own therapist as *in-house counsel.*

No, it's not the same as having a lover, a good friend or even a therapist verbalizing their belief in you. And the mean voices don't ever really just take a hike (I wish!). But like the justice system, at least there are always two sides permitted in every debate, and you're not just at the mercy of whatever the mean voices can think up (and they're very sly, because they have access to your personal *files!*). You can become your own advocate.

Later, I even started to write out both sides of my self-talk, where I could say all the meanest things I could think of, and then rebut them, one by one, with my (equally smart!) good voices.

And, slowly but surely, I started to treat myself like a friend instead of an enemy. And you know what, I'm a pretty good friend to have around!

So, to all of you out there who are mired in negative "self-talk," as they call it nowadays (we didn't even have words for it then), feel free to borrow from my experience.

It's not that hard.

Give yourself some affection, take a deep breath and say it like you mean it: "I love you, precious."

*   *   *

And after Maryanne left, I even appropriated it sometimes as the "finale" in my own bedtime ritual with the kids, and it never failed to elicit a smile.

Well, maybe not as big a smile as fish sticks and macaroni and cheese, but close.

The Mystery of
All Beginnings

It's a wise child that knows its own father.

And even more, it's a wise child that really *knows* its father or mother. Recently, I was talking to an older patient who was dealing with her own mother's decline: making decisions about care facilities, sorting through the boxes and boxes that were all that was physically left of her mother's life. It seems strange (and it is!) that a whole life ultimately comes down to someone rummaging through boxes and saying, "In," or "Out," while a rented dumpster yawns outside. It's enough to make you philosophical if you're an upbeat type, and downright sad if you have an unfortunate predilection for tragic sweep, as many of us do.

As she picked, sorted and differentiated what had been the treasures of her mother's life, she found herself pondering just how well she really even knew her mother. And this got both of us to wondering how well our children know us.

I suppose everyone is now familiar with the term "transference," the mainstay of traditional psychotherapy. In the Freudian interpretation of things, this means that the patient will transfer (i.e., project) onto the therapist elements of the relationships (internalized transactions, views and images) that the patient experienced with key figures from their past, usually parents.

But one begins to realize after years of doing therapy that this transference is also in play in how people relate to their own parents, as well. Very often the child's eye view of a parent is skewed and colored strongly by a myriad of factors, among them the one-off peculiarities of that child's relationship with the parent, the stage of life of the parent (and the parents' marriage or other significant relationship) when the child was young, specific issues that were going on at that time for the parent and things the child literally does not know about the parent and his or her life.

This is one of the reasons why I often make it a point to meet the patient's parents personally, if they are still alive. I sometimes hear things that astound me. No, not just, "There are two sides to everything," though that is certainly true, but things I could not have imagined.

Things like this:

A mom who was bitterly described as "always distracted and preoccupied" by her grown daughter (my patient). Then this mother told me, in strict confidence:

"Dr. B, I was battling cancer most of those years. I didn't want to burden the kids by telling them about it, especially since I was a single parent. Oh sure, I guess I was preoccupied, but you have to understand I was all alone with my pain, and terrified about what would happen to the kids if I died. And please don't tell her now, because after all we made it through, so let's just let sleeping dogs lie."

A father who was called "needy and over-involved" by his son, who confessed, tearfully:

"I have to tell you the truth now. My wife—may she rest in peace—was having an affair with our minister for at least twenty years before the diabetes got her. I knew it all along, but she didn't know I knew, and I never could confront her about it. Maybe I did wrong by taking comfort in closeness with the kids, but she was gone a lot of the time, supposedly on 'church business,' and I guess I covered up my hurt by throwing myself into being a dad. I know it sounds stupid, but I still loved that woman so much, I could never leave her. So maybe I was a fool for staying, and I was over-involved with the kids, but sometimes, that's life."

And often, parents say things that not only confirm what the patient has said, but confirm it in spades, such as this revelation by a woman in her fifties:

"I know I should never have had a child. I had no business getting pregnant, and should have taken care of business when I did, but I was too scared and conflicted to get an abortion, and I thought Joe would help out financially. But he disappeared right away. Honestly, it sounds horrible, but I resented every day I was saddled with that baby. I could have done something with my life, but instead I changed dirty diapers, did laundry and lived on hot dogs and beans. By the time the kid was gone, I was too old to train for doing anything worthwhile, so I got into a bad marriage, for financial security, which took even more years out of my life, and now, well, here I am."

Other parents are just as surprising, not so much in their words, but rather in their presence or personality. A man whom his son once described as "an overwhelming, towering presence" was in actuality a very slight, mousy man with a barely audible voice. A woman who was said to be harsh and cold described, with obvious warm feelings, how much she had enjoyed baking brownies for her children's friends.

Do I take all or any of this at face value? Of course not, but these things are all part of the *stew* that makes up the complexity of any parent. Often, when meeting the parent, I will notice, with pleasure, things that are not on the agenda, such as how much the patient's voice sounds like the parent's, or certain small mannerisms of the parent that are echoed in the patient. There are ways of saying things, expressions, attitudes, that have been inherited or appropriated by the child.

Sometimes the parent will reveal hidden stories and motivations that are deep-background clues to what happened, such as the woman who told me she married the patient's father on the rebound from her true love, or an accountant who told me that he was on his way to being a saxophonist with a top swing band when his father died and he had to forget his dreams and get a job to support his mother and three brothers. These things matter, because children pick them up on an unconscious level, and often, knowing this information, you can see how these undigested elements in the lives of the parents play out in the lives and choices of the children.

Another thing that flavors this stew is that families often operate on the level of mythology; supposed attributes of various family members, as well as unquestioned "family values," become distilled into a kind of handy, oversimplified shorthand:

"You know Dad—he's always happy-go-lucky."
"Jimmy's the brain, Johnny's the athletic one and Sally's always been the dreamer."
"Mom's obsessed with cleaning—it's all that matters to her."
"Well, everyone knows the baby of the family is always spoiled rotten."
"Mom and Dad never had a real argument in thirty-five years."

And on and on. While most of these things, like all stereotypes, have a basis in reality, we forget that they are merely short-cuts that *stand for* the person, but are not the actual entire person. In therapy, we often spend a lot of time helping patients break out of these internalized family stereotypes of themselves, these iron maidens of the soul, and sometimes we help them confront their parents about having these simplistic, limiting views of them. But children do this to their parents, too.

I have often heard patients say that, for example at holiday get-togethers, when wine is shared and old stories are told, they were shocked and surprised by the things they learned about their own parents.

"Uncle Joe told me Dad used to be the one who approached the girls first, because he was the one with all the sex appeal."
"My straight-arrow dad used to sneak into baseball games at Candlestick Park."
"Aunt Jane said Mom was a real hottie in her day."
"I found out Dad used to be the middleweight boxing champ of the First Division."

And sometimes we glean things that are not so benign, such as past criminal behavior, legal and financial troubles, past marriages and/or children and stories or whispers of rape, incest and other abuse as victim or perpetrator. Often these things don't fit in with our set ideas about who our parents are, or were, or should be.

Human beings like things to be seamless, wrapped up nicely and tied in a bow. But lives are not really like the movies—people are complicated and multidimensional, not all one thing or another. Therapy often involves helping people navigate the rapids of disturbing complexity: the woman who was molested by her own father, even though he was "the nice parent" (as opposed to the mother), and in some ways a wonderful person, or the mother who was always pleasant, but on closer inspection, turns out to have only shown a mask to the world, because she was in fact emotionally uninvolved.

Early in many people's treatment, therapists have a tendency to reinforce patients' key, monolithic views of their parents, in order to help the patient access and express all the unspoken, unprocessed negative feelings that have been crippling them. The patient must learn to recognize and claim the child's eye view of the situation, in order to establish a baseline self that they can build upon. At this early stage, if the therapist were to point out elements of the parent that run counter to what the patient is struggling to express, the patient might tend to retreat from manifesting the new self and say, "Oh, so you *are* saying I was crazy all along."

But later in the process, when a more consolidated self has been established, it sometimes becomes possible to broaden their conception of the parent without it threatening the self—to begin to see the parent as "only human" and to understand, in a new way, the actual reasons for the parents' harmful behavior toward the patient. This broader understanding doesn't provide an excuse or negate the harm done or the patient's hard-won feelings about it all. And sometimes this humanization of the parent can help the patient adopt a more humane attitude toward him or herself as well.

It is a hard thing to see your parent—the being who was once the center of your world, a titan bestriding the earth, the fountain that everything flowed from—begin to age and fade, to watch a once-transcendent, primary life force slouch toward obscurity and disconnection with "fortune and men's eyes."

It is hard, partly because it is such a confrontation with the reality of our own onrushing fate to see any life reduced to boxes.

At those times, it feels as if someone (maybe the Social Security Administration?) should provide a wonderful biographer for each and every person, to capture their struggles, their ups and downs, their failings and their dreams, realized or not, in order to properly document for posterity who this person really was.

Failing a wonderful biographer, we hope that we, as the children, have at least taken from them and their life stories that which held value, was significant and really mattered. We hope that we have at least been a witness to their times, a fair and caring witness who took to heart the meaningfulness behind whatever they had to give the world.

Because, though our aged parents' last chapters are, as often as not, banal and ignominious, we the living are the bearers of whatever small measure of glory they possessed, the keys to the mystery of our own beginnings.

The Memphis Moment

Deirdre Pomeroy was going to be my last patient of the day, my eight o'clock. I knew nothing about her, nothing but a terse voice on my answering machine saying, "I would like to discuss some things with someone." Hmm, she wouldn't be making the All-Transparency Team anytime soon.

I sighed and trudged across my office to jack up the controls of the fan and the window air conditioner to high, though I knew it wouldn't do much except make it harder to hear anyone talk. It was the tail end of one of those hot, sticky days that, when I lived in the South, I finally seemed to adjust to; but here in Oakland, when the heat and humidity came, it seemed to hit me harder, maybe because I wasn't "in training" anymore.

I checked the clock: 7:55. Good, I still had time. I trotted down the hall to use the facilities, then stood there at the sink washing my hands. The guy in the mirror looked as washed out as I felt. I splashed some cold water on his face and tried to make room in my mind for anything other than self-pity and fatigue.

Back in my office, the waiting room signal light flashed: game on.

I heard an explosive sigh before I even reached the waiting room. Was she just hot and tired like me, or was it more than that?

"I thought you'd be older."

I wanted to say, "It's okay, I'm wearing a disguise," but let it go. Her eyes searched me up, down and all around, and seemed to find me wanting in every respect. She was the very image of the hard-charging young businesswoman: dark green business suit, chic maroon heels and one of those initialed purses you don't get at Rite-Aid. Before I could even reach her, she stood up and charged past me down the hall, saying, "Now what?"

That was a first—you usually don't get a "now what" until the end of the first session. I spun around and called out, "Make a left at the second door," in time to stop her from sprinting the length of the hall, exiting out the back door and then yelling, "Now what?" from the parking lot.

By the time I entered my office, she was already seated and giving the place the once-over. I expected a Peggy Lee ("Is that all there is?"), but she just sat there, her legs crossed and her hands folded primly in her lap like the first day of class. She had pretty red hair, but it was yanked back to within an inch of its life in some kind of business-class bun. Finished with her initial inspection of the room, she fastened a pair of deep-green eyes intently on mine and sighed sharply again.

I was clearly at bat.

"Well, Ms. Pomeroy, what brings you to see me today?" I can be more clever and original than that, but in this case, I felt I'd better play it by Hoyle.

She tugged her skirt down, then licked her lips. "Well, as a matter of fact, I'm not exactly sure."

I angled my head. "Not sure?" Hoyle would be proud.

She nodded. "Not sure, that is, what *you* have to offer."

Hmm. I played nice for now. "Well, I would have to know what you need help with before I could even say what I have to offer."

"Surely it can't be that hard to tell me what you do for a living— doctor." Her eyes were on the move again. "By the way, your desk is a mess."

I cut Hoyle loose and let fly. "Look, Ms. Pomeroy, I don't have any-thing to offer if you're not willing to tell me what's troubling you."

After the shock treatment, the olive leaf: "Was it a crisis? A work-related situation? A relationship?"

It worked. She moistened her lips again, then crossed her legs in the other direction. "Okay, sorry if I sounded like I was doubting you—well, yes, I suppose I was doubting you, but it's not just you, it's more like, nobody can change reality."

I nodded. "What parts of reality are we talking about?"

Suddenly, her cell phone buzzed loudly. She stabbed around in her purse until she found it, then held up a "just a minute" finger to me. This is what I heard:

"I told you I'm on it! ... If I'm on it, I'm on it! ... Sigh ... All right then, next weekend... I've never said 'no,' have I? ... Sigh ... All right then, *this* weekend."

She hung up, looking like a beaten animal, then flung the phone back into her purse.

I pointed to the purse. "Is that part of the 'reality' you were talking about?"

She nodded stiffly, looking down. I could see her grinding her teeth. "It's all of it, but there's nothing you or anyone else can do about it." She looked up at me. "So why am I even here?"

I heard myself saying, with feeling, "You're here because your life isn't working for you, and you need some help." I noticed that I hadn't thought once about the heat, the humidity, the air conditioner or the fan. "And how do you know I can't do anything about it, or that we can't?"

Her body sagged. "Because I have to do what I have to do, and that's all there is to it."

I took a deep breath. "Look, Ms. Pomeroy—"

"Deirdre."

I was on first base; could I steal second? "Okay then, Deidre, suppose we start over from the beginning, and you tell me what this 'reality' is that's so bad it's even making you doubt your therapist?"

That got a grudging grin out of her, and brought those green eyes up again. "All right, we'll start over, then." She sighed, hard. "I have to travel for work—travel a *lot*, I mean." She nodded her head toward the phone in her purse. "That conversation I just had, for example. I thought I was off this weekend, for once, and now I find out I'm not only supposed to be in LA tomorrow, but straight through the following weekend, too." She paused. "Then Memphis, then Denver, then Minneapolis, then San Antonio. Do I need to go on?"

I held up my hands. "No, you don't need to go on, I get the *traveling* part of it, but if you could just tell me, why is it so particularly hard on you?"

Tears were forming in her eyes. "Look, I hate flying. I hate airplanes. I hate airport security. I hate change. I hate new things. I hate the kind of work I have to do when I travel. I hate living in hotels. I hate having nothing to do at night. I hate not seeing my friends. I hate being away from home. I hate strange places. And most of all," she was practically yelling now, "I hate traveling." She paused for breath. "Is that enough?"

I nodded. "Yes, I think that would qualify as 'enough' for any unbiased witness."

She continued. "And that's what I mean by 'reality': I have to do it, period, and that's it. Now what can anybody do to change reality?"

She was mad again. I knew she would snap my head off no matter what I said, but I'd already sent Hoyle to the showers, so what the hell. "No, you can't change reality, but you can change your *relationship* to reality."

She snorted with derision. "Oh, I see: 'Try doing some crossword puzzles on the plane, use your Valium as needed and call me in the morning'?"

I couldn't help but laugh; I love a worthy opponent. "Well no, not exactly, but before we can even get to any strategies, we need to gather some data."

"What do you want to know: height, weight, blood pressure, date of birth?" She ticked them off briskly on her fingers as she went down the list. Everything she did was fast, fast, fast, leaving no openings for emotion, or for being there with me at all.

Somehow, I had to slow down this freight train. "No, Deirdre, what I'm talking about is your feelings, your perceptions, your thoughts, while you're traveling—"

She interrupted me. "That's easy: I'm mad, I'm tired and I hate it. End of story."

I nodded. "Kind of like now?"

She did a double-take, then spat out, rapid-fire, "Yeah, as a matter of fact, *just* like now."

"So, you're traveling right now?"

"I might as well be."

"I agree. You're not even here; you're off in your head, not even experiencing what's going on at this very moment, sitting here with me." I could see her gearing up to spar with me. Then, just as quickly, her energy shifted. "You really think that?" she said, crestfallen. I could see that to her it meant failure.

I nodded, "Yes, I really think that." I paused. "That is, I thought that. Now, you seem like you're here."

She shook her head. "You tell me I'm not here, then you tell me I am here: get your story straight ... doctor."

"Gregg is fine."

"I'm glad Gregg is fine. Deirdre isn't." She tapped her foot a couple of times. "Okay, that was nasty, but look, I'm the type that needs to get things right, and if you don't tell me how, I'm no good." She looked at the clock nervously, aware our time was almost up. "So, what's my assignment, doc ... uh, Gregg?"

I wouldn't normally give an "assignment" to someone so duty-bound and rigid—or at least not right away—but since Deirdre traveled all the time and wouldn't be able to meet with me in person regularly anyway, I had to find a way to make some of the therapy happen on location. "Okay, then, you say you're in Los Angeles this weekend?" She was already packing up her stuff and rising, though I hadn't said a word about the session ending.

"Yeah, yeah, and straight on through to the next weekend." She threw a panicked look at the clock. "Hurry up, would you? We're almost out of time!"

I laughed. "If we run over a couple minutes, it's not the end of the world."

She was already at the door.

"Okay then, here's your assignment: go to Farmers Market, and ride Angels Flight."

She gave a start. "First of all, what are those? Second of all, what does going to whatever-it-is have to do with therapy, or anything else?"

I shrugged. "I guess we'll see. Oh yeah, I also want you to keep an email journal of your feelings about having to do those things, and also, write down what it felt like to do them, and then send it to me."

She snorted. "That shouldn't be hard. How do you spell idiocy?"

We exchanged email addresses. Then she threw the door open and sprinted down the hallway.

Two seconds later, my spine felt the front door slam.

*   *   *

A week later, I was sitting in my office chair shuffling through my mail when I saw a yellow envelope, one of those fancy-stationery jobs. The embossed return address said, "Ms. Deirdre Pomeroy." I sliced it open with the letter-opener and extracted a single yellow sheet of heavy bond paper:

"1) Farmers Market: boring, touristy. 2) Angels Flight: too far from hotel to waste my time. 3) My feelings: what's the point? 4) Next up: Memphis. 5) Assignment?"

I had to smile. Her personality certainly didn't suffer in the translation; it came through loud and clear. Not having any laid bond paper lying around, I brought up my email and wrote:
"1) Good clear authorial 'voice': no mistaking it's you! 2) Could use a little more local color: you know, talk about the weather, cloud formations, etc. 3) Excellent choice of paper. 4) Next Assignment: the Mississippi River, and Sun Studios (if it's not too far from your hotel); write about what it was like to get the assignment, and your feelings while doing the assignment."

The whole next week I didn't hear a word, though I found myself checking my mail, both snail and "e," regularly for the next installment. Finally, on Sunday, there it was in my email inbox:

"1) Still hate airplanes, still hate traveling, still hate hotel rooms. 2) I don't know if my job is working for me anymore. 3) 'On assignment,' I sat on a bench under an umbrella and looked at the Mississippi River in the rain. Watched barges and a riverboat go by. A scruffy-looking red-headed boy came up and asked me, 'What are they biting on?' My purse got wet. Felt like a fool. Well, you wanted local color. 4) Sun Studios was closed by the time I got there, but I found a cute restaurant nearby, and had some decent scampi. 5) Mind if I make up my own assignment for Denver?"

I immediately responded, "I would love it."

Late that night, which meant it was really late in Memphis, I received this email:

"This is so embarrassing, but you did say you wanted to know what I feel. Well, remember that red-headed boy I told you I met while I was on assignment at the river? I didn't tell you the rest of the conversation. After he asked me, of all people, 'What are they biting on?' I said, 'Shouldn't you be in school?' He just pointed down to the river and said, 'That river, lady—that's my school,' and walked away with his fishing pole and his backpack. Well, at the time I felt kind of sorry for him, and in a way, I still do, but later on I realized I was jealous of him, too. He seemed free, at home in the world and confident, in a way I never have been and probably never will be. And now, I can't seem to stop crying; about what, I don't know. Well, you did ask. Thanks for listening, if you are, even though this is probably stupid and boring for you, and one big fat cliché."

I continued to receive emails from Denver, Minneapolis, San Antonio, and finally her trip was over.

We had a session scheduled for a Wednesday evening. Once again, it was a scorcher, hot and humid. I had the fan and the air conditioner blasting as she entered the office.

Her red hair was down now and she was wearing a summer dress, but I could sense that wasn't all that was different about her.

She sat down and surveyed the office as before, then smiled. "Things don't change much with you, do they?"

I smiled. "Nope, I guess not."

She pointed. "Even your desk is still a mess."

I kidded back, "Hey, I didn't want to shock you; besides, change is supposed to be your department." I could see she didn't even hear me. She was clearly working on something.

She reached for a Kleenex. "This is our last session."

"Wow, speaking of shocks."

She looked at me with a level gaze. "I ... I quit my job." She continued, "Well, I might as well tell you all of it in one fell swoop: I already have a new one, that doesn't involve any traveling." She paused a moment. "And it's in New York. I'll be leaving tomorrow, my last *trip*."

I sat there, trying to take it all in. "You always were a fast worker."

She smiled, still dabbing her eyes. "Yeah, but this time I'm working fast on slowing down." She gazed out the window and took a long moment to gather herself. "You know, it's kind of ironic, but those stupid *assignments* of yours really changed me. Once I realized it was okay to explore the world a little and make those business trips more fun, I realized that I didn't have to travel all the time in the first place. I was a slave to that job, always terrified I wasn't going to be good enough. It's like being on a merry-go-round: you spend your whole life trying to adjust to living on the merry-go-round, and then, suddenly, you realize that all you have to do is just step off it, and you're free."

"Like that kid in Memphis—the fisherman?"

She nodded, thoughtfully. "Yes, that moment with him, he was my first inspiration." She smiled. "My Memphis moment." She shook her head. "God, I cried so hard that night." Then she looked up, smiling. "Guess all that stuff will be for my next therapist to figure out, huh?"

I smiled. "Yeah, the lucky stiff."

*   *   *

Deirdre would call me occasionally over the next few years, and always, we'd get around to the Memphis moment. And then we'd end like this:

I'd say, "So, what are they biting on, lady?"

And she'd laugh, and say, "Life!"

Just Passing Through

We live and we die
Like fireworks
We pull apart the dark
Compete against the stars
With all of our hearts
Till our temporary brilliance turns to ash
We pull apart the darkness while we can.

— "In the Embers," by Sleeping at Last

What's a nice species like us doing in a place like this? We live and we die, and we know it. We are glory, we are dust, and we know it. We are giants in the earth, we are a stack of bones, just passing through, and we know it. We are prisoners on death row, who don't even have the grace of knowing how death is coming, or when. But that, exactly, is our glory: here we are, in this impossible, ludicrous situation, but we make the best of it.

Oh sure, we live in denial of what's coming—of death, physical breakdown and the indignities of aging. Sometimes I think there should be a Dying Anonymous for all of us, where we have to get up in the meetings and say, "Hi, my name is Joe Jones, and I'm going to die."

In his book, *Living Your Dying*, author Stanley Keleman describes two normal phases in the great flow of human life: Self-expanding is expressive, reaching out beyond the physical body to newness and social interaction. Self-collecting gathers inward, withdrawing from the social world to define the self and its boundaries. We see these pulsations constantly in therapy.

New therapists are often surprised that, after a dynamic, boundary-stretching session, the following session is comparatively dead, quiet and uneventful. But this is exactly how growth and change occur, in pulses: expansion, then consolidation; rupture, then repair.

For example, in one session someone might experience deep despair, feeling meaningless, hopeless and hollow. If they are allowed to *drink deeply* of that despair, to experience it fully, to breathe into it, while being held emotionally by the therapist, the next session might seem relatively tame, disconnected and thoughtful, leading the therapist to wonder if he or she is doing something wrong.

But if the therapist stays with it, honoring the flow of experience, it pays off. On the way out the door, the patient might turn and say, "You know, I used to love dancing." What does this mean? It means, "Thank you." It means, "With your help, I'm remembering myself." It means that if we can stand up to despair together, like facing a bully, there might be a way out of this. Does the patient know this? No. Do you say any of this out loud? Of course not. But you file it away, you hold it emotionally for the patient and most likely, you sigh to yourself, thinking that maybe, like Scheherazade, you've earned the right to therapize another day.

So we face crazy, impossible things, like the unknown, our physical limitations, death and infirmity, sometimes alone, sometimes together. Where I used to work, in an alcohol rehab program, there was a poster up on the wall. It showed a picture of a mouse standing on the railroad tracks, giving the finger to an oncoming train. The caption was, "The last great act of defiance!"

In a way, we are all that mouse, insisting, in the face of overwhelming evidence all around us, that we matter. We pulse, expanding and consolidating, reaching out then ingathering, changing, changing again, as we try to make sense of it all. We search for our place in this life, even though there are no ultimate answers.

In Keleman's book he tells this tale:

"Plato, on his deathbed, was asked by a friend if he would summarize his great life's work, the Dialogues, in one statement. Plato, coming out of a reverie, looked at his friend and said, 'Practice dying.'"

But what does it mean, this "practice"? I think it means standing up to our emotional bullies within, breathing into change and not resisting the forces inside us that are trying to be born. In baseball, they talk of "making adjustments": A kid comes into the major leagues with a great reputation for batting. He has torn up the minor leagues, and now he is poised to bring terror to the hearts of major league pitchers. And for a while he does. But what happens? Major league pitchers are smart. They see his tendencies, and they adjust. They see that he is vulnerable to curve balls, low and away. Now what does the new kid do? If he is ordinary, he just continues to flail away at low-and-away curves, gradually becoming predictable and mediocre. But if he has greatness, he adjusts back. He learns to let those curves go, forcing pitchers to throw him something hittable. And he studies *them*, too. He learns their tendencies, their patterns, their weaknesses, and he uses all of it against them. Life is also a game of adjustments. Things change constantly. What we held on to for dear life yesterday is lost for good; what was our best "material" yesterday is irrelevant today.

So what does Plato mean by practicing dying? Perhaps having an open attitude to changes, the *little deaths* that happen to us throughout our lives. It means being light on our feet in the face of new information, not being unduly attached to ideas, images or the status quo, not having to have things a certain way, being willing to not be in control all the time. And maybe most of all, being committed to seeing things as they actually are. This doesn't mean being wishy-washy, passive or uncaring. It doesn't mean not being yourself. It means standing there and bringing your authentic self to each situation, meeting reality face to face and engaging it fully, in all its complexity. It means sitting with unsureness if necessary, until a greater whole presents itself.

We all have our tendencies, to be sure; these are the legacy, for better or worse, of our early family lives, our genetic predispositions and our unique interactive experiences with life. And to some extent, we are all prisoners of our tendencies. The famous psychologist Alice Miller once wrote a remarkable book, which she called *Prisoners of Childhood*. It discussed exactly this—how we are all shackled, to a greater or lesser degree, to our early childhood experiences. The book didn't sell well. Finally, she changed the name to *The Drama of the Gifted Child*. Sales took off and it became a best-selling classic. No need to explain why: we don't want to feel that we are prisoners of our past, knowing that we are always repeating tendencies, limitations and flaws. But if we are willing to face them, to "adjust back" to life, we can do great things. And even if we don't do great things, we can do ordinary things with a kind of greatness.

I have read quite a bit about prisoner-of-war experiences in World War II. One of the most surprising things I learned was the importance of rumors—incorrect rumors. In their memoirs former POWs wrote that rumors, most of them begun by the prisoners themselves, were a major source of hope and "entertainment." At first I was shocked: I would have thought it would make a prisoner enraged to hear that, say, "General MacArthur is forming a two-hundred-thousand-man army and is only two weeks from returning to free us," and then learn that it is wrong. But rumors were a cheap, available and defiant means of keeping up hope and morale, something the enemy guards could not control. They became an expression of creativity, a way of keeping the men open to possibility, a middle finger raised to the oncoming train.

So, yes, it's true that death is the oncoming train in all of our lives. We are all on death row, prisoners of childhood, living on rumors. Our position is laughable to some, ludicrous to others, and wholly absurd to anyone who is a fair witness to it all. If you ask heroes about their outrageous acts of bravery, they will invariably say, "I was just doing my job."

And that's what we do. If we are ludicrous, we are also magnificent. We "pull apart the darkness while we can," and if we do not live forever, well, we do our best to live now, and that is heroic.

That is our job.

The Diary of Anne Candid

Once, years ago, I was talking with Sarah, a young woman patient, about how to deal with narcissists and other people who are self-referent and always blaming others. These are the ones who end up making you feel wrong for any of your behaviors or personality characteristics that upset them. This led us into reflecting on single-minded family systems (like hers) that offer you two choices: either join us in thinking, feeling and acting "our way," and thereby be a part of something (ostensibly) wonderful, or have your own (wrong!) attitudes and be all alone.

What a God-awful Sophie's Choice, especially for a child, and most especially for a sweet, sincere child who wants and needs connection and who needs to feel a part of things.

Such a connection-oriented child, brought up in such a my-way-or-the-highway family, is at a terrible disadvantage. Desperate to fit in and not be an outsider in her own family, the child naturally (and unconsciously) learns to disregard and disbelieve her own perceptions. As Sarah and I continued talking we realized that, eventually, she was going to have to come up with a strategy for dealing with these types of monolithic people and systems.

But wait—though Sarah understood all this on an intellectual level, a strong part of her resisted it. That resistant part of her (the innocent child) still wanted to believe that everybody is basically honest and sincere and wants authenticity and connection as much as she does. Unfortunately, in our culture, that's called "asking for it," because believing unquestioningly in the "good of all mankind" means that sooner or later, and probably sooner, you're going to get beat up and dumped in an (emotional) alley somewhere.

Again and again.

Her continuing belief in the "goodness of all beings" led her to believe the self-referent people when they told her that she had upset them (i.e., by disagreeing with them or their ways, or simply by being herself). Therefore, she repeatedly ended up in situations where, in order to maintain the illusion of a connection or a working relationship with others, she had to doubt herself and her perceptions. Result? Feeling bad about herself and disbelieving herself, to the point where she sometimes thought she must be crazy. Oh, and did I mention suicidal thoughts and no self-confidence?

I tried again, mentioning gently that she was going to have to come up with a strategy that allowed her to maintain her own reality with these people, that when other people are lying, insincere or totally unable to perceive or value her reality, there had to be a way to detach from their demands, to stop giving them the power to define her.

Well, my pushing finally led to this outburst:

"But that's elitist and snobbish. Who am I to judge them? Besides, that implies that I think I'm better than them."

I tried to explain that, whether she knew it or not, this "detachment" is a function that most people perform internally, all the time. Let's say you're in a transaction with someone and it becomes clear that they're blaming you for something that's actually their own doing. You can say to yourself, "Hmm, I guess this person is too limited for me to pursue this exchange with them now." That is, you disengage to some degree and release the hope of carrying on a sincere, open transaction with them at that moment. No, it doesn't mean you write them off, or that you think you're "better" than they are. But it does mean that you decide, independently and unilaterally, that they are not able to continue things in a manner that honors your own reality.

Once again Sarah said, "But I don't like that!"

I responded, "Well, I don't like it either, but then, do you like thinking that you're a loser, crazy or wrong all the time? Are you willing to sacrifice yourself in order to maintain the illusion that you and this person are close, or on the same page? And remember, it *is* an illusion."

She looked agitated and truly dismayed. I could see the wrestling match going on in her mind:

In this corner, representing all that crap Dr. Bernstein is telling me about self-preservation by selective detachment: **Kid Change**!

And in that corner, representing the innocent child's belief in the Goodness of All Mankind, and the desperate need to stay connected with others at all costs: **The Resister**!

At this point, I could have pressed her to continue working on her feelings about all this, no matter how rational or irrational they might be, but instead I obeyed Bernstein's First Law of Psychotherapy: Shut up and listen!

And then, as so often happens when you shut up and listen, something creative and "self-y" happened. She finally looked up at me, a steely resolve in her blue eyes, and said, "But, what about Anne Frank?"

Well, I remembered that Anne Frank was one of her idols, someone she looked up to as a role model for innocence, authenticity and a belief in human nature. I wasn't positive where she was going with this, but I had a pretty good idea that what it meant, roughly, was, "If I accept your proposition that I have to decide on a case-by-case basis whether people are sincere and safe for me, or narcissistic and toxic to me, that would mean losing my charter membership in the Anne Frank Pure and Innocent Society."

Looking at Sarah's sad-shading-into-angry face, I also understood that, even beyond Anne Frank, she felt that accepting my "proposition" would also, in some sense, mean losing her charter membership in her own family. And the universally sad part is that growing up always means, in some sense, losing your charter membership in your own family—and absolutely so when your family is a monolithic cult that requires unquestioning agreement with what has been laid down by the elders.

As a child develops, and his or her uniqueness starts to become evident, a normal family says,

"That's interesting—you've brought some healthy diversity to our stock." Whereas a monolithic family says, "Kid, you'd better drop those new thoughts and feelings, but quick, or you're out of here."

Unfortunately, Sarah's family was the "drop it, quick" kind, though she had never really emotionally *owned* that fact. Not surprisingly, she had discovered and clung to Anne Frank as a symbol of openness and honesty, without fully realizing why Anne Frank meant so much to her.

Anne Frank is, deservedly, a symbol the world over of how the voice of life continues, even under the most severe repression and ugliness. But she is more than that, as well: her diary is not only the record of a family forced into hiding by the insanity of Nazi repression, but a testament to the struggles of a young girl to say, "I exist!" to the world at large, i.e. a universal teenage girl's shout-out of existence, of mattering, of uniqueness. Because the whole world had gone crazy, her story is not just the "usual" adolescent angst played out against her parents, but against society as a whole.

The challenge of a young girl entering her teens is to grow, to expand, to lay the emotional groundwork to eventually push her way out of her family system and take her place in the big, scary world beyond. And that, as we all know, is hard enough. But in the case of Anne Frank, we encounter a girl who, at the very developmental moment of gathering herself and her courage for the big push up and out of her childhood cocoon, was instead forced down and in, literally into hiding and secrecy and into an even smaller, quieter, more constricted world than her normal childhood life.

And so, her diary is not just the tenuous confessions and gropings-toward-adulthood of a normal preteen girl, but actually a piercing, heroic, countercoup scream to the world:

"I'm alive, damn you! I'm still here! I exist! You can't stop me from growing up!"

And the ultimate irony is that, if this type of diary had been written by, say, an ordinary Dutch girl of the same era, living out in the open, in a non-persecuted group, it wouldn't have nearly the same power.

Why?

Because at times we have to get mad (even if unconsciously) to force these things out of ourselves, to fling the words out there like spears, with abandon and full honesty. We have to be pushed to an emotional place where it almost doesn't matter what we write, or do, or feel. Almost like, "I'm lost anyway—so I'm going to go for it!" My guess, also, is that with the Nazis as a shared family enemy, it probably forced the developing Anne into a more appreciative stance toward her family than she would have embraced otherwise. She wasn't afforded the luxury of standard rebellion toward family authority!

The diary was not a careful record, or a childish outburst; it was more of a "Please, Lord, hear my cry!" Not that Anne recognized this, by any means, but the power of the diary is that it is the document of a girl in circumstances that stripped her of all pretense, posturing, preening and self-pity—a girl reduced, like a fine roux, down to her basic essence, and in the case of Anne Frank, an essence that carried a magnificent humanness and universality.

This courage, this magnificence, is what Sarah responded to in the writing of Anne Frank. And in lobbing the hand grenade of Anne Frank at me in the session, she was saying, "I don't have to face all this!"

She got *mad*.

I didn't say anything, waiting for her to make the next move; after all, it was her *show*. It was up to her to mobilize all that energy and pressure we had uncorked, like drilling down to a gusher.

Suddenly, she stood up, saying, "You can't take Anne Frank away from me! I won't stand for it!" and she stormed out of the room.

I could have stopped her in many different ways, but I wanted to give her her head, to let her loose in the world not being scared, not being careful, not caring anymore.

Like Anne Frank.

This was her break-out moment: hers alone, not to be carefulized or diluted by me or by anyone.

I waited.

The next night, I got a message on my voice mail from her:

"Dr. Bernstein, I'm going to leave a message here, but don't call me back. I need some time to deal with all this on my own ... Okay, I think I'm getting it: you're not trying to take Anne Frank away from me, are you? You're trying to get me to join her ... It's just so ... so sad, to have to leave my family like this—to, you know, outgrow them, I guess. I thought you were trying to get me to hate them, to reject them, but now I see that ... that it's not like that, is it? It's just sad, but kind of sad-proud, if you know what I mean ... Okay, that's all I can say, for now. I guess I'll see you next week ... since you're not a monster, after all." She gave a small laugh before saying, "Goodbye."

The next week I could feel, the moment she walked into my office, that something was different. Her posture was more erect, her bearing almost regal; she had always been a pretty girl, but now she was beautiful, radiant. I knew, without her saying a word, that she had crossed her own personal Rubicon; she would never be the same. You know, it's funny, being a therapist, because at times like this, part of you thinks, *Hey, what happened to the little Sarah? I'm not ready to lose her!* Loss and growth are hard for therapists, too! But you never say it—you just live with it, and smile.

The first thing she said was, "Dr. B, I never realized that one of the things about Anne Frank that is so perfect is her last name: you know, like frank means honest? And, in the last week or so, even though it's taken me a long time to get to it, I've started to be honest with myself. Well, actually, I've always been honest with myself. What's different is that I'm starting to be more honest with other people, and about other people. So I promoted myself."

I angled my head at her, confused. "What do you mean, 'promoted'?"

She laughed. "Well, you know how I always felt like Anne Frank was a sister—the sister I never had? But before, I never felt worthy of really being related to her. Well, now I've promoted myself to being her sister ... and, you're going to think this is crazy, but, secretly, I've started a diary, an honest diary, and I'm calling it 'The Diary of Anne Candid,' because that's my new nom de plume. And that's what I mean by 'promoted.'"

Sarah left a short time later to go to college. Her struggles weren't over by any means, but they were different. Now, instead of drowning in her troubles, she was swimming through them. Her therapy hadn't made her problems disappear, but it had taught her the Australian crawl.

Sarah got her degree, eventually got married, had kids and lives a nice life in a Midwestern town.

And every holiday season, she sends me a card, and it's always signed, "Anne Candid."

And every time I see that name, I smile and send up a silent prayer of thanks to Anne Frank, my assistant swimming instructor.

Ready to Fly

I am standing on the edge of the water,
And I am watching the wild birds fill the sky.
And I am longing to be lifted up among them,
I am not dying, I'm getting ready to fly.

— "Ready to Fly," by Calaveras

I'd like to talk about the deep, dark secret of Western civilization: *life ends.*

(Shh, don't tell! Of course, we can talk about it here though, because everything that happens in a book about therapy is confidential, right?)

So yes, it's true; we actually do have to die at some point. If we last long enough, we'll get old, then older, and then yep, we up and die. All of us! We don't know when; we don't know how. Kind of like roulette but without zero or double zero. Of course, we can take care of ourselves in the hopes that this will prolong our lives and provide "quality of life" for many years.

But that's kind of like what Robert Mitchum said in *Out of the Past* when his femme fatale was playing roulette and losing big:

Mitchum: That isn't the way to play it.
Girlfriend: Why not?
Mitchum: Because it isn't the way to win.

Girlfriend: Is there a way to win?

Mitchum: Well, there's a way to lose more slowly.

You can exercise and eat right. You can have so many air bags in your car that it would lift off if you had an accident. You can ingest vitamins and supplements and homeopathic remedies. You can stand on your head, gobble brewer's yeast, do puzzles to keep your brain sharp and meditate to achieve mindfulness. You can guzzle goji and açai berry juice and phosphatidylserine elixirs.

But in the end, there's still, well, the end.

There are plenty of books about it, from Stephen Levine's books, to Becker's *The Denial of Death* (not for the faint of heart, that one). But all the reading in the world won't change the fact that, in the final analysis, we're all taking that long walk on that short plank, and there are no reprieves, no last-minute pardons and no stays of execution for the likes of us.

So all of us are busy interviewing old people all the time, to find out how to do it, getting tips on what aging is like, right? Educating ourselves precisely on just what it is to have everyone you know gone, to have no one left who remembers you or your past. What it's like to feel all alone in the world, to hurt physically and lose it mentally, right? We just sit those wise elders right down and pick their brains endlessly about adjusting to times you don't understand, about your experience of not being valued anymore, and about how to deal with a world where everyone's younger than you are.

Right?

No.

What do you *mean*, no? You mean we're *not* all studying and talking to old people all the time for information and inspiration, for role modeling of grace and courage?

Are you telling me we just do a barrel-roll into old age—the hardest

thing most of us will ever do—on a wing and a prayer?
Not only do we not seek out older people to learn from their experience and wisdom, we actually avoid them and marginalize them. The truth is, they make us uncomfortable. They remind us of what we don't want to know: the inevitability of aging and death.

Maybe this story will help illustrate what I'm talking about. I know it did for me.

When I was seventeen or so, I was hospitalized so my doctor could do "studies" on my back pain. Nowadays, of course, I would be whisked into the hospital, shoved through an MRI like a buzz saw and whisked out before the ink could dry on my waiver-of-liability and proof-of-payment paperwork. But at that time, things were a little different. It was more like an "event": I remember my friends came—like a bon voyage party—and brought me a couple bottles of dry-roasted cashews—my favorite, then and now.
Finally, everyone left, friends and family, and there I lay, ensconced on my clean white sheets and my adjustable bed. I looked to my left. There was a bed there, but nobody in it. I didn't know from *private rooms*, but figured I had just lucked out and would have the whole suite to myself, for the duration—woo-hoo!

Around 5:00 p.m., an attractive "older" (maybe thirty-five) nurse came in and said, "Roll over."
Uh, okayyyy. What was all this about? I mean, did she think I was in for a hemorrhoidectomy, prostate trouble, or what? But what the heck, I did as directed.
Ooohh. Aaaaahhh. She started rubbing my back with some kind of nice-smelling cream. This was about the first time a grown woman had ever done anything so intimate to me, if you catch my drift.

I was just starting to think this hospital duty really wasn't so bad after all.

Then they wheeled him in.

I heard the orderly say, "Careful, Jimmy, he's in a lot of pain!" And then a drugged voice came from the gurney that was coming through the doorway: "That's okay, boys. You're doing fine."
I propped myself up and tried to watch, without being too crass about it. It looked like an older man, maybe late sixties—it's hard to tell when you're a kid—smallish, heavy-set, maybe a foreigner, judging from his slight accent.
The boys in white got him up off the gurney and situated on his bed, with only minimal groaning. But I had the impression that an ordinary person would have been screaming at the top of his lungs. Why? Because I heard one of the "boys" muttering, "Jesus, I can't believe he was quiet through that whole thing, and was apologizing to *us*, no less! The guy's amazing!"
Then came the shock troops: several nurses, hovering around him, giving him pills, hooking up IVs and electrical things until he looked like Frankenstein. And still, not a word of protest or complaint out of the guy.

Finally, everyone left except the two patients in 122-B: me and Mr. X.

I don't think he was even aware of me, because when everyone had gone, I heard some muffled groaning, crying to God and half-screams that you wouldn't normally hear outside of a battlefield. I remember it brought tears to my eyes, but I bit my lip because I already *knew* him well enough to know that if he heard me, he would stop immediately, and I didn't want him to have to hold it all in any longer—certainly not on my account.

Hours later, as I tried to settle down for the night, I still heard the occasional stifled scream escape from the poor guy's fitful sleep, a sound that was hard to ignore, or forget. I clearly remember realizing that, if I'd thought for a while there that a hospital stay was all back rubs and cashews, well, I was surely disabused of that now.

And I don't mind admitting, I was a little concerned about what the new day would bring with my new roomie.

*　　　*　　　*

"Vhat's your name?"

I struggled up from sleep, exhausted and confused about where I was. It took a moment to get myself oriented. "Huh? Who's there?"

"Me—the guy in the other bed."

I forced my eyelids apart. It was still pretty dark. "Oh, sorry, I was sound asleep."

"It's a new day. You don't want to miss the whole t'ing, do you?"

I sat up, twisting around in vain looking for a clock. "Why, what time is it, anyway?"

He kind of chuckled. "Seven forty-five."

"Oh, that late, huh?" I rubbed my eyes. I had been on summer vacation, getting up closer to 10:00 a.m. every day.

"Did I bother you last night?"

"Uh, no, no, not at all." In fact, his groans—and all the other unfamiliar clatter of the hospital—had kept me awake until a nurse came and gave him a sleeping pill, around 4:30 a.m. That was the moment I realized that you don't check into a hospital to rest!

"Good, I would hate to think I bothered you."

"Yeah, no problem. My name is Gregg Bernstein—how about you?"

"I am Mr. Davon."

He had a bit of a foreign accent, but also a world of dignity in how he spoke, enunciating carefully and separating all the words. I remember it reminded me of the way the TV horse said, "I am Mister Ed!"

Naturally, I wanted to ask the old prison line, "So, what are you in for?" but figured maybe that was a sore subject, so to speak.

But this guy certainly wasn't standing on any ceremony. He immediately said, "Stomach cancer, and you?"

Feeling a bit unworthy, I said, "Bad back. You know, studies?"

"Vhat? Your bad back is keeping you from the studies?"

"No, no, they're doing studies on it, you know, to figure out exactly what's wrong."

"Ah so, and it keeps you from dah vahr, too?"

"You mean a deferment? I don't know. I haven't been drafted yet."

"Ah so, vell, I hope it show some-ting bad, that don't hurt a bit, yes?" He laughed, though I could see it made him wince with pain.

I smiled, not wanting to be the cause of his pain. "Yes, yes, I guess you're right, there."

"I vent, you know."

"What? Oh, you mean…"

"Yes, to vahr. The first von, the big von." He laughed again, wincing. "I got hurt, bad. Dey send me home, and I had a good time vit all the girls that was left all alone on the … the, uh . . ."

"Home front?"

"Yes, the home front. I giff 'em all a good time." He chuckled to himself, and then paused. "Maybe same vit you, too? You giff 'em all a good time on the home front too, huh?" This cracked him up, but this time he had to suppress a scream.

I prayed to myself: *No more jokes, I'm not worth it!* I steered the subject back to less destabilizing topics. "So, where are you from, originally?"

He nodded. "Vhite Plains, New York, sonny." He nodded. "And now, I'm here in Studio City vit my kids, twenty-five, thirty years."

"Oh no, I mean, originally?"

He waved his hand dismissively. "Austria ... Hungary, we all over the place, like a whatchacallit..." His head went back and forth.

"Ping pong ball?"

"Yeah, dot's it, a ping pong ball, sonny. It go back and fort, who can keep up anymores? And who care, anymores? I got out of there, and dot's dot." He suddenly clutched his stomach and fell back.

I rang for the nurse, jabbing the red button over and over.

An older, stern, gray-haired nurse, looking like a prison matron, stood looking at me accusingly. "What's going on in here? What's he doing up? What's he talking like this for?"

I blanched. "Ma'am, I don't...I didn't..."

"Well, leave him alone. Can't you see he's..."

He's what, I thought. Or rather, *he's vhat?* I always had a tendency to take on the other person's characteristics, and inside me I had already "gone native" with Mr. Davon's patterns of speech. I wanted to cry, to say, "But he vas in de Big Von, don't you know? He can't die! He gave all de girls a good time. Don't you know anyt'ing? He's real!"

It was the first time it ever hit me. Real people die! Nice people die! People who are kind, and funny, and take the time to talk to stupid kids who were in the hospital for next to nothing, when they themselves are in agonizing pain—they die! I thought, *But he's my friend, my friend, Mr. Davon! Don't you get it?*

The nurse must have seen the look on my face. After fiddling with Mr. Davon's IV and easing him down gently, she tiptoed over to me. "Look, they did all they could for him. They opened him up and when they saw what was in there, they closed him up. It's all over. He's got maybe, oh, a day or so, at best."

I could barely breathe. I stammered, "But ... I thought he was here ... you know ... to get fixed up, and..."

She shook her head.

"But, does *he* know all this?"

She nodded. "Sure, he knows it."

I still couldn't grasp it. "But he was just talking to me. He, I mean, he woke up, and then he woke me up. He said, 'Get up. It's a new day and you don't want to miss it.'" I was babbling now. "He told me his story, he was a soldier, he...how *could* he, if he knew he was dying?"

She laid a hand on my arm. "Sounds like you got yourself a pretty good roommate, son." She walked off to do whatever nurses do for the next one, and the next one, and the next one.

Shortly after that, they came to wheel me out for my "studies." I whispered, "Goodbye," to Mr. Davon as I rolled by, just in case. I figured we had at least another day.

*   *   *

By the time they stuck all the needles in my leg, took all the pictures of my back, and I can't remember what all else, it was late afternoon. When they rolled me back into 122-B, the room was empty. I ate cashews and drank ginger ale till I thought I would bust, but it did nothing to fill the void Mr. Davon left in his wake. Later on, the older nurse came by and said to me, "Before he died, Mr. Davon told me, 'Say goodbye to sonny, in the other bed.'"

I felt honored. I said, "I guess his wife and kids'll be coming by later to claim his body?"

She frowned and shook her head. "No, he has no wife, no kids. He was all alone."

I was stunned, babbling out loud. "He called me sonny."

She nodded, patting my arm again. "I know." She moved over to strip his bed and get it ready for the new person.

I never forgot my brief encounter with Mr. Davon. Even looking back now over a lifetime of memories, I think it's the single most courageous and the kindest act I've ever witnessed. To sit there in agonizing pain, knowing it's your last day on earth, and still take the time to laugh and be real with some punk kid who means nothing to you—well, in my book, that's a real hero.

And so when I hear somebody say, "We can learn a lot from old people," I know exactly what they mean.

The Lady is a Bum

When you work in alcohol rehab, your clientele is overwhelmingly male. But that means that sometimes when there is a female, she is often an unusual person, an outlier, a wild child, a soul on the stray. And that was certainly the case with Lily Sondergaard—one of the most extraordinary people I have ever met.

Most of the folks who came to the treatment center where I worked were there because they had good insurance coverage; it's expensive to be in a thirty-day inpatient alcohol rehabilitation center. Very expensive. And at that time, this meant that most of my "customers" were union workers: teamsters, pipefitters, electricians, forklift drivers, and even a delivery man for Lay's Potato Chips. Or, rarely, their spouses, often women who had gotten started on drinking by trying to keep up with their husbands and ended up nipping at the bottle all day between dropping the kids off at school in the morning and picking them up in the afternoon. There were exceptions of course: women bar drinkers, librarians who lived alone and indulged in a wee dram or two while reading Shakespeare far into the night.

And then there was Lily Sondergaard. She never would have been in the program if it hadn't been for her rich brother, a shipping magnate in San Francisco, who fished her out of the drunk tank in a San Antonio jail one night, after she was picked up for mooning a Southern Pacific security guard from a passing freight car. Over her violent objections, the brother paid in full, in cash, and had her placed in our program.

Often when people were first brought in to the program, they were in the early stages of withdrawal, and none too happy about it. In the case of Lily, it took two burly male staff members to escort her to the dry-out ward, the first step in the program, while she, literally yowled, kicking and screaming, "I'll never dry out, and I'll never dry up!"

Several days later, when she had been detoxed, they released Lily, in all her sullen and angry glory, to the general population. She regarded most of her "fellow inmates," as she called them, with disdain, but especially the women. She would walk by the small group of three or so women in the program, sitting together, and say, "What are you old biddies doing here? Cluck, cluck, cluck, break up that hen party!" Then she'd saunter off, cackling to herself loudly.

Needless to say, her act didn't go over too well with the ladies, and the men had no idea what to do with her either.

In fact, that was the reason for my first meeting with her—the other patients had sent a representative to talk to the staff about how Lily was disrupting the whole group with her mockery and unwillingness to mix in. As the psychologist, I was elected to meet with her individually and see if I could settle her down and figure out her "trip." (Well, it *was* the seventies!)

As I entered the so-called therapy room, there she was, slouched down in a chair, her feet propped up on the table, bold as life. She was all of 5'3", tops. Her thick hair was straggly and unkempt, but shot through with incongruous streaks of blonde. Her skin was still a bit sallow from months of solid drinking, and her upper arms looked like pipe cleaners. And yet, there was something about her . . .

"Don't say it!"

I flinched at the unexpected outburst. "Uh, say what?" My mind raced to catch up, but drew a blank.

She just sat there in defiant silence, insolently looking up at the ceiling. Maybe so I could study her? I had never seen anyone with copper eyelashes before. They framed a pair of green eyes that had so many thready red veins traversing them, it looked like Christmas in there.

I sat in the chair facing her, wondering whether to play along or not. I finally threw in the towel. "Okay, I'll bite: don't say what?"

She tossed her head and cooed, in a sing-song, mocking voice, "Gee honey, you must have been so pretty," she gave a wry cackle before adding, "once."

Sure I could have said, "No, I wasn't thinking that at all," but it would've been a gratuitous cheap shot, and untrue. In fact, I realized that, cliché or not, that was exactly what I had been thinking when I first saw her sitting there. I'm always thinking of *comps* for everyone I meet— that is, what famous person they remind me of. It's something that seems to be built in to my wiring, for better or worse. As I flipped through my mental rolodex for Lily Sondergaard's comp (she was still looking away; it made it easy), I finally hit a match: Goldie Hawn, of all people!

I nodded and held up my hand. "We have better things to talk about than how you look."

She brought her legs down from the table, then flipped the chair around backwards and straddled it aggressively. "Such as?"

"Your behavior, your alienation of the other . . ."

"Inmates?" She grinned, looking again like a snotty Goldie Hawn, until she opened her mouth, exposing two missing front teeth, and two badly chipped ones. There went my comp.

"Look, we don't call them inmates here. This isn't a prison or a chain gang, but a place where people can begin to look at themselves and, maybe, get their lives back together again."

"I don't want my life 'back together again'—it was never apart."

I nodded. All right, maybe I had gone too far. I backpedaled, "Okay then, maybe you don't want to change your way of life, but surely . . ."

That mincing, sing-song voice again. "But surely you don't want to continue to be a slave to," she opened her green eyes wide, in mock horror, "Demon Rum?"

Before I could even get my mouth open to protest, she went on in a torrent of words.

"Look, mister, I don't want to be normal, and I'm not fuckin' Suzy Housewife, and I'm not fuckin' waiting for some fuckin' man to come fuckin' save me, okay? I like my 'way of life,' as you call it. I'm a lady bum, is what I am. By choice, see? Can you get that through your thick skull: by choice!"

Now she stood up and tossed her head at me again. "You, and all your 'straights' can call me a tramp, you can call me a hobo, you can call me a bohemian, a loser, a misfit, a fallen woman or a chronic wanderer; I don't really care. I call myself a lady bum, and whether you can put those two words together in a sentence or not, I don't give a good goddam, because it's good enough for me!"

And with that, she crossed the room, tore open the door, then slammed it on the way out.

I just sat there in the chair, processing the moment. After all, it's kind of memorable to be dressed down good and proper by an expert, even a misguided one.

And besides, she had told me so many things in that brief exchange, that it took me a while to begin to sort it all out: that she had a great deal of pride; that she was no dummy; that, true or not, she at least felt she had chosen her life, not merely fallen into it; that she had a fair amount of sophistication; that, in her own way, she felt she was a lady, and that it mattered to her; that she was sensitive; that she was angry as hell; and lastly, that underneath the bluster and the toughness, she was vulnerable.

I also sensed that she recognized something in me, something that made her care what I thought of her, enough to be worthy of draining her inner resources by going on such a rampage.

Sure, she had stormed off, but I knew we weren't done; like two fighters feeling each other out in a furious first-round exchange, we had established to one another the fact that we were adversaries worth bothering with.

She knew I was worth yelling at, and I knew ... what? *Was* I capable of putting the words "lady" and "bum" in the same sentence? Maybe she had me there.

I had my (mental) work cut out for me before we met again.

*   *   *

"So, what was all that about?"

The Director of Rehab was in my face, along with his coffee breath, insistent and anxious to find out what I had accomplished in my one-on-one with Lily. I couldn't blame him—Lily was disrupting the whole program with her snide remarks and standoffish behavior, and the Director needed things to run smoothly.

I thought carefully before I responded, knowing in advance what his response would be. "Look, I say we give her a couple days to cool off, before we force her into the group again. She's been on the road, on her own, for a long time. It's asking a lot to expect her to adapt immediately to a group of conventional people, what she would call 'straights.'"

As I expected, he angled his head at me skeptically and threw his arms out. "Hey look, she's an alcoholic, isn't she? That's what she's here for, and *we* run the program, not her." He waited, watching my face for signs of acquiescence, and didn't see any. Then he sighed and ran his hand down over his face. "Ah hell, you think you can do something with her in the interim, be my guest." He wagged his finger at me. "You've got two days, but by then, she better be up and running, or . . ."

"Or what? She's drummed out of the corps?"

He shook his head in disgust at me. "You goddam shrinks, always got some kind of complicated angle, don't you?" He started to leave, then turned back. "But . . ."

I nodded back to him. "Yeah I know, I've got two days, then heads are gonna roll."

"Damn straight."

Sure, I could smart-talk the Director, but what the hell had I just signed myself up for? I had no magic potions to offer, no hypnotic spells. The truth is, if she really just didn't want to be in the program, well then, she didn't have to be in the program. If she was happy being an alcoholic, and a "bum," then let the railroad guards, or the law, or the hospital, or even the coroner, have her. But she seemed to be worth a lot more than that to me; this was at least a chance to help her, in some way, and we couldn't just throw that chance, or her, away.

*   *   *

When I walked through the big double doors the next morning, the clerks and the treatment staff were staring at me like I was in a test tube. I walked up to Renee at the front desk, the intake clerk and the most level-headed person in the building, and said, "What the heck is going on here? Do I have two heads, or what?"

Renee lowered her head and said in a low voice, "They took her away in the middle of the night."

"What do you mean, 'her'?" One of the other female patients had heart problems, and another severe diabetes, but I had a sinking feeling it wasn't them.

"Your little friend." The words came from the Director, standing behind me.

I whirled around. "I don't appreciate that, Daniel."

He held up his hands protectively. "Okay then, your project. Is that better?" I could see him trying not to grin, and that didn't help matters.

I turned my back on him to face Renee again, steadying myself on the counter. "Where'd they take her?" The rehab program took up one entire floor of a several-story hospital, so I knew she was somewhere in the building.

Renee looked sad. "Fifth floor, doc." She put her hand over mine. "So sorry."

That "so sorry" sent my stomach to the ground floor. "Is she. . .?"

Renee nodded reassuringly. "She's alive, but they tell me it was touch and go there for a while."

I looked at the clock: nine on the dot. Shit, I had an hour-and-a-half group to run, and thirty patients waiting for me, right now.

At ten thirty-five, I grabbed the arm of a fifth-floor nurse I knew. "Sally, where is . . .?"

She nodded, then spun around and pointed down the hall. "501." As she walked off, she chirped, "They say she's your pet."

Damn, what the hell is going on around here anyway? I spend three minutes with the woman, and now we're Bonnie and Clyde?

The nurse in 501 was just leaving the room when I hit the doorway and made eye contact. "Are you Dr. Bernstein?" she said, almost jovially. *Shit.* Apparently, "word" had really gotten around.

I sighed and shook my head. "Yes."

"She'll be all right. Overdose, benzos." She put her hand on my arm, with exaggerated concern. "Are you all right?"

Christ, what did they think this was? A suicide pact? "Yes, nurse, I'm perfectly fine." I peeked over her shoulder. "Can I speak to her now?"

She rolled her eyes. "Oh sure, but she's fightin' mad that we brought her back." As she walked away, she tossed over her shoulder a sarcastic, "Good luuuuuuuuck!"

Lily was lying there like a sack of potatoes, her eyes half closed, the copper lashes fluttering. Tubes were running all over the place, and machines were blinking.

I pulled up a metal chair and sat there for a minute, just watching her, not wanting to wake or bother her. After a while, she began to writhe a bit, making small whimpering noises like someone having a bad dream.

Suddenly, her eyes popped open and her head came up. "Oh, it's only you."

I nodded, warily. "Yeah, just me."

She wet her dry lips with her tongue, then seemed to look around for the first time. She saw the tubes and the machines, and her head sank back on the pillow in resignation. "Damn, all I did was get myself in deeper."

I knew I was going to sound like a square, but I had to ask. "Lily, why did you do it?"

She shook her head as if to make my question go away, then kind of shrugged. "If I told you I did it to find the Holy Grail, would you believe me?"

I looked into her eyes and saw hurt. "No. People may drink to find the Holy Grail, but that's not why they O.D. on benzos."

She closed her eyes. "Stop making sense, would you? It's too early in the day for that. Just go away."

"Do you really want me to?"

I thought I saw a clear liquid leaking from her right eye. She picked up the top sheet and swiped at the offending moisture. "I said get outta here, before I . . ."

Something came to me. "You're like a trapped animal, aren't you?"

More liquid, more swiping.

"You know, like how an animal caught in a trap gets so desperate it will even gnaw off its own . . ."

At that moment a new nurse bustled in, square-bodied and middle-aged, holding out a small, white paper cup to Lily. "Now take your meds, and then we'll bring you some lunch. Now how's that sound dearie, good?"

It was time for me to leave. I started to rise, but suddenly something clutched my pants' leg, hard. I sat down again, tentatively.

The nurse saw my movements, then looked from me to Lily and back again. "Um, it might be best if visitors . . ."

"I'm a doctor."

A light seemed to dawn in her eyes. "Ohh, *you're* the one . . ."

I gritted my teeth. "Yeah, I'm the one. Now if you could just give us a few minutes alone, I'll be out of your hair."

The nurse knitted her brows in exaggerated concern. "Of course, hon-ney."

"Get me out of here." Lily's hand was still clutching my pants' leg.

I nodded. "I understand, I think, but after all, you did try to . . ."

She talked softly but fast, watching the doorway the whole time. "Look, I'm gonna level with you because I'm desperate, and because in some weird way, I feel I can trust you." She checked the doorway again before she went on. "I can't stand confinement. I can't stand being around so-called normal people. I don't want their talk, their ways, their clichés or their concern. I don't want to be in groups, and I don't want to stop drinking, or wandering, or bumming." She sighed, hard, and fixed me with her eyes. "Do you understand?"

I did, at least a little. "So, you're not really a suicide risk—it's just that . . ."

"It's just that I don't have any 'coping mechanisms,' as you would call 'em, to deal with straight life, and especially institutional life," she pointed to the blinking machines, "like this." She paused, then went on. "So, a long time ago, I ran, and I ran, and finally I found a way of life that I could stand." Her eyes were pleading now.

"And then we came along and ruined it all. Is that it?"

She nodded. "What you said about a wild animal caught in a trap . . ." She closed her eyes, then opened them again. "Well, that's it, exactly."

I met her eyes with mine. "Okay, I'll see what I can do."

Just then, a food staff lady breezed in, brimming with good cheer and lunch.

I stood up and headed for the door.

Lily called out, "Remember!"

*   *   *

"Are you crazy? We sign clients up. We don't send them away!"

The Director was aghast at my suggestion that we cut Lily loose.

I was determined. "But if we can't help somebody, what's the point . . ."

Daniel shook his head impatiently. He looked around and lowered his voice. "Look, Saint Theresa, we aren't here to save the world; we're here to making a living!" Seeing the disgust on my face, he arched back in his chair and added, in a conciliatory tone, "Well dammit, it's certainly not gonna *hurt* her any, right?"

"Dan, it already has! Look, last night she tried to commit suicide to get out of here. Doesn't that tell you anything?"

The Director nodded. "Sure, that she's depressed as well as alcoholic." He grinned evilly. "But we can deal with a switch hitter, right? Because we have a psychologist, right here on our staff!" "Switch hitter" is what he called a dual diagnosis patient. I didn't think it was cute.

Now I was really mad. "Look, we're gonna discharge her, or we're gonna discharge me. Now which is it?"

That brought him up short. I thought he was going to go the "Now, doctor, aren't you over-identifying with your patients?" route, but he surprised me. "What the hell are we going to tell her brother, the rich, influential, potential source of many, many, lucrative referrals, who I might remind you, paid in cash?"

I sighed. This one was easy. "Look, *I'll* talk to him, okay? And when I'm done he'll not only understand why we discharged her, he'll appreciate how we placed our principles above our pocketbooks."

The Director was still squirming.

"Look, she's a free spirit. When a wild bird flies into your living room, you don't try to make it appreciate life in the living room, do you? You let it go!'

He wasn't giving up that easily, and he surprised me again. "But couldn't you say that about all the patients we have in here?"

I nodded. "There's some truth in that, but it's a matter of degree; the folks in here are living conventional lives. Sure, they're using alcohol to escape, or numb, or feel free, but Lily is a different kind of animal altogether. She's found a life that maybe we wouldn't want, but it gives her a way to live outside of our system, to fly free and feel some pride in what she is. She calls herself a lady, and well, I believe her."

Daniel shook his head in surrender, then waved his hand at me. "Fine, she's gone, but don't try this crap again, or you might find yourself cut loose, too, Freud." He stood up to leave, before adding, "And don't forget—you owe me."

Well, I did talk to Lily's brother, the illustrious Mr. Sondergaard, and he did understand, and I did get Lily discharged from the hospital, and the program, after she was back on her feet again a couple days later. I walked her down to the hospital entrance, where a cab was waiting to take her to the train station.

She stood there for a moment looking uncomfortable, then just put her hand out to me and said, "I'm not much for thanks, but you done good, kid."

I shook her hand and our eyes met. Then she picked up her bag and thought for a moment before saying, "You know, you might have made a pretty good bum."

She hopped in the cab and was gone.

Red Sky

It was before the Walkman, before the Internet, the iPhone and way before Spotify; if you wanted to hear a song, you had to either buy the record—a financial stretch for me—or drive around all night in someone's car (yes, the wheel had been invented by 1965!) and hope they played it on the radio.

Oh sure, you could sit home in your room and lie on your bed staring at the radio, but that was no good. You had to be out and about with your friends, on the move, cruising, ready for anything, hoping they played "Satisfaction," "Like a Rolling Stone" or "We Gotta Get Out of This Place"—whichever one happened to be the soundtrack of your soul at the moment.

This particular night we were in Jim Berken's father's '58 Dodge, the one with the space-age, push-button transmission, and we had just pulled in next to the Santa Monica Pier, the once-vibrant amusement place that by the mid-sixties had become a seedy, rundown municipal eyesore.

We sat there, parked, for a moment, while Jim fiddled with the radio. Finally, I said, "What are we waiting for?"

Jim held up a hand to me. "Hang on. I have a feeling they're gonna play something good."

From the back seat, Bob Rubenstein crowed, "Yeah, hang on, as in 'Hang On, Sloopy'?"

I turned to the back seat and snickered—both Bob and I agreed that that song was dumb, though Jim for some odd reason had a special fondness for it.

I reached for my door latch. "Jim, let's go. We didn't come here to humor your bad taste in music."

Bob piped up again. "By the way, what *did* we come here for?" Then, as two drunken bums staggered into the street right in front of us, he added, "To get rolled?"

While Jim reluctantly shut off the radio and got out of the car, I gazed absently out toward the ocean.

"The sky's red."

Jim was pulling his jacket on as he looked up too. "Seems like the sky's always red out here. I think it has something to do with the salt air."

The three of us turned to start walking down the pier, as Bob said, "Yeah that's it all right, Jim. The salt air reaches all the way up to the ionosphere and makes the whole universe turn red."

Jim whirled on him. "Look, it doesn't have to reach the ionosphere to turn the sky red. It's low, see. I'm just talking about what's right above us." He snorted with finality. "It's a local disturbance."

Bob nudged me. "Now *there's* a local disturbance I could live with." He pointed his chin toward three women who were quite a way down the pier, but coming our way. Not girls, but women— they were all in high heels, had big, ratted hair and wore those long, tight skirts that were more the late-fifties barfly look than our generation of mini-skirted or post-folk, pre-hippie girls.

Bob licked his lips. He was always the most daring of us. I could see him breathing hard. "The night crackles with possibility. C'mon, I say we take 'em on."

Jim sounded scared. "Uh, yeah, in what? Thumb-wrestling?"

I put a steadying hand on his shoulder. "Hang on, Sloopy."

Bob gave a barking laugh, and then turned back to the women. "Hmm, they *are* kinda cute, in a certain sort of way."

I eyeballed the three carefully for the first time, and muttered, "Ten to one the gal on the right's got a shiv hidden in her beehive." They definitely weren't the kind of girls we knew.

Bob snorted, "I ain't lookin' at her beehive, Clyde."

Jim half turned to leave, hoping we'd follow. "I say we get out of here. They probably have pimps somewhere, backing 'em up."

Bob pulled Jim's arm to prevent him from leaving. "Knock it off—women can sense fear."

I laughed out loud at that, then turned back to look at Jim: I could definitely sense fear. "Look, let's stay here and just see what happens, if anything. I mean, what do we have to lose?"

Bob immediately shot back, "Our virginity, Clyde."

The women were fast approaching. In the harsh glare of the ratty old pier's towering light standards, I could make out their faces: indeterminate age, kind of average-pretty maybe, but hard. They'd definitely been around a few blocks, and in mixed company.

The women stopped right in front of us, cocking their hips and swinging their long handbag straps. I think most women, seeing three males together at the end of a creepy, dilapidated pier late at night would have been a little wary.

But not these three.

"Hi, boys. What are you three gay blades out for?"

"A good time." Bob's face sported a half leer I had never seen there before.

"Oh yeah?" The tall one on the right—the one with the shiv in her beehive—reached out and chucked Bob under the chin. "With what?"

Before I knew it, I'd said, "What do you mean?" I was always the curious, straightforward one.

Bob smacked his forehead. "Jesus."
I felt mortified.
The short one on the left swung her handbag toward Bob. "Don't mind him," she said, then turned back to me. "I think you're kind of sweet."
The tall one, ignoring all this byplay, turned again to Bob and repeated, "With what?"
Then Jim, suddenly finding his voice, said to me, knowingly, "She means booze."
I nodded, earnest as always. "Oh, I get it."
The tall one curled her lip at me. "Well hurrah for you, little man."

On cue, I felt mortified again. Then, before I took a breath, I stumbled into stupidity once more. "But, at this time of night, where are we going to get it?"

The one in the middle opened up her purse and produced a fifth of whiskey. "Right here."
Bob rubbed his hands together in glee. "Well then, we're all set."
The tall one shook her head in disgust at him. "Listen buddy, we don't give it away. It'll cost ya."

Once again, I was the designated dope. "You mean the party, or the booze?"

The short one threw back her head and laughed out loud. "The booze, silly. The party, well that all depends."
At least I didn't say, "On what?"
The short one reached out and took my hand. "I want the sweet one."
The tall one snickered, "No argument here."
I felt mortified—but you knew that.

The tall one leaned over and whispered something to Bob, then put her hand out.
Bob looked over at me and Jim. "Well?"
Of course, I said, "Well, what?"
He rolled his eyes. "Cough up, for God's sake! Brenda's waiting!"
"Oh yeah." Couldn't keep Brenda waiting. I reached in my pocket and extracted a precious fiver, and Jim did the same. We passed them over to Bob, who added some paper and put the whole wad in Brenda's outstretched hand. She counted it and nodded her approval. It made her beady eyes glitter.

And with that, we paired off: me with the short one, who turned out to actually have a name: Sally Lee (I never did find out whether Lee was her middle or last name); Jim, scared to death, with the one in the middle (I never did find out whether she had a name or not); and Bob, with the tall one, Brenda, who quickly stuffed the bottle back into her handbag like it was her most prized possession—and maybe it was.

*   *   *

Brenda took two or three big slugs for herself on the way down to the beach, then loosened up enough to share the wealth. None of us was used to drinking anything other than an occasional beer. But we were supposed to be men now, so we threw it down several times, like we had seen movie cowboys do it at the bar. We managed not to gag—barely, in my case.

I noticed that none of the ladies seemed to have any trouble putting it away.

"So, where are you kids from?"

I could tell Sally Lee was trying to be nice; after all, I was the designated "sweet one." By this time, we'd made it down to Santa Monica beach, and sat down on the sand, pairing off but staying close enough together to share the bottle. By now I could feel the infamous "warm glow" of the booze which I had only read about, coursing through my torso.

"North Hollywood," I answered.

She nodded, "High school?"

There was no way around the chagrin now. "Uh, yeah."

She passed me the bottle. I could feel it was almost empty, and pretended to drink a little, not wanting more anyway. Maybe I was drunk, but if I was, it was more from the adventure than the booze.

"How about you girls?"

Sally Lee stood up, kicked off her high heels, and twirled around under the red sky, pulling her long skirt up past her stocking tops so she could move freely. "Whee!"

I was mesmerized.

She reached out and pulled me up, and we joined hands and twirled around together. "Whee!" After a few times around, I was getting dizzy. Then, reeling and giddy, I pulled her to me and kissed her.

She moved away. "Hey, I don't even know you!"

"Oh, I'm sorry." As I backed off, I stumbled and fell down in the sand on my butt.

She looked down at me and laughed. "You're so funny. I was only kidding!"

I looked up at her and she was still spinning, even though she was standing still.

"Hey, you don't look so good." She knelt down and put a hand on my shoulder.

Everything was spinning together: her face, so close, her heavy eye makeup, the red sky, the crashing of the waves, her stocking tops, her saying, "I don't even know you!" the salt smell of the water, the croaking of the gulls . . .

*　　　*　　　*

"You all right?"
I pried an eye open. Bob was standing over me. He didn't look so good either.
My tongue was fighting me, but I managed to get out, "Uh, I guess so." I tried again to stand, and failed. "You?"
He nodded, "Yeah, sort of."
I struggled to stand again, fell back, then gave up and lay flat on my back in the sand.

I looked at the sea. The gunmetal-gray, crumpled waves were uninterested. I looked up. The red sky was gone; an ugly, grainy gray morning had taken its place. "What the hell happened . . .?"
Bob flopped down next to me and said, "We got rolled," in the flattest voice I ever heard.

I put my hands in my pockets: empty. I'd had a five and a twenty last night. I vaguely remembered giving the five to the girls for the bottle.

Bob mumbled, "I had a twenty, too. Jim's worse off; he lost forty bucks."

Bob picked up a piece of driftwood and threw it at the ocean. He missed. "For a minute there, we were hot stuff."

It struck me funny, and I started to laugh, thinking of our short career as "hot stuff."

Then Bob started laughing too. "Don't make me laugh; it hurts to move."

From out of nowhere, Jim crawled over to us on his hands and knees, shaking his finger at us. "I told you guys . . ."

Bob threw another piece of driftwood at the water. "Fetch, boy!"

"That isn't funny!" Jim always hated to have an I-told-you-so interrupted.

Now we were all lying flat on our backs in the sand, looking up at the grayness.
I croaked mournfully, "Red sky at night . . ."
Jim finished it. "Sailor's delight."
Bob laughed. "I guess that old saying isn't true."
Jim giggled. "The three of *them* were a sailor's delight, that's for sure."

Bob looked thoughtful. "You think it's possible they actually did want to be with us, that they didn't actually plan to roll us?

Then, when we all passed out, they just went through our pockets and did what came naturally?"

Jim shook his head. "Sure, Bobby, that must have been it. And maybe the Tooth Fairy's real, too. You make sure and put a quarter under your pillow tonight, if you even have one left." He cackled, enjoying himself, then added, "But be sure to do it with confidence—the Tooth Fairy can sense fear."

Bob cuffed him on the side of his head. "Shut the hell up."

I suddenly sat up and looked at Jim. "Did they get your car keys? Is it gone?"

Jim gasped and felt around in his pockets. "Oh no! My Dad will kill me!"

"You dipshit!" Bob threw some sand at Jim. Jim ducked it and grinned. Bob turned around to me. "He's only kidding—the car's fine."

I flopped back down and closed my eyes. "Please, nobody say, 'I was only kidding' for the next few months, if you don't mind! I'm full up."

*　　　*　　　*

We never mentioned the incident afterwards, as far as I can remember. I guess it went into the "live and learn" bin for all of us, self-explanatory and unremarked. But then, that's how getting to adulthood is, mostly, for all of us: you make a fool of yourself, you learn from it, you make a different kind of fool of yourself, you learn from that and so on.

So what did I learn from getting rolled on Santa Monica beach under a red sky? Well, even being taken seriously by a grown woman for a few minutes grew up a part of me, right then and there. Even if it was all a big con job. For a woman to hike up her skirt and show me her stockings, to stand and twirl around and around with her until I was dizzy, to be close enough to smell her sweet, boozy breath as I kissed her hard and to have her blue eyes look back at me, even in mock attraction, moved me a few steps down the road to the man I finally became.

Sure, Sally Lee left me with a hickey, a hangover and empty pockets, but that's okay, because those things all pass. Because when it comes right down to it, the real glory of crazy nights like this when you're a kid isn't about reality anyway; it's about possibilities—and memories.
And those you get to keep forever.

Red sky at night.
I guess maybe that old saying isn't so wrong after all.

Not Knowing

In America, we're supposed to *know*. We're supposed to be decisive, not wishy-washy; certain, not wimpy; active, not passive. Americans figure out what they want, and then they go get it. You hear it all the time, witness the iconic Nike slogan: "Just do it."

Of course, that's understandable in advertising. How many shoes, cars or widgets would a company sell with the slogan "Gee, it's all so confusing"? Or how about a political candidate who campaigned on "I do try to get it right—but then that's not always possible"?

We're supposed to be sure. We want to be told that a product is the best, period, or that a candidate is the greatest, period.

In the movie *U-571*, the head enlisted man lectures his captain, who has just been indecisive in front of the men:

"This is the Navy, where a commanding officer is a mighty and terrible thing—all knowing, all powerful...Those three words, 'I don't know', will kill a crew, dead as a depth charge...The skipper *always* knows what to do, whether he does or not."

Makes sense, maybe—in war. But do we have to live our lives as if we're at war? Do we all have to act like politicians, strutting around doing "great" all the time, pretending we know exactly what we're doing, definitive in our choices, and "weak" if we are confused, mistaken or not aggressive enough?

Years ago, George Carlin based a whole comedy routine on this, when he compared football to baseball:

"In football the object is for the quarterback, also known as the field general, to be on target with his aerial assault, riddling the defense by hitting his receivers with deadly accuracy in spite of the blitz, even if he has to use the shotgun. With short bullet passes and long bombs, he marches his troops into enemy territory, balancing this aerial assault with a sustained ground attack that punches holes in the forward wall of the enemy's defensive line.

In baseball, the object is to go home! And to be safe! I hope I'm safe at home!"

A funny routine. We laugh, particularly as men, because we can immediately recognize the militaristic, macho imperative under which we all labor, whether we admit it or not, and whether we ascribe to it or not. It is ingrained in our society and in all of us. The pot is constantly being stirred as we are reminded of our shared mythology: Our forefathers came here for freedom, to get away from the ingrown, hierarchical and effete British ways. We don't depend on others but get things done on our own. We fight at the drop of a hat because we know what we stand for, and we'll defend it to the last man. We know what's right and what's wrong, and we know what to do about it.

When there's a problem, we identify it, assess it and take immediate action: we know, and then we act.

Sound familiar? I constantly run across new therapy patients who ask the following questions about therapy, as if I am a personal trainer, or a physician treating the mumps:

"Exactly what are we going to do? Give me details."

"How long will this take? I don't want to get involved with anything that takes a long time."

"What can I read to make it go faster? What exercises can I do at home, what assignments? I need to get this thing over with."

But "this thing" is *them*! And the "it" in "make it go faster" is their own personal development! This way of thinking reduces a person to a defective product that needs to be fixed, and fixed quick. This way of thinking is fostered and encouraged by methods of therapy, self-help books and websites that are "sure" about what they do and certain that it will work for you. In fact, therapists are encouraged to "market" themselves (or their practice) in this manner:

"Find a specific niche and fill it."
"Brand yourself."
"Do solution-based, short-term therapy." (Not dithering, time-consuming therapy).
"Use proven, scientifically-validated therapeutic techniques."
"And of course, use Best Practices!" (The most terrifying, unassailable and over-hyped words in the medical lexicon).

Simply Google "Depression" and you come up with "The most proven techniques for fighting depression." Wow, not only proven, but *most* proven—impressive!
But consider this: every breakthrough, every new idea, every realization, must come after confusion or simply not knowing. There has to be unsureness and not knowing before there can be a higher order of integration. You rarely move from absolute certainty to any new realization, because you don't have to, since you (purportedly) already *know*, right? There is no reason to explore any further if you know it all, if you've already reached a final and complete understanding of the situation, or of your opinions, or of yourself.

So, uncertainty and confusion are mandatory for growth in any realm. They say that Einstein was the one who discovered relativity because he was the one who could tolerate "not knowing" for the longest, without coming to premature and incomplete conclusions, based on what "we (already) know."

The search for better, faster methods of treating human beings is laudable of course, and can bring relief to some people, some of the time. When I started my practice years ago, the standard attitude of a new patient was, "Okay, doc—so what do we do?" People didn't have access to the Internet when I started. There was no Googling "Therapy" in order to read up on techniques and proven techniques, much less most-proven techniques. People knew they felt bad and needed help. They had managed to find you somehow, some way, and you helped them. Sometimes I think those days weren't so bad after all. At least they had gotten to you because someone had said, "Hey, this guy is good," not "This guy does DBT" (or CBT, EFT or psychoanalysis). Not because these approaches don't have a great deal to offer, but because, in fact, "research shows" that to a great extent, *who* utilizes the technique is as important as the technique itself.

Much of what I've said above comes down to this: therapy patients (like other human beings) like to feel in control. They like to know what's going to happen, and when, and how. They want to know, not guess. To be sure, not doubtful.

Well, here's a news flash: therapists want to feel in control, too. People are complicated, unpredictable and changeable. Look, imagine having someone come to you for help. They are troubled, scared and probably a little desperate. They have already tried to improve things themselves. They have tried to use willpower, and they may have read numerous self-help books about their problem. They have talked to friends about it. They want help, now. They don't want to spend a lot of money and they don't want to spend a lot of time. The problem has most likely already taken a big chunk out of their lives and their potential happiness.

They tell you their story, then they look straight at you and say, "So, can you help me?"

You nod (looking confident, you hope).

But they're only warming up:

"How? And exactly what will you do to me? And exactly how long will it take? And, oh yeah, how much will it cost me?"

Imagine being the therapist at that moment. To some extent, they're putting their life in your hands, and they want (and deserve) answers. After all, they've already gotten a sack full of advice from friends, *Better Homes and Gardens, Omni, Workout Illustrated,* self-help books and the Internet. So now, finally, at long last, weary and anxious, they've come to you: The Real Deal. It's put-up-or-shut-up time.

So I ask, how would *you* feel? Well, if you're like most people, you'd want a *technique,* a *method.* A sure-fire approach, a proven one, a *most* proven one, if you could get it. Maybe even a (trumpets, please) Best Practice.

So therapists, too, want to be sure. It's hard to face someone and *not know.* After all, the old reliable medical model, from which we are all descended, will tell you that the patient has a specific disorder, and in case you're not sure about that, just check the Diagnostic and Statistical Manual, Version V (it's important to use Roman Numerals, like the Super Bowl—that way you know it's a big deal); the patient's "condition" is in there somewhere, for sure.

So now as the therapist you're finally on safe ground, because you not only know what you're going to do for them (your proven technique, remember?), you even know what condition they've got (don't worry—it's got a long, impressive number, and that's reassuring).

We're all suckers for sureness, for knowing. It's less scary and it gives us a form of security (hey, even false security is better than nothing, right?). As a therapist, it can feel, well, more professional. Most non-physician therapists have had the uncomfortable experience of talking to a patient's psychiatrist or family physician, the one who is licensed to dole out the medication. If they're even willing to talk to you—a non-physician—at all, they want to hear "the goods" and they want it in quick sound bites.

You want to say, with crisp efficiency, "I feel we're talking Bipolar I here, with a possible secondary Adjustment Reaction," not, "This guy doesn't seem to know himself at all—I mean, he undermines everything he tries to do, and, well, he just seems to sit there waiting for, you know, something." The latter would likely be followed by a sharp, disdainful silence, roughly translated, "And exactly what am I supposed to do with that, buddy? And by the way, where do you people get your training, if any?"

So, you want to have a technique, or approach, or method, going for you, and you want to know what they've "got." And they want you to have a proven technique or method, and they want you to know what they've "got".

So it's understandable why proven methods and diagnostic slots are so prevalent. Almost every young, or new, therapist I've ever had as a patient or a supervisee wanted to know exactly what to do, to fit in with a "school" of treatment, and to know how to slot their patients into diagnostic categories. They want to know who they are, and they want to know what to do.

This reminds me of a patient I worked with for years. He had been an engineer, and a good one, but he found it emotionally unfulfilling. Partly because of his therapy, he became interested in becoming a therapist himself, and over a period of years, he completed studies at a top psychology graduate program. He specialized in a behavioral technique that utilized a form of hypnosis for treating phobias and panic attacks. He prided himself on being more scientific than I, much more specific and exact in his approach, and he enjoyed pointing out to me that I was a throwback, groveling around in the dark ages of psychotherapy.

One day he was describing to me the treatment of a particularly difficult "case" of panic attacks with a male patient whom, I observed to myself, he seemed to enjoy and even identify with. At one point, he said, "Last time, we were in the middle of a session, and he kind of looks at me like we're, you know, friends. And the funny thing is, I could feel it too. I mean, I continued the procedure appropriately and everything, but I got a weird feeling that this other thing had a lot to do with what was happening. You know, like a wild card." With that, my patient looked at me in apparent confusion.

I smiled and said, "Uh oh, looks like you were busy doing a technique and a relationship broke out."

All responsible therapy has to have structure and even some technique; therapy is not just, "Let's hang out and see what happens." But all responsible therapy also has to leave room for surprise, creativity, relationship and "not knowing," because human beings are not the mumps, or an ingrown toenail, for which exact, repeatable treatments are known.

I understand the market forces that want to push therapy in that direction. It would be great, I suppose, if, after taking a course in a particular treatment modality, all therapists would be able to help their patients, regardless of their own personal shortcomings or the particulars of the patient's problems. It would be wonderful, I guess, if, through some exact measure of treatment efficacy, therapists would be able to show that their treatment modality actually was better, that their prowess as therapists was demonstrably superior, perhaps even "most proven."

But people are complex and complicated, and fortunately or unfortunately, when treating psychological problems, one size does not fit all. There are factors in play that mitigate against the repeatability of an approach from patient to patient, or easy slotting of problems by the numbers, or even Roman numerals. For example, there is the immediate sense of personal compatibility, or not, between a patient and the therapist.

What if, when the patient walks into the room for the first session and starts talking, it feels like cats and dogs? What if the person reminds you of your Aunt Minnie, the one who always gave you an icy stare and treated you like a subhuman? Or your ex-spouse, the one who cheated on you, spent all the money, then kidnapped your child? Of course, as therapists we are trained to be "objective," to put aside our personal prejudices and we all do our best to do so, but in the cases above, or related situations, doesn't the patient perhaps deserve someone who does not have to overcome these things to be with him or her?

So, if you're being honest with yourself, you are unsure about whether you are the right person for the job, or maybe about whether you can work with this particular problem. But we are supposed to be sure, to know. How can we not know and still be a good therapist? But the truth is, you don't know, and how can you expect the patient to have the courage to face the unknown when you can't, or won't?

How do you not know and still go forward? Well, there are at least three possible approaches:

1. Ignore the feelings, trust your "technique" and blast forward, hoping it all works out, and that the feelings are irrelevant wild cards.

2. Refer the person to someone else, someone who, perhaps, would be more compatible or less triggered by the patient.

3. Hold the issues (i.e., the possible incompatibility, or the feeling of being out of your depth) lightly, but importantly, and continue ahead, watching (inside and out) for what happens next. This way, you're like a tennis player awaiting the serve: nimble, balanced and ready to move in whatever direction is needed.

Approach #3 is exactly what I did with a very difficult person I used to work with. He was an overwhelming, force-of-nature type: very insecure, very loud, very sure of himself, a "type A, alpha male," in his own words. Even though he was very bright (he dropped "Harvard" bombs on me at least three times in the first hour), he had been fired from several jobs in recent years, each time for his personality, not his work per se.

The first time he came in, it was clear he hated being there, in the position of a supplicant (his word)—that is, not in control and having to depend on me. He quickly tried to take control, criticizing my office and my education ("So, no Ivy League for you, eh? Ha ha, what did you major in? Remediation?")

Once he had gotten those preliminary shots out of the way, he began his interrogation:

"So, what do you have to say for yourself?"

At this point, I was angry and a little overwhelmed. I truly wanted to say, "I don't know. I guess I haven't had enough remediation," but I couldn't join him in his game of "Who's the top dog?" if I wanted him to improve. I could feel the intensity of the forces that were driving him: the insecurity, the fear of being in a subordinate position ("one down"), and what he must have gone through to bring himself to seek help. But most of all, I could see he was trapped in an inner world of *always* having to know, like a dinosaur stuck in the tar pits. If he lured me into competing with him, then even if I "won" we would both lose.

I knew my next statement could make or break the whole enterprise. I took a deep breath. "I don't know what I have to say for myself, but I would like to help you. I'm not sure if I can, but I'd like the chance to try."

He snorted in disgust, but then looked down and cleared this throat. His foot stopped wiggling impatiently for a moment and, still looking down, he said, "Well, at least you aren't pretending to be God in his heaven, like the others."

"Oh, you've seen others?"

"Yeah, *experts*." He named a couple of well-known local practitioners. His foot started wiggling again. "At least they're supposed to be."

I could feel the air in the room being let out, a little at a time. It felt like a relief to me, though his face was falling. He had given me an opening, a bone, though he probably didn't realize it then, and I wanted to capitalize on it without alienating him.

"Wow, you must be pretty far gone, if even the experts can't help you." Oops—had I gone too far?

His foot stopped again, and he gave a reluctant chuckle and smile, behind which I could see, for the first time, a vulnerable young boy. "Wise ass," he said, standing up to take off his fancy blazer with the coat-of-arms buttons on it (his first layer of armor) and settle in for a while.

"Fair enough," I replied.

We had begun our journey.

The "I don't know" (a.k.a. inadequacy) had been flying around the room like a hot potato before I first spoke, waiting for someone to grab it. Once I caught it, with that, "if I can" opening, we were in business. Now, we both "didn't know," but we had non-verbally agreed to not know together, wherever it took us.

Eventually, much of the pain that was locked up behind his superior attitude came to light, and he was able to be less defended, in front of both himself and me. His behavior in the world became more flexible and fitting to the actual situation, and, importantly, he began to have more space for other people's needs and feelings, so that his intelligence and perceptiveness could become a tool instead of a weapon.

He could say, "I don't know," and he could appreciate it without disdain when others didn't know. And when you can do both of these things, you can get to places beyond the known—places where only creativity, imagination and heart can take you.

Grow Up, But Stay Small

The other day I had a weird experience. True, it was an experience I've had many times before, but for some reason this time it struck me differently. Maybe because I'm getting older, maybe because I'm getting more grandfatherly. Maybe because as you age, you tend to hold on more tightly to the familiar, to the old days and what has become so precious.

A patient whom I've been working with for a while had her last session before she embarked upon a long trip that somehow I knew would be transformative.

As she got ready to leave, I found myself saying, "See you on the other side."

She cocked her head at me and said, "Yes, and it may really *be* the other side."

What did all that mean? I don't know. I just know that something compelled me to use that phrase, "the other side"—some part of me that knew something that I didn't consciously know, until I said it. And she clearly got it and responded in kind.
It was one of those magical moments that give you a little zing up your spine.
What did I know? I'm not positive. I just knew that she would be different when I saw her next. Different in a good way, an expanded way.

And that's great.

But it's also hard.

Anyone who's had children knows what I mean. You work hard day and night to get your kids through their youth, to help them grow up, to reach those all-important milestones: first day of pre-school (oh, the heart-rending cries!); first day of "real" school; first sleep-over at a friend's house; the Halloween costumes, changing through the years; junior high; high school; dates; driving; broken hearts; homework; tests, term papers; sex; college; and then, leaving.

I often tell the over-involved parents I work with that you have to think of yourself as a mother lion, nursing your cubs, catching their food for them, teaching them to hunt with you, hunting on their own, and finally, leaving.

Leaving—that's always the primary goal, the purpose of the whole thing.

So I tell the parents that, and they get it, and they try. They do the right thing and let go; let go of the baby they gave birth to, let go of the expectations, the hopes and dreams they have, let go of the closeness they felt with that sweet, innocent little bundle of softness they brought into the world. They try to let go of it all.

But I know how hard it is.

And every parent knows exactly what I'm talking about when I say that every step toward growing up, every step toward leaving, is hard. No matter how proud you are, or how glad, it's still hard.

You want to make a deal with the child, or with fate, or God: Can't there be two of my child? Let my "baby" stay the way she is, always be that cute, that close to me, that precious, while the "other one" grows up, as I want her to?

Can't there be two? One for me, and one for the world?

Kids are always embarrassed and annoyed when parents drag out the photo album to show family members, or new girlfriends, or grandchildren, pictures of Little Johnny or Joanie in childhood.

Mind you, "Little Johnny" may now be the forty-five-year-old own-er-operator of a fleet of cement mixers. He may have five kids of his own, a big mortgage, tax problems, arthritis and a cocaine habit.

It doesn't matter; he'll always be Little Johnny to them.

He'll always be Little Johnny because those early days of connection and innocence are a *big deal* to parents. To be that involved, that needed, that close to a fellow creature is a rare and miraculous thing. I mean, what else do you do in life that's more important? It informs and shapes every aspect of your life, and every aspect of your life affects the child: your job, your marriage, your hobbies, your interests, how you feel about your life, your friends, your own past life as a child.

They all matter; they all form the child, because to your child, you are the only game in town. He or she is watching you intently, to find out what life is all about, to find out if things are okay, and always wondering, wondering:

What do you really think of me?
Do you want me here?
Do you love me?
Am I a joy, or a pain in the neck?
Do you like me, or just put up with me because you have to?
Are we alike?

Notice that every one of those questions has "you" as the focus. To the child, you are her everything, her pole star, the one constant in life: you, you, you. And that's heady stuff for anybody—to be that important, that much of a big deal, to somebody who really matters to you. Aside from being in love, that's the only time in life that one can matter that much to another person.

Sure, it's a lot of responsibility, but then it's also a lot of power and importance.

Okay, for a moment let's get back to my patient who's leaving on a long trip.

What does all this have to do with her?

Well, a lot, actually. If you're being honest with yourself, and you give a damn as a therapist, you begin to feel about your patients some of the things a parent feels about a child. After all, if the core of "transference" is that patients are projecting onto you the things they felt toward their parents, and using the therapy as a crucible to work those unresolved issues out, it follows that the same is just as true of the "countertransference" the therapist feels back toward the patient. It involves many of the same things parents feel toward their children:

How am I doing?
Could I be doing more?

Are they reaching their therapy milestones? ("Baby's" first eruption of the unconscious, first being late to a session, first strong disagreement with you, first acknowledgment of the connection, first obvious pushing away from the connection, first obvious claiming of the self, first worry about losing you, first thoughts of leaving you ... and on and on.)

Countertransference in therapy, as a general phenomenon, has of course been extensively documented and discussed. But what about the "normal" parental feeling of loss, of sadness, and even of hurt, anger and abandonment, that therapists feel when patients do get better? Many therapists—and I've supervised and consulted with many in my day—aren't even aware of these feelings, because they're in addition to the typical countertransference issues. These are the personalized emotional reactions a therapist feels toward patients with whom he or she has sat so closely for long periods of time:

My God, he's a mouse, just like my cousin Saul!
My God, he's a died-in-the-wool Republican capitalist. How am I sup-
posed to be sympathetic that he's firing half his workforce to cut costs?
My God, her arrogant self-centeredness is so much like my mother it
makes me want to yell, "You're not the only person in the world!"

Yep, bet on it, therapy patients: your own therapist really does have
his or her very own authentic feelings about you, both positive and
negative feelings that often come from "some time before." Just
hope that he or she is conscientiously noting them, claiming them
in a conscious way, working with them, getting consultation about
them if needed and using this awareness to further the work.
What do I mean by using this awareness? Well, here is an example
from my own practice.

I had been seeing this big, beefy, fifty-ish guy for quite a while. He
was what you might call the hail-fellow-well-met type, a corporate
salesman who had a story or a joke for every occasion. He made
sure he "bonded" with me about everything he could dig out of me:
baseball (I'm always a sucker for being sidetracked by baseball talk,
and I have to watch myself like a hawk!), talking about our kids,
my interest in World War II (his father had won the Navy Cross as
a Marine, and he figured out, correctly, that he could really get me
going on that one), old movies (don't even get me started!), stories
about how he'd gone marlin fishing in Mexico—you get the picture.
He was charming, he was funny, and there was a pull toward just
yakking the session away with him every time, being "buds."

Except that he hadn't come to me to become best buds!
His marriage was falling apart, he was estranged from his grown
kids, he was in trouble at work, and he had no real friends, even
though, of course, everyone was his "friend." He had grown up on

a farm in rural Indiana, a lonely, isolated farm, an only child, with cold, distant parents. So his solution was to shed all that isolation by becoming a big-city backslapper, bonding and *hail-fellowing* with everyone he met, proving that he was no hick and was surrounded by people.

And the anger, the despair and the hurt? He kept it all stuffed down, deep inside. It's a well-known thing that therapy patients will present the parts of themselves that they believe in, that they know will "work," in order to get you to like them, to relate to them in ways they are familiar with, thereby maintaining control over the relationship. Unfortunately, if you allow yourself to go for these ploys, both you and the client lose out.

Well, it was like that with this man and his big personality: if he could get me to hang out and "chill" with him, listen to his stories, laugh at his jokes and be charmed by his charisma, then he was on his own turf. But he came to me because always being on his own turf wasn't working! He was alone, isolated, in trouble and failing, at work and home.

So I had to head him off at every turn, frustrating and ultimately infuriating him. Every time he would launch into another story, I would say, "But what's happening right now, here?" When he would try to lure me into the weeds by talking about the time he met Willie Mays, I (reluctantly!) had to drag him back by saying, "We're not here to talk about Willie Mays."

At first, he would just try another tack—a better story, a funnier joke. Then, when he saw that that wasn't going to work, he would lapse into sullen silence, looking at his watch (translation: "I've got better things to do, and a lot better audiences than this!").

One day, he finally said, "Look, whatever your game is, I don't know how to play it."

I said, "Of course you don't. You're not here to practice what you do know how to do. You're here to work on things you *don't* know how to do. Are you willing to trust me enough to hang in with this for a while, and see where it takes us? I love your jokes and your stories. And, believe me, I'd love to talk about Willie Mays all day long, but it wouldn't do a thing for you. I think you're worth more than that, a lot more. And as for 'playing my game' goes, that's not really accurate. What I'm suggesting is that we *stop* playing games—your games—and see what happens. Sure, it's uncomfortable: all you know is your game, and it works on almost everybody. Hell, it works on me, too, but there's more to you than jokes and stories, even though you don't know it. I'm telling you that *I* know it. Give me a chance to prove it. Okay?"

I held out my hand.

I wish I could say that I saved his marriage, healed his rift with his children and raised the dead. But I will say this (with apologies to baseball fans everywhere): Stan became a *man*. He actually became an organizational consultant (as he called it, a "therapist for businesses"), using his interpersonal gifts to help people forge workable and functional relationships. It was too late for his marriage, but he did eventually remarry, to a warm, kind woman with whom he achieved genuine closeness.

He isn't "alone in a crowd" anymore, and though nowadays everyone isn't his best friend, he does have a few real friends, whom he doesn't feel he has to entertain constantly.

So, what about the woman patient I talked about, the one who's going off on a trip that I know will change her?

Like a doting parent with a child who's growing up, I want there to be two of her: one to be the person I have come to know, respect and treasure, and the other to be the one who goes off, has great adventures, expands her life in wonderful ways and maybe comes back to teach *me* a few things!

But regardless of what comes next, I will always have the "first one" in my heart—the things we went through, the demons she faced, her journey to the "starting gate."

She's at the starting gate of her great adventure.

If you listen closely, you can hear the trumpets playing "Call to the Post."

And . . . they're off!

See you on the other side.

The Professor Earns Tenure

"Well," she said, as her roaming eyes found my framed diploma, "doc-tor." The word dripped with acerbic acid. "I'm not entirely sure that I even care to be in your purview."

Wow, I wasn't even aware that I *had* a purview. But all the same, I felt kind of proud that she thought I might. Autumn Ariel Auchincloss, Ph.D., classics professor at UC Berkeley, had been referred to me by Suzy Rogers, a long-ago client of mine—also a Berkeley professor. Suzy swam at the same club as Dr. A, and so she had a ringside seat for the spectacle of Autumn's weight loss, which had been consistent and considerable over the past year-and-a-half.

Suzy had approached her in the club locker room a few weeks earlier, and braving Dr. A's electrified grid of a persona, said, "Do you want to talk about it?"
"I beg your pardon? Why are you approaching me in such a manner?"
Yes, Autumn Auchincloss really talked that way, like she was on the bustle-and-pantaloon circuit, dismissing her interlocutor with an arrogant swish of her fan.
"Come on, Autumn, you've been losing weight for quite a while, and I was just wondering what's going on, and if you're seeing anybody for it." Suzy shrugged. "It's called help, in case you've never heard of it."

Bless that Suzy Rogers—you can tell *she'd* been in therapy!

But Autumn, she just snatched up her towel and bolted upright. "Have you been spying on me?"

Suzy rolled her eyes. "Yeah, Autumn, me and the NSA, we've been deep into the case for months now."
Then, as Autumn's emaciated body disappeared down the row of lockers, Suzy called out, "Look, I'm just offering a sympathetic ear. I'm here if you want to talk."

Autumn just barked, "Leave me alone!" over her shoulder as she turned the corner to the shower room.

That's where things stood for another month or so. Suzy didn't see Autumn at the club anymore after that, and found herself questioning the wisdom of having brought the whole thing up in the first place.
Then, during a break in a Humanities Department committee meeting just before the end of spring quarter, Suzy was standing at the sink washing her hands in the rest room when Autumn sidled up next to her and whispered one word. "Who?"
Suzy felt like saying, "Don't look around, I have to clear it with my operatives," but played it straight. "Dr. Gregg Bernstein. He's over near Piedmont Avenue, if that's what you're asking."
By the time Suzy reached for a hand towel from the dispenser, Autumn was off, in a streak of sensible brown tweed.

So you can begin to see what I was dealing with as I sat across from her in that first session. I could see and feel that this was going to be one of those, "I'm here; now you do the rest" arrangements, where the patient wasn't going to give up the reins, even while seemingly handing them to me.
I began carefully, willing to take responsibility, but not to buy in to the proving-myself mode that she was obviously setting me up for.

I nodded, I hoped in an amiable manner. "So, tell me why you're here today." Safe enough, though she clearly had the ability and the personality to twist and ridicule anything I said. Oh, one more thing: I had once seen a shrunken head, but her whole body looked like that, her outfit hanging on her like a child playing dress-up in mommy's clothes.

"Why, didn't Professor Rogers tell you all about me?"
Man, she could really arch an eyebrow.
I shook my head. "No, Suzy only said that you had lost some weight, and maybe wanted to talk to someone about it." I let a beat go by. "I don't talk to patients about other patients."
She shook her head in seeming disgust. "So, it's up to *me* to tell you the whole thing, is that it?"
"Yes, I guess it is at that. After all, it is your story, Autumn." I looked up from my note-taking. "I may call you Autumn, mayn't I?" (Heh heh, I'm allowed to have a little fun, right?)
She heaved a dramatic sigh of noblesse oblige. "Well, I suppose you'll get to it eventually, anyway, so ... you may as well go ahead."
I did. "All right then, Autumn, just tell me in your own words what's been going on, so I can begin to understand."
She did that eyebrow thing again. "Cliché much?"
I arched mine back, still not biting. "If you'll just continue, please."

"Well, it all started about two years ago." She stopped and looked over at me, painfully self-conscious, expecting me to twist her words, to criticize her, all the things she had tried to do to me.
I shrugged. "Well, it's better than 'once upon a time,' so please go on."
"I'm afraid it's all going to sound so ... insignificant, shall we say."
"I promise you it'll matter to me, so just do your best to keep going."
She traded legs under the brown tweed, still looking dubious.
I gave her my patented forbearing smile. "Look, if I have something

really disparaging to say, I'll get it in there, so let me take care of that end of things, okay?"

Did I detect a teensy grin? In any case, she sighed again, and began. "About two years ago, on a Friday, I was preparing to retire for the night," she looked over at me, but got nothing, "when there was a knock at the door. I put on my wrap and asked, 'Who is it?' A man's voice said, 'It's a lack of sugar, crying in the night.'" Her eyes were closed now, remembering. "Well, that wasn't very amusing, but it sounded safe enough, so I opened the door a crack, still leaving the chain on. There was a man there, holding out an empty cup. He said, 'Open up please, sugar. Or rather, 'Open up please: sugar?'

"Well, I thought that quite annoying, but said, 'Hand me the cup and I'll see what I have.' I took the cup to the kitchen and filled it up. On the way back, it occurred to me that this whole thing might just be an excuse to meet me, in which case I wasn't interested. I handed the cup to him through the doorway. 'Here you go; sweet dreams.' Before he could say anything, I closed the door in his face. I had essays to grade over the weekend, and I was tired.

"I had finally gotten back in bed when I heard, 'Knock knock!', loudly. Oh for goodness sake, now what? I straggled to the door again and opened it a crack, as before.

"The neighbor man was standing there in the hallway, his eyes narrowed to slits. 'Thank you!' he yelled, and then grabbed the outside knob and yanked the door shut with a loud slam, right in my face."

Autumn crossed her legs fiercely, arched everything that could be arched and then stared out the window for a full minute as I waited. "So, uh, what did you do then?" Sure, it was banal as eggs for breakfast, but sometimes a question is just a question.

She twisted her head back to me and spat, "What do you think? I went back to bed, hoping against hope I never saw him again."

I let the silence breathe for a while. Sure, I could have taken a what-the-hell position; I had a fare and the meter was running, so what did I care? Plus, her nastiness kind of invited *disdain ping pong,* you know, like: "Well, same to you!"

But that's not the way I play the game. Because, unlike a taxi driver, I'm not just being paid to take someone from A to B, but to make sure that by the time they get there, they've been enriched by the experience. Some people, like Autumn, make that difficult, because they fight you tooth and nail every foot of the way. But then if they were easy, they wouldn't be in therapy. So it's really more like being a cab driver who specializes in fares who hate cab drivers, and get sick in taxis! If I didn't want vomit all over my back seat, I had to drive very carefully.

On the other hand, I always do have that one ace in the hole: *they* asked *me* for help. So when they act like, "What are you doing in my life?" I can always say, "You asked me into your life!"

And when they say, "Get out of my business!" I can always say, "Your business *is* my business!"

Does all that make it any easier? Not really. But remembering those things does help me hang in there, because when someone acts like "Butt out!" and I feel like saying "Fine, you're free to leave at any time!" I do stay mindful of the things I said above, because I am the one who needs to remember that I have a right to be in "their business" even when I'm not wanted. It can be a lot harder to hang in there than it is to withdraw one's energies from the whole project. But as a therapist, digging in my heels in the face of hurricane-force winds is sometimes what I'm being paid to do.

I was still competing with the view out the window for Autumn's attention, but my next line was a gimme. "So, I take it you did end up seeing him again?"

Slowly, she turned her head in my general direction, but with a blank stare. "Uh, what? What did you say?"

"I said, I gather you did end up seeing him again."

Still blank.

"Him, as in the not-very-funny sugar man?"

She snapped back to the room. "Oh, yes . . ." she gathered herself now, along with her arrogance. "Well of course I saw him again; why else would I be here?"

I tried not to roll my eyes, but not very hard. "Please go on Autumn, so that all of us can know what happened."

This was it, the in-or-out moment that comes for every therapy patient. Either she was going to go down that road with me, or play games and then blame me because "nothing happened."

"Looking back, I guess I was already headed for the edge of the cliff by the time he left that first night." She stole a glance out the window again, and then kind of slumped and gave up fighting it. "I barely slept after he slammed the door in my face. It seemed like every time I closed my eyes, all I could see was his eyes, drilling through me, with that ... that ... expression."

"What expression?"

"Like he owned me or something." She actually looked me in the eye for the first time. "It's so blasted embarrassing, even to tell ... you know ... you."

I couldn't help laughing a little.

She added, "Oh no, I don't mean that you're inconsequential or anything, just that, well, even telling a therapist, it all seems ... more than faintly ridiculous, and a bit ... sordid." She tugged her brown tweed skirt down over concentration-camp knees, then twisted her neck scarf back and forth like a little girl.

I was at bat, but all that was called for was a sacrifice bunt. "I don't really see what's so ridiculous about developing a crush on . . ."

"A *crush*? You call that a crush?"

Arrogant/vulnerable, arrogant/vulnerable—we were doing the UC professor two-step. But that was okay; I knew it well, Horatio. I continued. "At this point, I don't really know what to call it. Why don't you fill me in on how far it went, I mean, beyond a crush?"

She hung her head. "Humiliation ... degradation ... mortification . . ." Roget's death-spiral. "Submission ... domination . . ."

She seemed played out, so I finished the litany. "Malnutrition ... starvation ... emaciation?"

She gave a mirthless cackle and pulled her blouse away from her body. There was a lot more blouse than body. "Well it would be pretty silly to deny it, wouldn't it?"

We sat in silence again, then she licked her lips and cut to the chase. "Do you think I have a death wish?"

I smiled. "I wouldn't say a death wish, more like an I-don't-want-to-go-on-like-this wish."

Autumn nodded in acknowledgment, then bowed her head, and it struck me that she looked like a madonna. Then the light caught some streaks in her hair that I had never seen before. It didn't surprise me, but it pleased me. At times like this, when a person is becoming more human right in front of your eyes, special touches like this often seem to make their appearance, like, "Can I come out, now?"

This emboldened me to take a chance—a risk that she was ready to drop another layer of her defenses and connect more deeply with me. I said, "You know, you remind me of a story. I used to run a group home for teenage girls who were runaways and what they called 'beyond parental control.' Well, one day I was working with one of the girls when she was in the process of changing like this, confiding in me and becoming more vulnerable, and I said, 'There's something happening to you.'

"The girl considered it for a moment, then her face lit up and she said, 'Oh yeah, you mean like the Velveeta Rabbit?'"

Autumn laughed, really laughed, right out loud, and I guess I don't have to add that as she did, even more beauty showed through.

We were a team, and brown tweed was on its way out.

Of course, a lot more happened as time went by, and we plowed through what was behind the humiliation, the degradation and the mortification. But once inner beauty shows itself, the rest is all just details. Therapy is a lot like slowly and painstakingly untying a knot: experiences and emotions become entwined and locked together so that they are not subject to change. Like a knot, the more you pull the ends, the tighter the knot becomes. So the job of the therapist is to gently, carefully, loosen things up until there is no more knot, and the underlying emotions are once again free to flow and be acted upon by normal experience.

In Autumn's case, there was an arrogant, unavailable professor father in her background, who lashed out at her unpredictably, criticized her for everything and therefore made her desperate to please him, which she could only do by intellectual accomplishments. And even then not very often, or very much.

So she grew up haughty and removed—a chip off the old block—until the sugar man appeared, fitting the old pattern like a key in a lock. He degraded, controlled and debased her until there was literally not much left of her, then discarded her like the pile of bones she had become.

One of the most destructive aspects of this type of experience is not just "what happened" itself, but the feeling of losing control over your own behavior, the feeling of *How could I have let this happen to myself?* You feel that you can no longer trust yourself, that someone, or something else, other than you, is in control of your life. And if you can't even trust yourself, there is no place to live your life from.

So the primary task we faced was to restore a sense of authorship, a sense that Autumn was running her own life.

As time went on and trust in self was restored, and trust in me was ventured, Autumn did become more and more herself. And as often happens, the qualities that had once been off-putting and harsh, morphed into softer, richer versions of themselves. The arrogance became something close to stateliness, the underlying insecurity became humility and the arched eyebrows became playful punctuators of mood and tone.

The last time we saw each other was just before Autumn moved to New York to pursue the peripatetic life of a young, tenure-seeking professor. (Of course I just had to say, "Autumn in New York" to her, which got an especially arched eyebrow!) I told her I was proud of her, but by then she knew all that stuff, so it was mostly a lot of nodding, well-wishing and remembering the times we'd shared together, good and bad.

Toward the end of the session, I asked her to kneel on my office carpet, and then I touched her head ceremoniously with my pen and intoned:

"By the purview vested in me, I do hereby confer upon thee Therapy Tenure, with all rights and privileges pertaining thereto."

We both laughed, and then she was off.

I heard from her a bit now and then, but no big deal. Then, come Christmas time, I received a package from New York with no return address or name on it. I saved it for Christmas morning, as I always do, and after I'd opened my other presents, I turned to the mystery gift, if it even was a gift. Well, after I pulled off the brown postal wrap and then the gift wrap, I peeled away all the tissue paper and lo and behold, there it was.

My family looked at me like I was crazy.

After all, what kind of a dope would go all misty-eyed over a box of Velveeta?

Do You Believe in Magic?

One's destination is never a place, but rather a new way of looking at things.

—Henry Miller

Everyone in therapy wants to change. We hear it every day, from new patients and old. They come in with a problem, that frequently sounds like this:

"I'm _____ (fill in a way of being), but I want to be _____ (fill in a "better" version of way of being). Where do we start?"

It reminds me of an old comic strip I used to read, in which there was a character who obtained plastic surgery. I can't remember whether the person wanted to hide or just look better, but I do remember the premise was this: plastic surgery can make you look any way you want. All you have to do is point to the right picture, and let's go!

In other words, magic. People love magic. Another favorite magic fantasy is hypnosis. I can't tell you how many people have said to me, "Can't you just hypnotize me, and when I come out of it, I'll be different?" Magic lurks everywhere in our society, but we don't always call it magic.

Think about these claims:

"Lose ten pounds from your thighs in two days, without having to diet!"

"Send \$29.99 for step-by-step instructions on how to have power over other people!"

"Make up to \$5999 per month, from home: no sales, no calls, no products!"

"Take my weekend seminar, and never be shy again!"

I love magic, too—heck, most art is based on magic, on teleportation; it *transports* you. For two hours, I can watch a movie and be somewhere else. For days I can read a book and be someone else. I can watch a music video and be swept up in the energy, sadness, joy or wildness of a song. We all want to be somewhere else, someone else, and we want life to be different than it is—better. We want all things to be possible, and in art or fantasy, all things *are* possible.

We don't want to have to work for it. We want it good, and we want it now.

Sounds like a child, doesn't it?

"Mommy, I want a pony!"

In a movie or a book, as soon as little Johnny says, "I want a pony," we know that somehow, some way, he's getting a pony. In real life, not so much. One of the things we like about movies and books is that the story makes sense. It *goes* somewhere, almost like there is a God watching over the whole story, because there is: the director, and the writer!

We want there to be a God, a higher power, watching over us, too, but all too often, when a child in real life says, "I want a pony," the response is, "Do you realize we live in a city?" or "Do you think we're made of money?"

And this is assuming there is even anyone there to listen. More often than not, and so very unlike the movies, our wishes are met by the other person's being preoccupied, distracted, or even cynical. We express a wish, and we're simply told, as in the old English nursery rhyme, "If wishes were horses, beggars would ride."

So we learn that to wish for something unrealistic leads to being mocked, put down or ignored. We learn that this is for "babies" (though for many of us, it wasn't even okay as babies!).

Why are people so mean about irrational wishes? Here are a few possibilities:

First, many people have never had anyone treat their irrational wishes with respect, either, so they have no role model for this. Also, if you didn't get something yourself, you often have no way of accepting that others may need it.

Second, people feel that to "encourage" irrational wishes is to lead the child (or person) down the wrong path; i.e., that our job as parents is to teach the child about real life.

Further, it makes parents (especially those who actually care) feel inadequate: Jeez, now what? How am I supposed to get this kid a pony?

And feelings of inadequacy lead to anger: You made me feel inadequate, so to show that I'm not inadequate, now I have to make your wish seem ridiculous and paint you as a spoiled baby.

In fact, the skillful handling of irrational wishes is one of the most important jobs of a parent. Unfortunately, most parents are ill prepared for the task. Consequently, the child learns to ditch all the elements of "wishful thinking," and it's a case of throwing out the baby with the bathwater, because in wishing lies great power.

Almost all meaningful change starts with a wish:

"Why can't I be taller?"
"I want to be rich and famous."
"I want to be young again."
"I want to love my life."

Yes, these may all be irrational wishes, or at least not reachable by mere wishing (i.e., magic). But is the recognition of irrationality the "end of the line" for a wish? It doesn't have to be, and much is lost if it is. Because any wish, even if it's a wish for magic, can be just the beginning of the line and not the end, as most therapists can attest to. Wishing, hoping, dreaming, are direct pipelines to what's inside of us, and fantasy is one of the most profound (and useful) of the signal qualities that sets us apart from the rest of the animal kingdom.

But how do we use it?

As I mentioned earlier, parents spend an inordinate amount of time drumming into their kids that they have to be realistic in life. So it's safe to assume that most people, by the time they're even young children, actually know the score:

You can't attain anything without work.
Money doesn't grow on trees.
Don't wish your life away.
Wanting something, or even deserving it, doesn't mean you're going to get it.

Okay, so they know these things on some level, but what does that actually mean? In most cases, what it means is that while they've learned these (admittedly) valuable lessons about reality, they may also have learned to suppress their irrational wishes entirely, maybe even lose touch with them.

Then what?

For most people, having ditched everything irrational, all that's left is the humdrum, the ordinary, the boring, i.e., "going straight." But somehow, a lifetime of being good, of being realistic, of not wanting more than you can have, of settling for the regular stuff, doesn't seem that thrilling, exciting or worth fighting for.

And there's something else, too: living life that way doesn't seem to fit with your insides. You hear a great song, see a great movie, read a great book, and you feel something inside you, something above and beyond the normal, the safe, the regular. It makes you want more out of life than just playing it by the book and being good, and it makes you want more out of yourself than just falling into that long, gray line behind everyone else.

And what about those *weird* feelings that come up inside, especially when you're young, the ones that no one really talks about? Wanting to hurt yourself, or other people? Sexual feelings or desires that aren't the norm? Crazy thoughts about all kinds of things: running away, experimenting with drugs and alcohol, living an alternative life, being different? You've been taught that these things are ridiculous, wrong, bad. Yes, you understand all that, but the thoughts, the wishes, are still there. Are you supposed to just squash them, push them away and march along with the crowd, acting normal, keeping your secrets inside?

Whom do you talk to about it? Your school guidance counselor, the nice one who's trying to get you on track for college and a good future?

Nope.

Your parents, who would just be worried, or mad, that you're going against everything they've tried to instill in you all these years?

Nope.

You keep it to yourself. Maybe space out, alone in your room late at night, trying to get away from all the pressures to conform.

And if you're already an adult, already grooved into regular life, what do you do? Maybe you drink alone in the living room, late at night. Maybe you have an affair, and then feel crummy about it. Maybe you try to lose yourself in sports, activities, interests, raising kids, work.

And maybe, just maybe, you see a therapist, to figure out, *What's wrong with me?*

Well, very often what's "wrong" with you is that your dreams are under lock and key, exiled deep in a bunker inside of you. And even if you somehow got access to them, you wouldn't know what to do with them anyway. You're not really going to run off and join the French Foreign Legion, or become a hobo, or immediately act on any of your dreams anyway, so being in touch with them just hurts, right?

But a therapist knows what to do with your dreams. When we can haul them out together and take a look at them in a safe and accepting environment, they can work for you in ways that might surprise you. It is possible to lead a life that doesn't feel staid, constricted and boring, and sometimes it isn't that different from your current life. But it requires the therapist doing what your parents couldn't: letting your dreams breathe, so that they can interact with and be affected by reality, without being mocked or squashed. They need to evolve, and, like growing a plant, this involves water (attention), good soil (a safe environment), and time.

How does this work? Well, it could look something like this:

Sometime in the mid-eighties, Terry, a big, burly guy in his early forties, came in to see me. At first glance, he looked like he could be the owner of a bustling Italian restaurant, or maybe a "mad" sculptor (a lovable mad sculptor, that is).
But what was he?
An accountant.
He told me that he came from a very difficult family background, in which his father was an alcoholic, his mother ("She was wonderful") died when he was seven, and his "mean stepmother" was

always yelling at his father for being a weakling and a failure.

So where did this leave Terry? On his own mainly, unless his father wanted someone to make a quick run to the liquor store for him when his stepmother wasn't looking. Not only did procuring a bottle of whiskey for Dad bring him a "Thanks, old boy," but even a pat on the head and sometimes a quarter: "Here ya go kid, get yourself a Snickers." When you're starving for attention, even a pat on the head and a couple of Snickers can be a big deal.

There was no planning for Terry's future, no encouragement, nothing but staying out of range of his stepmother. One day in high school, Terry was called in to the office of the school guidance counselor, the infamous Miss Schwartz. Apparently it was a requirement that every student had to see her once a year.

She was a tall, reedy woman in her fifties, and she had a reputation for being mean and scary. Terry was dreading the meeting, remembering that once Miss Schwartz had come up to him in the hallway and said, "Do you even *have* parents?" telling him that she had tried to contact them, repeatedly, for some reason, and struck out. His Dad had never been to any of his schools, not once, and his stepmother—well, it was best to keep her away from any part of his life.

He sat there quietly at Miss Schwartz's desk, while she leafed slowly through his records and his test results, until she finally put the paperwork down and looked at him, with a small, pitying expression. Then she sighed heavily and said, "Terry, here's the deal. You come from a difficult situation and you're probably on your way to nothing, but I'm going to say this anyway, because I'm supposed to offer you guidance, whether you use it or not. You're not a bad kid—not a particularly bright kid, either—but all in all, you might make something of yourself, because you're mostly quiet and you get your work done. And I'm guessing you get it all done with no help from anyone, either."

Terry squirmed in his seat, unused to being talked about at all. Even though her words kind of hurt and made him uncomfortable, he also liked it, a lot, that she was acknowledging his existence. He nodded, "Yes, ma'am."

She sighed again and continued, chewing on her pencil thoughtfully between words. "So, here's what I think. As I'm sure you've figured out by now, the world revolves around money. Now, there are two ways to get it, legally. First come the people who are smart enough to make a lot of it. Then come the people who help the smart people take care of what they've made."

She paused, chewing thoughtfully again. "I'm thinking you're the second kind, the helpers."

Terry wasn't sure if he should be insulted or grateful. They sat there in silence for a moment, until he managed to sputter, "So, what does that mean, you know, about me?"

She waved her hand at him. "Quiet, I'm thinking."

Wow, imagine that: someone was actually taking time to think about him. He knew, somehow that her next words would shape his whole life. He noticed he was holding his breath.

Finally, she tapped the pencil on her desk decisively, three times. "An accountant, I think." She paused, chewing the pencil again and looking at the ceiling. "Yes, that's it." She carefully placed the pencil back in her desk tray, with finality. "Terry, I don't know if you have it in you or not, but that's what you should shoot for. If you don't make it, well, you'll still have a college education to fall back on. And a quiet kid like you, who does his work, can always manage to scrape by."

She looked at him with a not-unkind expression. "I think we're done here."

So that was it: the gods had spoken. He was supposed to be an accountant. That is, if he was smart enough and hard-working enough to make it. If it wasn't exactly thrilling, at least he guessed she was right about that money stuff: anyone who could help the smart people who made lots of money take care of their money, would always have a job, somewhere.

Well, Terry rode that interview for the rest of his life. He attended a local community college, and then transferred to a state college, majoring in accounting. He graduated, not with honors, maybe, but then he'd had to wait tables practically full time. And eventually he went all the way through and became a CPA. He got married, had three children, owned his own home and had a German shepherd he called Miss S, in honor of you-know-who.

All in all, a "nice life."

So what did it mean that one day he walked into my office for the first time and said, "My life isn't enough"?

That his whole life was a sham, a mistake or a mess?

No. To me, it just meant that he had reached the next stage, the stage where he could take everything he'd worked for thus far (successfully) and add to it. He had enough experience now, and enough self-esteem, to recognize that fifteen minutes of guidance, given him twenty-five years before, was not enough to carry him through the rest of his life.

I didn't feel we needed to tear down Terry's life, just build on what was already there. So often, the "problem" is not the existing family relationships, or the existing job, but a person's inability to see and access what is already there, both outside and inside, and put it to good use, in a way that also preserves what they have built up over the years. For so many people, they're (unknowingly) still seeing the world from a child's eye view.

The *Wizard of Oz* is a classic example of this. Dorothy leads a (purportedly) drab life on a drab farm with drab people, until she has a kind of spiritual awakening, that enables her to "see" her life in a new, colorful, richer way than before.

If Dorothy had come to therapy at the beginning of the story, many counselors would have agreed with her initial take on the situation and recommended her leaving the farm as the solution, i.e., that she had a lot more going for her than the other people on the farm, that she had greater dreams and more potential—needs that (supposedly) couldn't have been met on the farm.

But what was the actual solution? It was Dorothy's "stepping up" to take a more empowered view of the people on the farm—her own view. Instead of being the little, passive girl who lived amongst all these adults who were beyond her ken, she (or at least her unconscious) became able to see each of them as they actually were—flawed beings, each of them needing something specific to be complete. In seeing these adults as full human beings, like herself, she was able to join them in the human race, to feel like she and they were all in the same boat. And of course, in seeing their flaws, she was able to see their true value, and her own.

She didn't have to leave the farm after all in order to be her real self: but she did need a transformative experience (*therapy*) to reach her empowered self, and to develop a truly adult life.

So, the therapist's job is to help people find, and follow, their own yellow brick road to inner consciousness and empowerment, not help them run away.

It is said, "Wherever you go, there you are," and that's true, as far as it goes. But what's more true is this: If you're not "there" here, you're not "there" *anywhere*.

Movement in space isn't the answer; movement inside is the answer. So, the next time you "wish for a pony," don't squash that dream. Take a closer look: with a little help, you might find some version of that pony! It's not magic; it's a willingness to explore, and respect, what's already there, inside you.

And Terry? Well, he's still an accountant, but after a few months of therapy, he suddenly remembered that he'd always wanted to sing in a barbershop quartet. These days, you might see Terry on the weekends in a church or a retirement home, or even on a stage, singing "Sweet Adeline" with three of his closest friends.

I went to see them once, when they won a local barbershop contest.

Terry came up to me later, a big smile on his face, and said, "It's like magic!"

Grist for the Mill

Down by the old
(Not the new, but the old)
Mill stream,
(Not the river, but the stream)
Where I first
(Not the second, but the first)
Met you,
(Not me, but you)

—"Down by the Old Mill Stream," by Tell Taylor*

The condition known as ADHD—fact or fiction?
Fact.
Ritalin and other ADHD meds—dangerous fad or helpful tools?
Helpful tools.
Good, now that we've gotten the drama out of the way, let's get down to actually talking about ADHD, and not agonizing over how many Adderalls can dance on the head of a pin, which is what much of the "discussion" about ADHD has been for decades.
I remember a time when I was on the phone with a patient's psychiatrist, and I suggested that he evaluate our shared patient for ADD (as it was then called) and possible medication.
After an ominous silence, he sneered, "There's no such thing as ADD, and if you were a therapist of any repute, you'd know that."
I said, "I'm sorry, but I couldn't disagree with you more strongly.

Aaron can't concentrate on the reading he was assigned for school, and he needs some help."

He said, "You change your tune right now, young man, or I'm hanging up this phone."

Change my tune?

I said, "Okay, how about, 'Down by the Old Mill Stream'?"

Sure enough, he hung up. Oh well, I doubt that he could have done justice to the second-lead patter that makes that song any fun at all (see above). And really, as someone wise once said (I'm pretty sure it was either Rumi or a TED talk), any psychiatrist who doesn't even offer to sing second lead on "Down by the Old Mill Stream" is not worth the paper his prescription pad is printed on.

But back to ADHD. Unfortunately, this is one of those disorders that carries special stigmas and complications, partly because the mythology surrounding it has passed into popular culture, to the misfortune of anyone who has it. It became good copy, provocatively adorning the cover of *Time* and other major news magazines. It was denigrated as an "excuse" for students who would not do their homework, an unethical bonanza for doctors who prescribed medications for it and a cop-out for anyone who was disorganized, scattered or had difficulty concentrating and staying on task. People were told if they just ate the right things, it would miraculously go away. They were assured, and scolded, that it was caused by food additives, too much sugar, too much TV or video games, not enough exercise, and other societal ills du jour.

The net result—people who have it are often ashamed and confused. They feel inferior to "regular" people, and wonder:

What's wrong with me? Why can't I read a book like other people, or get through a movie, or pay attention in class? Why can't I stop jumping around all the time? Why do I get so many parking tickets, and why can't I pay my bills, or even find my bills? Why can't I finish a term paper, or start studying before the last minute? Why does my room look like a federal disaster area? Why am I always forgetting everything? Why do I always make everyone mad? Why am I always late? I don't think I'm a bad person, but what's wrong with me? Am I stupid, lazy, emotionally disturbed or what?

Thank goodness, in recent years ADHD has been thought of less as a religious cult and more of an actual working diagnosis. The Americans with Disabilities Act helped. Now anyone with a legitimate diagnosis of ADHD can have extra time to complete tests, for example. Why? Is it because they're stupid, lazy and emotionally disturbed? No, it's because they have a brain function disorder that can actually be seen on functional brain scans (SPECT; PET). As Dr. Daniel Amen and many others have shown repeatedly for years, it can be demonstrated that, when many people with ADHD are asked to do math problems in their heads for example, activity in their frontal cortex actually can slow down, rather than speed up, as in "normal" people. This means that when confronted with certain kinds of problems in real life, including academic ones, many people with ADHD actually can't "think straight," regardless of their IQ. It means they may space out when contemplating starting a term paper, instead of making and carrying out plans to begin the paper. I have heard this phrase countless times: "I can't trust myself."

Imagine living with this:

You're talking to someone about something sensitive, and suddenly you blurt out something inappropriate.

Or you're talking to someone, and suddenly you notice they have a glazed look in their eyes because, as you suddenly realize, you've been rambling tangentially about everything under the sun for the last five minutes.

You're sitting in class, being quiet and facing front. Suddenly, everybody is getting out paper and pen, preparing to do something important. Why? You realize you've been gazing out the window for the last five minutes, though you thought you were attending to the teacher's every word.

You vow to start working on your taxes early this time, but first you're going to allow yourself just a few minutes of watching your favorite TV program. You even set the timer on your iPhone for fifteen minutes, to make sure you don't forget. You "come to" two-and-a-half hours later, wondering what the hell happened. You realize you set the timer for 8:00 a.m. instead of 8:00 p.m., your wife is yelling at you because you promised to put the dishes in the dishwasher and feed the dog, and when you finally do get to work on the taxes, you can't find the paper bag where you put all the receipts for the past year.

Your life becomes a constant storm of forgetting, failures, disappointing others, embarrassment, inability to trust yourself, and wondering: *Shoot, what was it I promised to do? It's on that list somewhere. Where is that damn list anyway—the new one, not the one that got lost somewhere in the car last week? Where's that phone number—you know, the one for that guy I was supposed to call to explain why I was late with the information he wanted, the information about, damn, what was it again?*

This—this storm of forgetfulness, this barrage of unfinished business, this litany of people mad at you—this is your life. So what do you do? You develop compensatory mechanisms to help you get through it, things most people wouldn't understand, things that are private, alone. Most all of these mechanisms are developed "in house" by people who are alone, ashamed, confused, frustrated. They are not well-known principles that are taught in school by anyone, but Rube Goldberg devices of the mind that help you get through time, that help you survive. Things like:

- Getting high on marijuana or alcohol. ("Thank God. For a few minutes or hours I can forget all my problems, slow down a little, appreciate the moment and not feel bad about myself".)

Of course, it ends up not only worsening the problems (because, though you may feel better for the short term, you have just put off real life that much longer, making returning to real life more difficult, requiring more dope and more booze), but now you have a problem with dope and booze on top of your ADHD problems. And now everyone's mad at you for that, too, requiring more dope and booze to deal with it all.

- Becoming adept at excuse-making. This is a whole internal subculture unto itself, including developing a persona where you laugh at yourself for others' benefit (while hurting inside), saying things like, "There goes Old Faithful again: every hour on the hour, I have to forget something important," or "They say I was dropped on my head a lot as a baby." You spend inordinate amounts of time trying to think up plausible excuses for things undone, things forgotten, things you "didn't have time for," although secretly you know that you wasted infinitely more time avoiding the task than you would have spent actually doing it.

- Lying to others about "what happened," and what's worse, lying to yourself. Eventually, you begin to believe your own lies and excuses and blaming, until they all run together and you can't tell them apart anymore.

- Saying to yourself, "Screw it, I don't really care anymore. I'll just be a rebel and go my own way, and damn the consequences. 'Their' world is all screwed up anyway. I don't want to be a part of it. Bunch of compulsive, anal, neat freaks and perfectionists anyway. Who the hell needs it?"

All around you, you see people doing well, doing what they're supposed to be doing, paying their bills and taxes on time, not being terrified because they might be pulled over for an expired car registration and brake lights that don't work. They're getting raises and promotions. Everyone isn't mad at them. Somehow, they seem able to do things right, do things on time, take care of business. How do they do it? Are they better than me? Smarter than me? They don't blurt things out, or embarrass themselves, or have to lie to live, or have to remember their lies so they all match up.

What's *wrong* with me, anyway?

This is usually when those who seek therapy, seek therapy. If they are young, it most likely involves school performance, the infamous "not working up to potential," and comes complete with disappointed, angry, frustrated parents who also wonder what they did wrong to produce this obstinate, maddening low achiever.

If they are adults, they come in trailing a stream of sabotaged opportunities, missed deadlines, legal troubles and wrecked relationships. Nowadays, most will add, parenthetically, after they've listed their "real" problems, "Oh, and I'm pretty sure I have ADD, too," as if they are reporting, for the sake of completeness, that in addition to cancer, they also have dandruff.

So the first thing we talk about is that ADHD isn't just something "else" you have, in addition to your real problems: it is a primary problem that affects the entire range and scope of your life, from school, to work, to relationships, to your personality and most importantly, your self-esteem, your dreams and your hopes. This is *big*, and it needs to be dealt with, if not first, then soon. We talk about how ADHD is not a moral disorder, and not a genetic propensity to being a lazy slob, a liar or a procrastinator. It is not caused by having a deprived childhood, though of course it interacts with whatever emotional problems, and whatever other disabilities, are also present. It is not about being stupid, though high intelligence can mask it until later in school, perhaps college, grad school or beyond, or the point at which the mental work required of you can't just be faked, fudged or tossed off at the last minute anymore.

So we talk about self-image, which by this time is usually down in "loser/failure" territory. Most people seem to operate on the implicit assumption that they, along with everyone else, have "free choice" in what they do. Much later, after a lot of therapy, most of them look back and see that they were in fact hobbled by emotional wounds and damaging assumptions, and that they were irrationally harsh on themselves, holding themselves to standards they couldn't possibly have reached, operating as they were with both hands tied behind their backs. But at the beginning, waving the free choice banner, they have no other option but to see themselves, personally, as the reason for their failures.

As a patient, they want to know: "Why can't I get it together, like everyone else does? Lots of people have problems, and even worse backgrounds than me, but they seem to be able to function, and live up to their potential. Why not me?"

Why not you? Because your brain isn't working right. And because your brain isn't working right, you've developed a chip on your shoulder and resistance to doing the things you can't do as well as you should (schoolwork, sitting still, paying attention, reading, being patient about anything). Plus, you believe on some level that you're some kind of a second-class citizen who's born to fail, or at least disappoint.

So we often start with education—reading (though of course reading is hard sometimes) books like *Driven to Distraction*, by Edward Hallowell, books by Daniel Amen—that show graphically the functional deficits in performance on the basis of actual brain scans, and describe the subtypes of ADHD that are suggested by these studies.

We also study books that take a creative, even refreshingly radical view of ADHD, books like *Attention Deficit Disorder*, written by Thom Hartmann (it used to be called *Hunter in a Farmer's World!*). Hartmann, the parent of an ADHD child, advances a theory that in the early days of human existence, the ADHD brain was actually optimally suited to survival in a hunter-gatherer society, when an active, ever-changing approach to interaction with the natural world was required in order to recognize possible prey and move boldly toward risk in obtaining sustenance.

We discuss possible medications that can help, and also the resistance to such help: "I shouldn't need that." "Pills are just a crutch." "I'm not that bad." "It'll make me a zombie." We talk about how the proper medications, far from making one a "zombie," can make one feel: "This is more like it—now I feel like myself; now I can use my brain, instead of fighting it all the time."

No, "pills" are not the entire answer, and sometimes they are not part of the answer at all, but they can often provide a dramatic shift in the ability to utilize what the person has—to get the car on the road, instead of being stuck in neutral, which is how it feels to many ADHD sufferers.

We also talk about ways to keep to-do lists that work. Lately, there are several apps for cell phones that are remarkably good at helping people organize their lives, not only keeping tasks in order, but reminding them of upcoming needs and helping them keep track of elapsed time. A young patient of mine says his app is like having a "smart valet" to help him address the tasks of life, without judgment or blame.

And what is the outcome of all this? Well, I'll just say that there is nothing more meaningful than having someone who was angry and resentful, disillusioned with the whole idea of doing anything with their life, sit before me and say, with tears in his eyes: "I'm not stupid, after all. I'm not lazy, and I'm not a bum. I can do things. I just have to give my brain some help, and when I do, I can accomplish all kinds of things. I'm not afraid anymore of what's going to come out of my mouth, or of what I'm going to do next. I don't wake up in the morning dreading remembering what I did, or didn't do, yesterday. I don't have to make up excuses and lies to cover my screw-ups. Do you have any idea what it's like to be able to trust yourself again?"

Turns out there's a lot more at stake in treating ADHD than proper mental functioning.
The real treasure at the end of all the work?
Self-respect.

*"Down by the Old Mill Stream" was published by Tell Taylor in 1910. He wrote it in 1908, but his friends tried to persuade him not to publish it, as they felt it had "no commercial value." Whoops, it became one of the most popular songs of the early twentieth century, sold four million copies in sheet music and is still a staple of campfires and barbershop quartets more than a hundred years later. The moral? If it feels true to you, go with it.
Self-respect.

Is Rain an
Inanimate Object?

Part One

Meagan Minor came into my life on a wistful, wispy note. That first voicemail went something like this: "Do you see people, and if so, can you see me? ... Can *anybody* see me?"

By that time I was an experienced therapist, a grizzled veteran of the outpatient therapy wars with borderlines, bipolars, obsessives, rageaholics, love junkies, hate junkies, snipers, clingers, distancers and the chronically uncommitted. To be brutally honest, most older therapists tend to get to a point where, when they hear an incoming message that sounds like trouble, or even questionable, they say to themselves, *Dude, I don't need this stuff anymore.*

But there was something about her tone of voice that was so...plaintive, so ingenuous, that I decided to give it a whirl. God knows I've always been a sucker for originals, for one-offs. So I called her back a couple hours later, and this is how the whole thing began:

Me: Is this Meagan?
Meagan: I'm not sure anymore.
Me: Not sure that you're you, or that you're Meagan?
Meagan: My driver's license says Meagan Minor. Does that help?
Me: Well it helps me, but I guess it doesn't do much for you.
Meagan: Just who *is* a person anyway? I mean, a name can only take you so far.

Me: It's a nice name, but I think I get your meaning.

Meagan: That's more than I can say. In fact, I don't think I even have a meaning.

Me: C'mon now, everyone has a meaning. How about coming in and talking it over?

Meagan: If that's what you want.

Me: (*What do you mean: what I want? You're the one who called me!... Gregg, shut up and listen.*) Yes, for now, I guess it's what I want. How about Wednesday night at eight?

Meagan: Aye, sir.

What did all this tell me? That she had "selfing" issues, that she had boundary problems, that she was unable to fully *inhabit* her own sense of personal place, that it was easier for her to accede to my wishes than to guess what her own might be, and that underneath there was probably a ton of rage and resentment. And as for personality and persona? She almost reminded me of the good old hippie days—you know, the, "I don't know anything; does anyone?" school of experience. But in any case, kind of dreamy and vague, maybe one of those who meditates and believes in Eastern no-self philosophy as a cover for actually having no self? I was already half-preparing myself—quite happily—for yoga pants, long swirling skirts, peasant blouses, and maybe, a discreet butterfly tat inside one ankle.

But wait, where did that whole, "Aye, sir" thing come in? Maybe a Navy brat, with a hard-core admiral for a father, setting off a massive rebellion that left her. . .

Blah, blah, and blah—speculation is fine, but as always, it really comes down to meeting the person with an open mind, being ready for the unexpected and a willingness to do whatever it takes. And for some reason, with her, I was ready and willing.

Whether I was able ... well, time would tell.

*   *   *

I had no idea what would greet me in the waiting room that first Wednesday, having purged the hippie concept from my mind ten minutes after that first conversation. (Well, that's not quite true; having made a sincere *effort* to.) I hadn't really asked anything about her, and anyway, I actually prefer to be surprised rather than having my mindset already established when I first meet someone. Beginner's mind—that's the goal.

And this time I was definitely surprised. Sitting there in the chair was a Navy enlisted woman in full uniform, spit-shined, squared away and shipshape.

She shot to her feet, ramrod straight, and gave an official-looking nod. "Sir."

I couldn't help emitting a small, muffled laugh. "At ease, trooper."

"Uh, we don't say trooper."

I smiled again. "Yeah, I know. It was just kind of a joke. I mean, you were so formal. . ."

She looked distressed. "Would you prefer 'doctor'?"

At that, an older woman sitting across the waiting room peered at us over her *Elle*.

Wherever this was going, it needed to be in private. "Tell you what—why don't we go back into my office, where we can continue the conversation in a more confidential setting?" I indicated the back hallway with my arm and stepped back to let her pass. But she pulled up short, indicating with her own hand, "After you, sir," with a little bow.

Hmm, by this point, "Sir" was getting a little concerned about exactly what this lady wanted from therapy. Was it going to be hippie, or squared-away Navy? Either way, it was certainly shaping up as a challenge. And I like to be challenged, and surprised.

"So, you're probably wondering what I'm doing here."

"That would be a fair assessment."

She held her purse to her stomach and started twisting the handle back and forth. "Well, it's all about the Navy."

I waited in silence.

She fiddled with her purse some more, before adding, "Oh, should I go on?"

Hoo boy. I almost said, "Permission to speak freely," but only nodded, "Yes, please go on, so I can find out what you're doing here, as you said before."

She looked puzzled, then nodded back, "Oh, you mean, just go on and tell the whole story?"

"Exactly." *What the hell?*

She took a deep breath and looked down at her dazzlingly shiny black sensible Navy shoes. "Okay then, here goes. I joined the Navy five years ago, after my father died, because I had nothing else to do, no life, no direction, nothing. You see, after my father died, there was no one to tell me what to do, and well, I heard the Navy's pretty good at that." She scanned me with intense gray eyes. "Am I boring you?"

"What makes you think that?"

"Oh nothing. I just hope I'm not taking up too much of your time. You know, like, 'Get to the point already?'"

"Meagan, you just got here. You've said maybe two sentences. Now please go on. I'm interested, really." I raised my pen again to write.

"Sure you're not mad?"

Damn, was this a *Candid Camera* stunt, or what? "No, I'm sure I'm not mad. Now please go on," I attempted a small smile, "so my pen has something to do tonight."

She ground her lips together a while, then just when I thought she might ask if someone in the *next* office might be mad, she sighed and went on. "Well, I know how to take orders, and for a long time, that was fine. In fact, for five years it was fine. But then two years ago, after I made E-3, that's when all this stuff started."

I kind of knew that E-3 indicated her enlisted rating, but wanting to make sure I knew what she meant by it, I prompted, "E-3?"

"Oh, I forgot. Well there's Recruit, then Apprentice Seaman. Then just Seaman—and that's called an E-3." She put her head down again. "And like I say, that's where the trouble started. Because the next step up is," she took a breath and looked at me with scrambled eyes, "Petty Officer."

I nodded, beginning, slowly, to get the picture. "You mean, when you go from taking orders to giving them?"

She was looking down again. "Yes, but it's more than that. It's responsibility, and leadership, and . . ." She was blinking like crazy now, fighting to stay centered. "And all those other things that I . . .that I can't do." She felt for the clasp of her purse and jammed her hand in, groping around for something. I had a pretty good idea what it was.

"Just try and stay focused on what you're telling me. You're safe; you're just sitting here with me, talking. Nobody here is asking you to do anything you can't do, okay?"

When she looked up at me, I took the opportunity to reemphasize the point, holding her with my eyes. "We're right here, right now; you came here for help, remember? I'm here to help you, not judge you or make you do things you don't want to do, or feel you can't do." Her gray eyes were still pinballing, so I took a wild chance on a mode she might understand better, adding in a stern voice, "Are we clear on that?"

That did it. Meagan took two deep breaths, and then settled down. "Yes sir, clear." For a moment she was still, and then she cocked her head at me, puzzled. "But how do we eliminate the bad parts?"

I filed away "eliminate" for later. "What do you mean, the bad parts?"

"You know, the weaknesses, the self-doubts, the termite-infested wood underneath? The rotten core?"

Now that was a new one on me: I had never heard an inadequate sense of self described as "termite-infested wood." Well, I guess maybe it's better than "foul rag and boneyard of the heart," but not by much. It started to give me an idea of how she saw herself, as a demolition project, with an inherently weak, crumbling underpinning that needed to go, inadequate and inherently no good.

"Sorry, did I upset you?"

That brought my head up. "What are you talking about?"

"Oh, just that you looked kind of overwhelmed when I said that, like maybe I'm too . . .too fouled up to help, beyond . . ."

"Beyond all recognition?"

The ends of her compressed lips might have turned up a micron or so. "Yes, sir, beyond all recognition."

But I was still chewing on that one word from a few sentences ago: "eliminate." As in, "How do we eliminate the bad parts?" Well actually, both "eliminate" and "the bad parts" worried me, because they told me she saw herself as unsalvageable and unserviceable. It reminded me of that old John Bradshaw program on PBS where he talked about the experience of shame, in which a person felt not "I made a mistake," but "I *am* a mistake."

Meagan returned to rooting around in her purse until she finally found what she had been looking for, and held it up: a pill. A tranquilizer, I guessed, some kind of "-pam," to ward off the panic. She cast her eyes around the office in flustered desperation, of course not saying a word, until I finally put her out of her misery.

"Meagan, are you looking for water, and something to put the water in?"

"Uh, yes sir: hydration."

"Then why not just say, 'Hey Gregg, get me some damn water,

please?'" (I was role-modeling, priming the pump, leading the receiver, whatever you want to call it.)

Her eyes were pinballing again. "Oh, I could never say that—not to you!"

"Why not? Who am I supposed to be: the Buddha, the Dalai Lama, or maybe, your father?" I paused one beat, then added, "And why do you need a pill now anyway? Heck, everyone's a little nervous seeing a therapist for the first time, and I think you're doing just fine."

"I don't feel fine. I feel like I'm the world's biggest screw-up. My C.O. said to me, 'What the hell's wrong with you anyway? What seaman wouldn't want to strike for a higher rating, especially up to E-4? Do you want to be a worm all your life?'" She hung her head. "Nope, there's no getting around it: I am a worm, and a candyass, and always will be." She bit her lip, then twisted her face up at me. "Uh, you do know what that is, right?"

I smiled. "Candyass? Yes, although I think in my day it might have been feather merchant." I shrugged and nodded appraisingly. "But sure, candyass works, too."

I was ready to make a move, and by that I mean forcing her to *shift*. I regarded her for a moment, watching the panic brewing, and then said, "Hang on a minute. Since you insisted that I get you some damn water, I'm going to go to the head and get some for you. In the meantime, I want you to sit here and think about the fact that right here, right now, at . . ." I checked my watch, dramatically, "eight thirty-five and twenty seconds, you are safe. Not only safe, but about to have not only some damn water, but a damn pill, too."

Without another word I got up, turned and headed for the office door and down the hallway to the bathroom, smiling to myself at the expression of horror those two damns must have put on her face. But that's all right: the shock of cold water on your face is a lot better than panic.

I returned with the cup of water, but when I handed it to her, she merely drank it down, straight.

"What? No pill?"

"No, I decided I don't need it after all."

I sat down and sighed, hard and loud. "Whew, well now, after all that running around to fulfill your endless demands, I forget where we were."

Did I detect a tiny smile behind that pale pink lipstick?

Her eyes crinkled a little. "So I begin to see what your plan is: I'll have my hands so full dealing with you that I'll forget all my other problems. Is that it?"

I threw up my hands. "What have I done? I'm just trying to conduct a standard intake interview, and you have me running from pillar to post. Then, when I finally get back, you accuse me of being difficult." I pointed my finger at her. "You're a lot trickier than I expected, Seaman Minor." I had a crazy idea, and let fly. "I may have to bring in a consultant to deal with your case."

Her eyes went wide again. "A consultant? Am I that bad?"

"Yes, my dog Angus often helps out when I have to deal with difficult and baffling characters. I may have to tell him about you, but don't worry; it's all confidential—terriers don't talk. Any objections?"

She clapped her hands. "I love dogs! Could I see him?"

I nodded slowly. "Hmm, I suppose it would be all right. That is, if you think you could stand up under a grilling by a Scottish terrier."

Now she was definitely smiling. "Could you bring him next week?"

"What makes you think there will be a next week? After the water incident, the termite-riddled wood incident, and all the rest of it, why would I want to see you again, especially now, with the added expense of a consultant in the bargain?"

"What if I bring a chew toy. . .in the bargain?"

"Never touch the stuff."

"No, for your damn dog!"

"Well, all I can do is ask him."

She looked at the clock. It read 8:45. "Are we done?"

"Yes, so next Wednesday at eight?"

"All right."

"What happened to, 'Aye aye, sir'?"

"I don't know; I feel more like a civilian now."

"Welcome back."

After she left, I sat for a long time in my office, trying to puzzle out one thing that still bothered me. Where was the "hippie" in the E-3? Was I relying too much on my intuition (I had been accused of that before), or was I correct that the woman I talked to on the phone wasn't the same woman whom I talked to in my office? No, none of that "split personality" stuff—in fact, I haven't run across a genuine multiple personality in over forty years of practice—but I know the person I talked to on the phone had a very different "vibe" than the lady whom I met in person. How aware was she of this, or was it so unconscious that she wouldn't know what I was talking about if I brought it up to her?

But it was way too early to delve into that yet. First I needed to establish basic trust. People don't realize this, and therapists don't talk about it much, but regardless of how many amazing techniques a therapist has, it takes time for a patient to trust you, especially when the original interactions, emotional assumptions and expectations they "downloaded" from early interactions with their parents, were not exactly stellar. A long-time patient of mine recently told me, looking back on his therapy: "I now see that it took me most of two years before I even actually got the concept that you were here for me."

Well, I wasn't getting anywhere sitting there in my chair and analyzing it all. It's ironic that therapists so blandly reassure their patients, "Just hang in there; the answers will come in time," then go home and anxiously try to figure out what comes next, instead of realizing that "only experience can reveal the answers" applies to themselves, as well. I knew the answers (if any) would only come from sitting with Meagan, so I just filed away the hippie avatar for future reference, and drove home to bed and Angus, grateful for his company, and expertise, on this case.

*   *   *

The following Wednesday, there was Meagan again, in her Navy uniform. She snapped to attention. "Sir."

"Stand easy, trooper."

She smiled, "Uh, we don't say troop—hey, where's Angus?"

"Angus is on the consulting couch, waiting for us."

She followed me back to my office and took a seat in the patient's chair while Angus, lying down on the couch, wagged his whole body, then rushed over to introduce himself, standing on his hind legs as she reached down and picked him up to her lap, handing him the cute rubber bone she'd brought.

"Angus, I'd like you to meet E-3 Meagan Minor."

She stroked and petted Angus, as he licked her face, then turned around a few times and sprawled out on her lap to shake the rubber bone into submission. "Is it okay if he stays here during the session?"

"Well, he can't very well get a feel for your personality without having some contact, can he?"

She frowned, for the moment unsure of just how serious I was being. Then she looked at me blankly and said, "So, what do we do now?"

I was reluctant to jump in and tell her what to do, but so far I really didn't even know anything about her, so I gave her a kick-start. "Tell me a little about yourself."

"You mean my history?"

"Sure, your history, the things that have happened to you, what matters to you—everything that someone who wants to know you needs to know."

She hung her head. "Sorry, I don't know how to answer all that."

Okay, I could see this was going to have to be done by the book. I said, "Well, where were you born? Where did you grow up?"

"Sacramento ... Alameda."

I nodded. "Go on."

She frowned. "Go on with what?"

I was beginning to see now what she meant about only being able to take orders, not give them. She literally had no ability to go one iota beyond what was demanded or expected of her. I could also see that I was going to have to change my own style and ethic of doing therapy if I wanted to help her. Yes, it went contrary to my principles and my comfort zone, but sometimes you have to sacrifice your principles, temporarily, to serve the patient's long-term needs. If I didn't "turn to" and get my act together pretty quick here, I was going to lose the good start I had made with Seaman Minor.

"Tell me about your mother." (I decided to start with Mom, figuring we would eventually work up to good ol' Dad, if you still remember my fears about there being an admiral in the woodpile.)

"What about her?"

"What was her name? Where did she come from?"

Meagan nodded sharply. "Rebecca Stratwood ... Marion, Ohio."

"Did she work? Or was she a stay-at-home mom?"

"No ... Yes."

My God, this was gonna be brutal. But I plowed on, trying to make it sound like something other than an interrogation. Most patients, after a series of specific questions like this, would say, "Don't I ever get to say anything?" But Meagan seemed to thrive on it, petting Angus and looking more relaxed as it went on. Oh well, at least I was getting some information without alienating her.

By eight twenty-five, I had found out that she was raised in a quiet area of Alameda, that Mom was "nice, but strict," that she did "okay, but not great" in school, had never gotten in trouble, was always a "good kid" and that she'd had a brother, ten years older, who was the family star, and was attending the U.S. Naval Academy until he was killed in a training accident during a summer deployment.

And yes, it didn't take a Sherlock Holmes to figure out that it was Meagan's job to take the place of the missing son in the family constellation.

By eight thirty I was ready to tackle Dad. For a moment, I forgot myself and dared to ask, "So, where did your father fit, in all of this?"

"Uh, what do you mean by that?"

Oops, stupid me. Back to paint-by-numbers. "Where did he come from? What did he do for a living?"

"Minneapolis ... Engineer."

Here we go again. "What kind of engineer?"

"Aeronautical."

At that point, Angus jumped down and headed for the couch. I had the feeling that even he had had it with all this small-steps-for-tiny-feet jazz. Or maybe he just needed the consulting couch to figure his next move. I certainly didn't know mine, until suddenly I had a flash and said, "And he always wanted to be a . . .?"

She nodded, "Naval officer. You know, a pilot. But he washed out of flight training."

Wow, two whole sentences in a row! I felt like giving Angus a high-paw. Again, something told me to ask, "And what happened then?"

A crisp nod. "He, uh, well, he . . ."

"He what?"

"He was discharged, for, uh, medical reasons."

Another flash. "A nervous breakdown?"

She ground her lips together and looked toward Angus, who was still sleeping off the interrogation. Finally, she whispered, "Yes, that's about right, sir."

I took another shot. "And at home, did he run a tight ship?"

Her eyes pinballed again. Uh oh, was I too full of myself, too confident, blowing her fuses before she was ready? She licked her lips and offered, "That's fair, sir, I would say." Then she held her hands out to me and added, "But doctor, understand, I don't consider that a bad thing. God knows, I wouldn't have made it if he hadn't pushed me, and ... well, directed me."

"Did he direct you into the Navy?"

"No sir! That was my own decision; all my own."

It dawned on me that she had no idea whatsoever that her career choice was in any way living out her father's dreams or pinch-hitting for his dead son. It was hard for me to believe, but then, when you've been a therapist as long as I have, you sometimes lose track of the fact that most people don't think of their lives psychologically and can be staggeringly unaware of even the most obvious connections. I had to honor that fact and remember that it wasn't about what I could see, but what she could handle, and use. Sometimes enough is enough, and what we had done tonight definitely felt like enough. Oh yes, one more thing: just because somebody is unconscious of something, it doesn't mean their unconscious isn't working on it.

I gestured to the black Big Ben clock sitting on the table next to Angus. "It looks like our time is about up for tonight. See you next week."

She threw a quick, intense, longing look at Angus, then shot to her feet, determined, I suppose, not to take up one more second of my time than was officially owed to her. For a moment there, I just knew that some part of her wanted to ask, "Can you bring Angus again next time?" But of course that would have been totally out of bounds for her to even feel, at least for her persona as Meagan Minor, Good Kid.

But I registered it and smiled to myself, knowing that my long-range task was to befriend and make a space for the part of her that wanted Angus, the child part of her that needed and wanted things, re-gardless of whether they were reasonable, fair or "asking too much." I think Angus knew it too, as he gave his rubber bone one more spirited thrashing, for the road.

*   *   *

Meagan called a few days later to say she wouldn't be able to make our next Wednesday meeting, that she had "mandatory, all-day meetings," but that she'd be there on the following Wednesday. Okay, no problem, except that a couple of days later I was just locking up my office on a Thursday night as I finished up the week's work (I don't work on Fridays) when I checked my machine and there was *that voice* again, and by that voice I mean my old friend, the hippie. Or was I crazy? Here, I'll let you judge for yourself:

"Doctor, I'm floating away ... Oh, no, I don't mean like a deployment cruise or anything, I just don't feel like I'm part of the earth anymore ... Like, you know, all of the atoms that make up who I was, are being dispersed and floating away from each other. Oh man, how can I make you understand? ... Uh, do you know what a bardo is? Like an intermediate state, an indeterminate state, kind of discon-tinuous and porous? So, I think it might be a bardo, but of course I don't know anything, and I'm probably boring you anyway. Sorry to bother you."

Well sure, I kind of knew what a bardo was. Heck, "back in the day," *The Tibetan Book of the Dead* was pretty much de rigueur on ev-ery hippie's bookshelf. In my smattering-of-knowledge way, I knew that a bardo is a transitional phase, where something has ended, but you're not over the hump yet into the following phase, so it feels uprooted, unfamiliar, disoriented and maybe, like Meagan said, a bit airy, as if your atoms were spaced too far apart. What concerned me (or rather, intrigued me) about her message was not, "Oh no, what do I do now?" I knew what to do: Meagan was shaping up as a classic "selfing" job—if anything, my specialty.

No, what intrigued me was this alternate persona she seemed to have, underneath the good girl, the conventional girl, the by-the-numbers girl. And the good news was that, at least on some level, her unconscious was willing to share it with me, show it to me, even though the "regular Meagan" might not be fully aware of it, or at least not able to bring it out into the light of everyday life.

Part Two

Of course I immediately called Meagan back. And I confess, with some chagrin, that I was as interested in who she was going to be in the conversation as I was in the actual content of the conversation. But before I go any further, let me just tell you how I remember that phone call:

Me: So, I understand you're not feeling very solid tonight.

Meagan: I ... I'm sorry I bothered you. I should've waited till next Wednesday.

Me: What for? Life doesn't just happen on Wednesdays, you know. I want to be there for you.

Meagan: I know you say that—you have to say that—but you have your own life to live, too, without me burdening you with all of my little worries.

Me: I don't consider those little worries; it sounded as if you felt like centrifugal forces were tearing you apart.

Meagan: (Long pause, then a long sigh) Yeah, something like that. (Another pause, another sigh) Is that normal?

Me: Well, it can be, for someone in therapy. After all, just to come in and ask for help is a huge affront to your demons.

Meagan: Demons? Oh my God, am I possessed?

Me: No, no, nothing like that. I'm just talking about the parts of you that think they're looking out for your best interests, by making sure you don't bother anybody else with your problems, that think you should be totally self-sufficient, that think you should be self-contained and never burden anyone.

Meagan: Well, what's wrong with that?

Me: It short-changes you, that's what's wrong with it. You deserve better. You deserve more. You deserve someone to care, to help you, to notice you.

Meagan: (Sounds of crying)

Me: I mean, if we were talking about your best friend, wouldn't you say *she* deserved all those things?

Meagan: Well, I guess, sure, of course, but. . .but that's different.

Me: It's only different because you don't see yourself as worthy of all those things—yet.

Meagan: You don't understand. I can't expect those things; I'd only be disappointed and hurt. And people would be mad at me all the time, for being a whiner, a baby, and, you know, a . . .

Me: A candyass?

Meagan: You said it, not me. And my C.O. said it, too.

Me: Look, you have to understand something: the Navy is probably not the best place to find a supportive environment for what you're going through.

Meagan: What *am* I going through . . .?

Me: (I felt what was coming next)

Meagan: A nervous breakdown?

Me: *Bingo.* No, not a nervous breakdown. Let's go with your own terminology and call it a rearrangement of your emotional atoms.

Meagan: Is that why I feel like I'm in a fuckin' centrifuge?

Me: *Woo-hoo to that "fuckin'"!* Yes. That's why it feels like a fuckin' centrifuge. We're in the process of breaking free from the emotional patterns that have been in place for all these years, and when things break free, they do feel a bit. . .well, free-floating.

Meagan: I notice you said, "we." But I don't see *you* doing any panicking.

Me: I said "we" because we're in this together. And I'm not panicking because I know what's going on, and I've been on this journey many times before with my other. . .

Meagan: Victims?

Me: Now, what would Angus say to that?

Meagan: I guess he'd say it was pretty mean.

Me: That'll cost you one chew toy.

Long silence.

Meagan: Why do I feel better now?

Me: That's for me to know and you to find out.

Meagan: Okay, I'd better shut up and stop bothering you now.

Me: I'm not going to take that bait. See you next Wednesday, unless you're a candyass and I hear from you before then.

Meagan: Oh, you won't; I promise!

Hmm, no "bardo" talk, right? Fascinating—or at least I found it so. Where did that part of her go when she was in her "straight" mode? I really should have been seeing her at least twice a week at this point, but like most patients she couldn't afford that, so I would continue to try and supplement by being open to contact between sessions, until she had enough of a sense of herself to bridge the sessions using her own resources. If you consider that in these situations a therapist is basically working with a young, wounded child, it's amazing that such patients (and therapists) are able to get the job done on the basis of only one limited contact every seven days. The courage and trust required of a patient to go to such places and do such work, with such little support, is truly remarkable. For those who condemn therapy as "hand-holding" or babysitting for the weak and feckless, I'd like to say right here that doing therapy is a lot less like babysitting than it is like running a SEALS training, or an Outward Bound program for adults, where people learn to cross rivers on a rope bridge and spend days alone in the wilderness, living by their wits with very little contact with "base camp." So, hooyah! to you therapy patients out there: you rock!

But back to Meagan's story. I didn't hear anything further for the next two weeks, but her various manifestations (the hippie, the shippie, and the bardo state) were on my mind a lot as I focused on holding a mental space for all of her. I know it sounds stupid, but I believe it helps the process if I hold a mental space for all aspects of a patient's being, in my consciousness, even between sessions; after all, the least it could do is function as a kind of stretching exercise for my mind, keeping it limber, wide (as in "bandwidth") and open to all possibilities.

And that Wednesday night, when I walked into the waiting room, I was glad I had done those mental stretching exercises, because Meagan was sitting there (yes sitting: not jumping to attention!) dressed in faded, holey jeans, sandals, a black t-shirt with that famous Rolling Stones red-tongue logo and a green Oakland A's baseball cap, turned backwards.
While I was taking all this in she said hopefully, "Where's Angus?"
I almost said, "The heck with that. Where's Meagan?" but fortunately I had done my stretching exercises, so I just nodded, "He's in the back, on the consulting couch."
She rose and walked back down the hallway, with me following, still trying to clear my head.
Meagan strode into the office and took a seat in the chair, looking

over at Angus.

Predictably, Angus hesitated at first—as you may know, dogs are exquisitely sensitive to the overall look of a person, and may not fully recognize someone as a friend, when they're used to seeing the person in a particular mode of dress. But after a moment of suspicious sniffing and staring, Angus hopped down and presented himself to her in that classic Scottie okay-you-may-now-love-me pose.

But there were still more surprises to come. After greeting Angus and settling him down on her lap, Meagan's face seemed to fall.

When I cocked my head questioningly at her, she just looked down silently, sadness leaking out of every pore.

"Meagan, what's wrong? What happened?"

In response, she just stood up, basically dumping Angus onto the floor, then went over and pulled the Indian blanket off the couch and brought it back to the chair, drew her legs up under her and just sat there, hugging the blanket to her chest.

Angus gave a Scottie snort of disapproval, then hopped back up to the couch to puzzle the whole thing out; after all, how could somebody who had a chance to hold him, not want to hold him?

Angus wasn't the only one who was puzzled. Part of me wanted to poke her, do something aggressive, but I settled for silence, never the worst choice.

A full two minutes went by—an eternity in therapy. Then, just when I was starting to wonder if all I was doing was letting her sit in misery and confusion, she said, "Tell me, is rain an inanimate object?"

I tried to put on my hippie hat, but maybe the sixties were too far back for me to recapture. Besides, I kind of intuited that this was going to be more rhetorical, maybe even allegorical, than literal.

Then, just when I opened my mouth to take a stab at something, she said, very sadly, "Just because something moves, does that mean it's alive?"

Suddenly, I was glad I hadn't mentioned the change in her clothes.

I could now sense that she had several levels (i.e. selves) going on at the same time. As opposed to a bardo, which would be a disoriented state, she now had several differentiated selves going on at the same time, but my guess is they weren't speaking to each other yet. Whoever had "dressed her" probably wasn't the same one who had reached out for the blanket and curled her feet up under her. And the angry girl who had dumped Angus on the floor could be yet another manifestation of her unintegrated Meagan-ness. I sensed that these "people" all wanted to know each other, but needed a proper introduction, a translator and a master of ceremonies.

Guess who?

But wait, let's circle back a moment. The "raindrops" question was clearly her way of metaphorically saying that she doesn't feel alive, or rather, that she cannot access the aliveness that is in her.

Okay, now back to the action:

"What's going to happen to me?"

I needed to be careful now, gentle. "We're going to start connecting the dots—on the inside."

She snarled, "What's *that* shit supposed to mean?"

The "angry girl" strikes again: great news! (She would never have been able to be so open with me at first, even from an unintegrated self like this.) I said, "It means that there are different parts of you that are showing themselves, and we're gradually going to see if we can help them all have a place at the table."

She hugged the blanket to herself harder, grinding her lips again. In a small voice, she said "Can I do this?"

I smiled. "We can do this."

"Are you really going to help me? Do you. . .?" Her voice trailed off. Then she took a breath and, lips trembling, tried again, "Do you know what you're doing?"

I smiled again. "Well, it's not exactly like cracking a combination lock, but I know we can figure it out together, over time."

She cringed. "What if I don't do it right?" She added, "What if. . .I screw it all up?"

"Look, you're not a candyass or a screw-up, Meagan. You're a smart, competent woman who just needs a safe place, and some help, to put all the pieces together. That's all."

She cringed again. "And you'll be patient?"

"Yes. It's not hard to be patient with you. You're a fast learner, and besides, I have a lot of admiration for your courage and determination." (Again, leading the receiver—people will follow genuine praise toward their higher capabilities. It's just a matter of creating a safe place for the built-in growth process to function.)

And with that I sensed a shift in her, with less fear and more determination. "Where do we start?"

"We've already started." I took a quick glance at the clock: 8:39. She'd probably done what she could do for tonight, but I didn't want to leave her in tatters. Clock management is just as important for a therapist as it is for an NFL coach. I felt for a way to wrap it up while still figuratively holding her and keeping the forward momentum. "Wow, you did so much tonight; I'm really impressed."

She gave me a sort of frown-smile. "Me? I didn't do anything, except maybe ditch Angus, poor baby." She got up and went over to pet Angus, who was very forgiving. By doing this, her unconscious helped me out in wrapping things up by shifting back to her "caring" mode, the bread and butter of her regular persona.

I also knew that her unconscious knew I had noted her change of clothing, and it was expecting some acknowledgment. I was getting to it, but the time wasn't ready yet.

As she continued to pet Angus, I nodded toward the clock. "Well, I see we're going to have to stop, for now. Does next Wednesday work for you?"

She turned toward me, now safely back in "regular Meagan" mode, and nodded.

Now I needed to remind her insides that I remembered the session, and meant what I'd said. "Just remember: we're going to do this, together."

She sighed hard, ground her lips together again and said, "Okay." Then she folded the blanket and stood up to leave.

One, two, three—now! "I like your shoes."

She smiled, big. My old professor used to call it "the smile of the unconscious," and it stayed on her face all the way out of the room. Then, just as she went through the door, she tossed back, "I threw all my tranquilizers away."

These are the little joys of being a therapist.

Part Three

Her subsequent visits told me that we had broken the back of Meagan's "selfing" problem in the "civilian clothing session" (as I always called it, to myself).

That doesn't mean the work wasn't hard, or that I was sure of every move I made; just that, together, we had pushed our way through that first big dark night of the soul, where the patient's bare posterior is hanging out over a cliff and the therapist has to come through or else lose the chance to be trusted enough to finish the job.

She did her part, and I did mine, and gradually, the sub-parts all came together into a smart, funny, sensitive, remarkable, big-hearted woman.

I always wondered whether she even remembered the bardo message she had left me that one night.

Then, toward the end of a session one night, she suddenly tossed this out: "When I was a child, I used to read a copy of *The Tibetan Book of the Dead* under my sheets at night, with a flashlight. My father would have killed me for having such 'trash' in the house, but our landlady gave me a copy that her son left behind when he moved out to live in a commune. For some reason, to me it represented the larger world, beyond my father's control, where there were other, bigger ways of looking at things. And it became something I could hang on to, that was my own private property, my own private world." She looked down, in thought. "Maybe something like a ... a parent."

That was the last time she mentioned it, but I immediately understood what it had meant to her. We all need things to hang on to, things that can't be taken away from us, that are always there to draw on.

As time went on, Meagan came in uniform, or out of it; it didn't matter so much anymore. There were even a few long, swirly skirts and, yes, even a discreet foot tattoo. But rather than a tiny butterfly it was…wait for it…Winnie the Pooh, riding an anchor!

And even the uniform changed. Yes, one early spring evening, about two years later, she showed up and really got me good, the little sneak. Without a word to me, she had taken her Petty Officer test, and there, on her right shoulder, was an eagle! I could only stand there as my eyes welled up. It felt like Christmas and the Fourth of July all rolled into one. And then she stood up, snapped off a formal salute and handed me a small, wax-paper envelope. When I angled my head at her, she smiled and said, "Go ahead, open it."

Inside were two identical silver eagles, each one standing atop a red chevron. "Those are my new E-4 collar devices. I, uh, left them off deliberately." Her eyes were shining now, too. "Would you ... could you, pin them on me... doc?"

I had to blink back tears as I fumbled them out of the envelope. "But, how do I . . .?"

She chuckled. "Well, I figured as a civilian you couldn't sew, so I just brought this, for now." She reached into her purse and handed me two of those little gummed squares you use to stick posters to the wall.

I pulled the backing off the first one and fixed it on her right collar, and then did the same with the left. Then I stood back and saluted her. "Congratulations, trooper."

She laughed out loud.

"Well, I didn't want to say, 'Petty Officer,' because you're anything but petty, to me."

"Yes," she said, nodding slowly and looking me straight in the eye. "I know."

I nodded to her, deeply moved, and thought to myself that our exchange was over.

But after a moment, she added, "And then there's this: you taught me a few other things, too, that my father never taught me—in fact, that I never even knew I needed to know. You showed me that leadership isn't about giving orders or telling people what to do. It's about using your position to help others, to inspire them to believe in themselves." She paused. "Because that's what you did for me."

I felt like an E-4 too.

The Steamer

In a local cemetery where my deceased son Brett now lives, there also lives another boy, whose headstone I always pass on my way to visit Brett. I don't remember his real name, and wouldn't share it if I could, out of respect for his family members.

However, I do want to share this: his headstone has a picture of a locomotive on it, and in big letters, the boy's nickname: "Steamer."

Now don't ask me why, but every time I see that headstone, or even think about it, I start bawling shamelessly like a baby, often right out loud. Sometimes I even reach out and touch "his" train, like a holy relic; I trace its indentations lovingly, with my finger, trying to connect, and I actually say, "I love you Steamer, you're my kinda guy," and, "I'll never forget you," as I stand there like a dope with big, fat tears running down my cheeks. All for a kid I never even knew. Sometimes, I try to salute him, like a train, "Whoo! Whoo!" but most of the time I can't get the words out for the crying.

And when I get ready to leave, at first, I forget, but then I catch myself, I turn and say, "Oh yeah, Brett says hi."

I mean, they must know each other by now, right, having been neighbors for years?

I know it's not fair. Every person in that cemetery is technically "equal," and deserves a moment of thoughtfulness and maybe even a tear, from me—in fact from everyone who passes. But to me, a kid who was so cool, so lively, so joyous, so spunky and so much into trains that they called him Steamer? Now that's a kid I would have wanted to know, and (dare I say it?) a kid who really deserved to live, dammit!

Now I don't claim that all this is anything more than a projection on my part. Heck, maybe Steamer was actually an obnoxious brat who drove everyone crazy wherever he went, who wore on your nerves something fierce and gave his parents nothing but a hard time.

But I don't really believe that.

You don't either, do you?

Hell no; the Steamer was cool, and fun. Spunky, like I said before. He made you smile. He ran around the house with a sheet over his head and pretended to be a ghost. He lined up the chairs in the living room, pulled blankets over them and made it his secret club-house. He begged you until you finally gave in and took him to the scale-model Live Steam Trains up in Tilden Park, and then he rode 'em all day long, idolizing the old geezers in red bandanas who were always up there, working on 'em with grease guns and all kinds of special tools, talking that insider railroad lingo that you have to be in the fraternity to understand.

And when the train barreled around the curves, Steamer would lean far out to touch the branches of the trees along the tracks, just because he couldn't stand not to, until the old conductor back in the caboose had to call out and warn him, with an understanding smile, to keep his hands in the car.

And then later, you'd go to the Smokehouse for chili dogs and fries, and maybe pineapple shakes. And then on the way home, after all the excitement, Steamer would fall asleep in the back of the car, and in the rearview mirror you could still see the baby boy that he used to be, that trusting, open, vulnerable face with the adorable features—that baby face that tore more and more love out of you until it hurt.

But that's all over now—the rides, the clubhouses, the ghost-sheets, the hot dogs—all of it.

Why? What sense does it make, any of it?

I want to say, "We need you, Steamer; come back!" I want to say, "Why did it have to be you?" I want to scold God, to yell at Him, "Why wasn't Steamer even allowed to reach out and touch the branches, but You were allowed to cut him down in his glory and the boundless joy of his youth?" I want to shake my fists at the sky, and say to Him, "What's wrong with you, anyway? The least you could do is write in the clouds above the cemetery: *'Brett and Steamer, I am so, so very sorry for what happened to you!'*"

But, back in the cemetery, I do the mature thing of course, the rational thing: I turn away from Steamer's grave. I dry my eyes, I go and visit with Brett. I kneel down and tell him all about Steamer, in case he doesn't know, although I think he does: the steam trains, the branches, the hot dogs at the Smokehouse—all of it.
And he smiles and says, "Yeah Deeta, I know," or at least I think he does, as I bend down to caress his new stone house, built sturdy and strong, like the one built by the smart brother in *The Three Little Pigs*, which we used to watch on Saturday mornings.

God, I sure hope my rational mind is wrong, and that what really happens in the graveyard at night is that kids like Brett and Steamer rise up and come out to play football with pine cones, skipping stones along the wide pathways, maybe even sometimes pushing over the gravestones of some old Civil War veterans, who smile indulgently, remembering what it was like to be a kid—a live kid.

Does it matter what I think—about Steamer, about the cemetery, about fairness, about anything? Does it matter what any of us thinks? Probably not. But if thinking these things, crying over Steamer, smiling about the steam trains, imagining "my" two dead cemetery boys playing at night, helps us to go on, to make sense of the world, even if it is a crack-brained sense, then it has a meaningful reality of its own that we needn't be ashamed of.

Yeah, I know that death is final and that God always wins in the end. But at least in the cemetery, between me, Brett and the ol' Steaminator, we're pushing back a little and giving Him a run for His money:

All aboard!

We are handed a world and a reality that is sometimes hard—sometimes too hard—to bear. And all we have to fight back with is imagination and heart, and what some call spirit, and some call God. Maybe it's not enough, but then would anything ever be enough to face up to something as staggering as death?

I'm still working on my experience of the cemetery, but up until now, I've only gotten this far:

I love you, Steamer.

I love you, Brett.

And I'm trying to find a way to love you too, God, if you'll just help me out a little bit.

I'll be watching the clouds.

Doin' What Comes Natur'lly

A therapist is asked many questions.

Some of them are easy, cut and dried: "How much do you charge?" "How long are the sessions?" Some are harder—not to understand, but to answer: "How long will this take?" "When will I feel better?" "What will I be like when we're done?" And then there's the hardest one of all (for me): "So, what kind of therapy do you practice?" Aarghh, errr, that is, well . . .

I always think about Marlon Brando in *The Wild One*, when his gang comes to terrorize the town, and he's asked, "Hey, Johnny, what are you rebelling against?"

And he says, "Whaddya got?"

Why is this? Because the real answer is, "It depends on what you got." And in the beginning when the patient is asking the question, I usually don't really know yet what they "got." I also can't really determine yet how what they've got is going to look in a week, or a month or a year.

Sure, they might "have" alcoholism, or a bad relationship, or depression, or anxiety, or no job, but how are they going to respond to what I do? Are they going to listen if and when I offer advice? Are they going to be able to tolerate sitting in a room alone with me, and use that time to explore themselves in a deeper way? Are they going to do most of the work outside the room with other people, in other situations? Will we be problem-solving, practicing, rehearsing, dramatizing, exploring dreams, free-associating, deepening our relationship, or just checking in about the outside world?

I think most patients would be very surprised about how I work with other people I see—what we talk about, what we do, where they sit (or lie), even how we "use" the office space.

There are people who come in, sit in the same place and get to work immediately. For others, I prepare the space by setting out blankets and pillows, or re-arranging the seating. Some have asked me to turn away from them, some to move closer, some to move back, back, back.

I have taken walks with some people, done walking meditations together in the office, yelled at people, whispered, cajoled, begged, inspired, encouraged, apologized, confronted, talked a lot and sometimes just shut the heck up.

Some do the work primarily through feelings, some through ideas, some through pictures. Some write between sessions, a little or a lot, to me or to themselves, to God, to dead parents, to their Higher Power, to their demons.

For one woman, I kept videotapes of a TV series on hand so she could watch them when she got into rage-storms during sessions, to calm her down so we could get back to work. I have gone with patients to a nearby cemetery to visit dead relatives, to talk to them, and about them together, and to serve as a mute witness.

I flew in a small private plane with one person, to help her face her fear of flying.

Some people lie on the floor, on the couch or on a yoga mat.

Some have brought pets to be with them, to show me or to introduce to me, or just to feel safe.

One man brought in a poodle to "approve" of me, or not—I passed. Guess that's what they call the sniff test!

I have met sons, daughters, parents, siblings, wives, husbands, neighbors, landlords, physicians, past therapists, friends, business partners, lovers, ex-lovers, affair-mates, teachers, prospective spouses, ex-spouses, roommates, employers and lawyers. I've accompanied patients to see psychics and hypnotists. I've gone together with them to see what a mess their place was. We've looked at photograph albums, trophies and artwork. Sat together looking at a tempting booze bottle, sat together writing bills, calling creditors, writing resumes. At times we've sorted through bags of receipts and tax records. Looked at old family videotapes, listened to old family audio tapes, perused old report cards and bug collections, listened to music composed, poems written, journal entries.

I've heard wild tales of debauchery, poignant tales of sitting in a room alone for years.

Some people cry almost every session, some never. With some I cry, with some never. With some I feel powerful, with some hapless and ineffectual. I've "been" a genius, a dope, funny as hell, boring, original, obvious. My office has been called amazing, warm, cozy, inviting and safe, and also messy, banal, cluttered, depressing, upsetting, brooding.

Mostly we sit, we focus on the present and we pay close attention. And mostly, contrary to popular conceptions about self-absorption, though people want to talk about themselves, they don't want to sit with themselves.

And mostly, contrary to cultural mythology, even though people want real closeness, connection and intimacy, many cannot tolerate it in real time, with a real person.

With some people we establish our own language and terminology, references and in-jokes. We laugh a lot, talk about books, movies, sports, music and what it's like to be alive. We bond, sometimes for life.

With others, I feel more like toilet paper—there for the moment to handle the shit, and then discarded.

And it's all all right.

Yes, you heard me: It's *all* all right.

My job is to take whatever I'm given and make the most of it, whether it would look like a "big deal" to an outsider or not. Maybe the best I can do with someone is to empower them so that they go on to win a Nobel Prize. With others, it might be a heroic triumph that I got them to shift from using me as toilet paper to using me as a hand towel. I'm not being glib here. This is what happens in therapy, without marketing claims, jargon, quick-fix bullshit or empty promises.

Why do I stress this? Because therapy is one area where "buyer beware" is almost meaningless. How could a prospective client possibly know whether a therapist is any good or not—any good, that is, for their particular problems, for their particular personality, their particular historical context? They don't. They can't.

And the therapist him or herself doesn't know at that point either—not really. Any therapist who promises big change up front is deluded, or a liar, because the therapist can't possibly know either. Anyone who says anything more than, "Come on in and let's see," is guilty of wishful marketing. It's disrespectful to act like you know what's going to happen; people are more complex than that, a lot harder to figure, more unpredictable.

What's going to work?

The fact is, you don't know, until it works.

Or not.

As a therapist, you follow *trends* in your professional experience—it's only human.

You gave a particular book to a particular patient and it changed their life? Great! Now, you eagerly want to give it to your other patients, too: "Wow, give 'em this book, change their life! Why didn't I think of this before?"

Whoops.

They'll say, "I got through two pages and fell asleep," or "It reminded me of my cousin, whom I hate," or "I felt totally insulted and patronized through the whole thing, so now I'm actually kind of disappointed in you too."

Back to the drawing board. Like trying to hit a major league base-ball, much of therapy is failure. And much of the success in doing therapy comes from what was once called "listening with the third ear." What does this mean? Originally, I think it meant being willing to tune in to your own unconscious, your intuition, your empathy, to listen to the overtones, the subtext, the undercurrents, the un-stated, the unfiltered "back and forth" of what is happening between you and the patient. And it is that, but how do you get to the third ear? You get there by not forming clinical impressions premature-ly, by not playing the smart guy, by not coming up with brilliant connections and formulations, by not talking too much, by being willing to not know what's going on.

In my day, there used to be a book called *Don't Push the River (It Flows by Itself)*. Well, that's it: be still and pay close attention. The information you're looking for will come to you in good time, if you will be still and listen, to the patient and to yourself. Sure, you're anxious to understand exactly what's going on with the patient, anxious to do a good job, to succeed, to not fail. But you can't afford to fall prey to that anxiety and let it push you to rush your half-baked ideas into the sacred space that is therapy.

You don't tell them; they tell you!

When the process gets you there, insights will be revealed, and not before.

All you have to do is make the therapy space a place where the truth is safe, and make *yourself* a place where the truth is safe. Yeah, that's *all* you have to do! Try it sometime; it's one of the hardest things I've ever done, and one of the most rewarding. Think of it this way—it's not about getting the patient to trust you, it's about you trusting the patient. If they feel respected, listened to, honored, empowered and safe, things will happen.

I remember when I first started to do therapy, in my twenties. I was working with an African-American veteran named Spencer, who was ten years older than me and had a big chip on his shoulder about "the system" and how he'd been screwed over by it, and by all the other therapists who had tried to help him.

Our first session, he started right out in high gear. "Boy, what the hell do you know about being black?"

I fired right back. "Look, I think I can relate to what you've gone through, whether I'm black or not."

He just shook his head, stood up and walked out the door.

Failure.

The next time, I was smarter. I wasn't going to get into it with him. I would just try to understand. Here's how it went:

Me: So, can you try and tell me what's been so hard for you?

Spencer: Hard? What would you know about hard?

Me: I'm just interested in trying to help you express some of what's inside of you.

Spencer: Kind of like pulling the wings off a fly, then watching to see what it does?

Me: No, I just mean. . .

Spencer: You ever heard the word "condescending"?

Me: Yes, but I don't think . . .

Spencer: You got that right, kid; you don't think.

With that, he stood up and walked out again.

Failure; if you want to be a therapist, get used to it.

But I was learning.

The next session went like this:

Spencer: Now what do you want with me?

Me: (Silent)

Spencer: (Agitated): You going to tell me all the shit you've read about the black experience? Maybe quote Malcolm, maybe tell me some of your best friends are black?

Me: No.

Spencer: So, what do you know about being black, about being me?
Me: Nothing.
Spencer: Then what are you doing here?
Me: I was hoping you could teach me.
Silence.
Spencer: Hmmm ... Cracker, you might not be a lost cause after all.

And with that, we made a start.
What did I do? I helped to make the space safe. I established that we were both people. Yes, I was on the therapist side of the room this time, but it could just as easily be switched in the next lifetime. And I had no way of knowing what he was made of without doing a lot of listening and learning. It's not about proving anything to the patient. It's about taking up the challenge of getting to know, a little at a time, who they are and what matters to them.
And having made the space safe (or at least safer), his insides could come out and play a little, without fear of my judgment, my "expertise," my arrogance or my superiority. And from there, we could find out that we both liked Fats Waller, that the song "The Folks Who Live On the Hill" made us both cry, that we both loved lonesome train whistles late at night, that both our fathers fought in World War II and that he had lost a beloved dog when he was twelve.
Is this therapy? You bet it is, because the meeting of the minds we made, as human beings, allowed him to talk to me about how much he hurt, and it allowed me to tune my listening to his frequency, so that I could let it come to me, instead of forcing it with my pretended expertise.
Was he "cured"? No. For one thing, we only had the chance to meet maybe ten or twelve times. But I do know that by the time we were finished he felt respected, because he told me so. And I know that, in helping him reclaim something of himself, I took a step toward becoming a therapist.

He would always know that at least one white man thought he was really something.

And me? I'll always have the honor of knowing that, for a cracker, I'm not a completely lost cause.

So, what kind of therapy do I practice?

I don't know. Tell me what you got, and we'll figure it out, together. We won't get it from books, or impressing each other, or applying a technique, or enforcing "patient compliance."

We'll figure it out by listening carefully with no preconceived notions, and then watching and waiting until something emerges out of the fog.

Then, if we're lucky, like Bogie and Claude Rains at the end of *Casablanca*, maybe we'll walk together into that fog and say, "Louie, I think this is the beginning of a beautiful friendship."

I'll Be There

A fella ain't got a soul of his own—just a little piece of a big soul, the one big soul that belongs to everybody. I'll be all around in the dark. I'll be everywhere. Wherever you can look—wherever there's a fight, so hungry people can eat, I'll be there. Wherever there's a cop beatin' up a guy, I'll be there. I'll be in the way guys yell when they're mad. I'll be in the way kids laugh when they're hungry and they know supper's ready. And when the people are eatin' the stuff they raise and livin' in the houses they build—I'll be there, too.

These stirring words by John Steinbeck, spoken by Tom Joad (Henry Fonda) in the classic film *The Grapes of Wrath*, have immense power because, like all great art, they resonate on several different levels at once. In the film, Tom Joad is planning to leave the family, and his mother wants to know where he'll be. He is a young man whose family ("Okies," in the argot of the times) has just completed an arduous trek to the West, escaping the grimness and despair of the Dust Bowl, for what they hope is a better life in California. It doesn't turn out that way. Instead of milk and honey, they find hordes of other displaced people just like themselves, arriving from all over the country. They find the police of angry communities, trying to keep out, or beat out, these unwanted newcomers. And they find greedy landowners, taking advantage of this desperation to try and get their crops picked for next to nothing.

So Tom Joad decides he's had enough. He's pulling out. He doesn't have the slightest idea where he's going—it's enough to know that it's not where he's been. He wants something new, something different. And like all young men, he wants a life of his own making. And like all concerned mothers, Ma Joad is anxious and worried about her son leaving the family. So when she asks the question, she is simply distressed and wondering where he is going to go.

But his answer "jumps the tracks" to a place so universal it has rightfully earned a kind of immortality in movie (and literary) lore. On one level, Tom is talking about what we would call his spirit. He is saying something transcendent:

"The things (moral and political principles) that I stand for, are me. I am the spirit of fairness; I am the spirit of the fight for a decent life for all. I am joy; I am righteous anger; I am the spirit of every man who is trying to fend for himself or make a life for himself in this rough world. Where these things are, there I will be."

Compare to this passage, from *The Little Prince*, by Saint-Exupery: "People have stars, but they aren't the same. For travelers, the stars are guides. For other people, they're nothing but tiny lights. And for still others, for scholars, they're problems. For my businessman, they were gold. But all those stars are silent stars. You, though, you'll have stars like nobody else."

"What do you mean?"

"When you look up at the sky at night, since I'll be living on one of them, since I'll be laughing on one of them, for you, it'll be as if all the stars are laughing. You'll have stars that can laugh!"

And he laughed again.

"And when you're consoled, you'll be glad you've known me. You'll always be my friend. You'll feel like laughing with me. And you'll open your windows sometimes just for the fun of it. And your friends will be amazed to see you laughing while you're looking up at the sky. Then you'll tell them, 'Yes, it's the stars. They always make me laugh!'"

On one level, Tom Joad is saying, "The things I am associated with will remind you of me." But on another level, I believe he is, in effect, speaking as an agent of The Divine, of Infinite Spirit: "I am everywhere, witnessing and representing all that is good, fair, and righteous—protecting the little guy, those who are not powerful and need my help, in their struggle to survive in the world."

In its overall meaning, this manifesto sounds like it could be from the Bible—perhaps Jesus addressing a crowd of people. In its majesty and scope, Steinbeck also channels and appropriates the same authorial voice as Walt Whitman in *Leaves of Grass*—a kind of populist humanism that moves us deeply because it has always been associated with America, and with the idealized American character.

But what is left unspoken here, though nonetheless evident on an unconscious level, is yet another layer of meaning: that Tom (like Jesus) is leaving his immediate family in order to pursue a calling, to right the wrongs, to fight the good fight, to speak to the downtrodden and devote his life to his larger family—the family of humanity. The grandeur, the selflessness and the eloquence of Tom's spoken words at the moment of his leaving show a man transformed, a man transcendent, with an unshakeable vision.
Like Christ, this is a man on a mission, and the mission is bigger than his personal life.

Ma Joad unconsciously comprehends this and it terrifies her, as well it should. One gets the sense that Tom will not be coming back home, ever—that he no longer places much, if any, importance on his own personal outcomes in all of this.

So, what does all this have to do with the process of therapy? A great deal, if you look closely.

First of all, a therapist is also an evangelist of sorts; one who pursues a vocation to empower the unempowered, to restore functionality to the (emotionally) disenfranchised, to help people find an expanded sense of self, to rise above their limited, harmful and sometimes abusive surroundings, to become the person they were born to be.

Long ago I had a friend, a fellow graduate student, whom I admired greatly. He used to say, "A therapist is a salesman—a salesman for mental health." At the time I thought that statement was kind of underrating the grand profession of psychology, as I saw it then. But now I see that he was right—a therapist *is* a salesman, because he is "selling" the patient on doing the (hard!) work required to transcend the harm done by a difficult early environment, selling a belief in overcoming whatever barriers—social, neurological, biochemical—life has put in the patient's pathway to self, selling a belief in one's own possibility.

Sure, you can know your theory and be very experienced and well-schooled, but eventually most therapy comes down to getting the patient to "buy in" to what you're trying to do. After all, if the patient's not there, there's no therapy.

When therapy fails, why does it fail? Mostly, for not very dramatic reasons, in not very dramatic ways. The person decides they can't afford it. They feel they don't have the time. They don't understand what's happening. They don't see why they should keep coming. It hurts too badly. It doesn't make sense to them. They're afraid of getting too dependent. They feel it's not helping them in the way they first hoped it would.

These mundane, ordinary reasons all relate back to the therapist being unable to sell the person on the importance of therapy, to make her believe in it, to empower the person enough to talk "out loud" to the therapist about her most difficult questions and doubts. The patient was desperate enough at one point to pick up the phone or email you and call for help. But now, perhaps the crisis has calmed down (temporarily), or resolved in some short-term way (a break-up, or staying sober for a few weeks, a new medication that is helping, or just blown over), and the reasons for spending the money, taking the time and going through the difficulties of therapy don't seem as compelling. And so, the person gradually falls away. Perhaps they request meeting every other week, or once a month, or they say, "Nothing personal—I just feel like taking a break," or "I guess it's not what I thought it was going to be," or "Thanks. I'm feeling a little better now. Maybe I'll come back when/if things get worse again."

But it is the therapist's job to help the person stay with it as long as it takes to really resolve the problem, or at least to help the patient get to the point where the problem will not recur in the same way, as intensely, or as frequently.

Is this *creepy*? It can be. In the minds of many therapy patients: *You just want to keep me coming forever, for your own pocketbook.*

A patient once accused me of using her as an "annuity." And to be fair, I think that can happen in therapy. The therapist gets used to meeting with the person regularly. They talk and talk and talk about the problem, with the therapist spinning out theories about why it all happened. Many patients have come to see me after having spent months or years with another therapist—talking, talking, endlessly about the problem, speculating about what caused it, only to end up with the classic patient's lament: "I understand perfectly what caused my problems, but I still have them!"

And I always ask, "And did you talk to Dr. _____ about all these

feelings, including what you were thinking about the therapy?"
And the answer is almost always, "No, well, not really."

And this is a shame, because it tells me the therapist didn't manage to convey to the patient the one indispensable thing—that honesty and openness in the therapy relationship itself is crucial to the success of the whole enterprise. And it also tells me that the therapist failed to help the patient feel safe enough to express these doubts and questions to him or her. And this is ironic, because a big part of why people end up in therapy is that their parents (and others) did not encourage them to express themselves honestly (especially about the parents, to the parents) and didn't make it safe to do so. Thus, the patient's silence in the therapy relationship merely becomes a repetition (and sadly, a confirmation) of the original hurt.

If there was only one thing I had the opportunity to emphasize to therapists, beginning and experienced alike, it would be this: to stress to the patient, from the very beginning, that it is crucial (and safe) for the patient to openly express his or her changing and challenging thoughts about the therapy process itself, whether those thoughts seem rational, or fair, or not.
One of the saddest things I frequently hear from patients in failed therapies is that when the patient finally did try to express his frustrations, or doubts, or disappointments about the therapy, the therapist became defensive, angry and even attacking, such as the situation wherein a therapist finally erupted: "Listen, I'm doing my best. If you don't like it, you're free to leave!"

All of this is what I mean by the evangelistic aspect of being a therapist. You're conveying to the person that he or she can "get better," but that it's going to take a lot of work and a lot of honesty on both your parts. Can this lead to a conflict of interest? Absolutely! Consider this: you can be a good salesman with a bad product. There is virtually no way for a new therapy patient to know whether his new therapist is really any good or not, so a therapist who is a good salesman (or even an unethical manipulator) could induce a patient to stay in a sterile, barren, or even harmful therapy situation.

But what's worse is what happens much more frequently: a good, well-meaning therapist loses a patient for lack of conveying to the patient how important, how crucial, it is to talk openly about the patient's feelings about the therapy.

Yet another aspect of what happens when a patient quits without a word is that the patient can end up feeling the therapist just let it go at that, instead of fighting for the patient and the therapy. And by fighting, I don't mean coercion, but passion, engagement and caring. So often, patients in these circumstances don't even appreciate these issues until much later in their therapy with me, because it is only later that they realize they are (and were!) worth fighting for. Many times they will say, in retrospect, "Wow, now I realize that my previous therapist just let me walk away without a word and didn't really care enough to help me talk like this about it first."

And, of course, one of the main reasons people seek therapy in the first place is that they didn't feel valued by their parents—by parents who didn't connect with them, or fight for them, or stay there (emotionally) through disagreements and difficulties.

A therapy patient is a person who has lost her heart, and even the path to her heart. I think this quote from the author Robert Walser expresses this condition beautifully: "A person who does not know how to preserve his heart is unwise, because he is robbing himself of an endless source of sweet inexhaustible strength ... a warmth that, if he wants to remain human, he will never be able to do without."

And for a person who has lost her heart (and therefore, her way), the "prescription" is connection. Again, Walser says: "The heart needs a kindred, familiar heart, like a little clearing in the forest, a place to rest and lie down and chat."

And that precious clearing, that familiar heart, that safe place to chat? That is psychotherapy.

Is saying such a thing naïve? Is it unscientific? Is it soft-brained pap? James McMahon, an esteemed psychotherapist, feels this about the importance of "theory" by itself: "We write more and more esoteric journal articles and we quote each other and discuss theory with each other in conferences and meetings. But how practical is it all? How much does it help? What can we bring into our consulting room that helps us make true contact with our patients? I think it often actually stands in our way. We do the good work we do in spite of it!"

Note that he says, "But how practical is it all?" He's not saying, "C'mon, people, be nice; be kind and understanding toward your patients because it's the right thing to do." He is saying this: to do anything that doesn't constitute "true contact" does not work.

Why is this? Because working back through all the layers of pain and emotional damage hurts. And if you're not truly caring or involved with the patient, it isn't worth it for the damaged part of them. They don't know this, of course. They've already accepted, on some un-conscious level, that there is no such thing as "real caring," or at least real caring directed toward them. As far as they know, whether you really care about them or not is irrelevant, because they have no first-hand experience that another person's caring (about them) even makes a difference.

What matters (they think!) is for you to give them the magic words: words that explain their problems, words that tell them the magic stuff to do about their problems, words that will magically undo the harm. Since they think magic words are the answer, they feel that your caring for them is merely an extraneous factor they don't know what to do with anyway. What they don't realize is that the child in them needs someone to hold them (figuratively) through the work of exhuming their lost self from the dead, that if there isn't anyone "there" to care and see them through it all, they can't do it.

They don't know that they can't do it alone, and they don't know that the fact that there was no one really there is the reason for the whole problem. They don't know this, but you do! Because the truth is that the child in them can perform miracles, but only if you hold their hand through it, and hold it the right way.

Is this the dreaded *dependency*? Yes, it is temporary dependency, for a purpose, or what they used to call "regression in the service of the ego." It isn't an end point, however. It is a (normal) stage of development that the patient will pass through, using you, and then be able to do for themselves just as other "normal" people can.

After all, we don't become disturbed that an infant, or a toddler, or any young child, is dependent, do we? It's normal for that stage of development. So why do we think the process of therapy would be any different? Since normal development was sidetracked and stunted for lack of a reliable partner, the *cure* comes through the appearance of a reliable partner, for now. Later, having gone through it all with you, they internalize (i.e., download) the functions of the parental figure, so that they can do it for themselves. This internal "selfing" process is the real hoped-for outcome. And note, I don't say that understanding is the real hoped-for outcome. You do not teach the patient tricks, or explanations, techniques or anything else: you *go through* something with them, until finally the "something" is inside them, to stay. It's just that the unreliable experiences people have previously gone through in early life (and sometimes later) give dependency a bad name, so to speak, so that any hint of really needing someone is terrifying.

And so, to return to Tom Joad's speech in *The Grapes of Wrath*—what is really happening here, emotionally? He is moving beyond his everyday identity with his original family, to his membership in the family of humanity. He is expanding his small, personal identity (I am this guy, from this family, who is on the run from despair and degradation) to a larger identity, as a human being, then as a living being, and then as spirit made manifest.

And this act of expansion, this expanded identity (I am part of humankind>I am part of something bigger>I am spirit incarnate) gives him the "holding" experience: I am not alone. I was never alone. I am a part of something bigger than me. And this holding (just like the holding in the therapy relationship) is what gives him the courage to strike out into the world boldly, to prosecute aims that are bigger than "I want a job; I want security" (i.e., the things his family is seeking).

This is a spiritual awakening, which really means an identity expansion and the joining of a bigger family, not just the family of humankind, but the family of living beings, and ultimately the family of spirit.

The aim of psychotherapy may or may not involve an expansion that large, into the realm of spirit (although it can). But it must involve an expansion beyond the stunted personal identity that was frozen by key experiences in the family of origin. And it always, always, involves an expansion of personal identity from a personality system that is motivated by fear to one that is about the encountering, the experiencing and the expression of self. From self-protection, to self-manifestation.

And that takes a partner.

And that's what psychotherapy is all about: providing that partner.

Because "selfing" is a two-person job.

So, when someone struggles in to see you, heart-sick, soul-battered, and weary beyond telling, what you are really offering, beyond the theories, beyond the techniques, beyond the expertise, is simply this:

I'll be there.

A House Full of Girls

Part One

I finished my internship in Los Angeles.
Check.
Then I flew back to Tennessee to defend my dissertation.
Double check.

What was the next check mark?

Well, you needed to get fifteen hundred hours of post-internship "supervised experience" in an approved setting before you could sit for your licensing exam, but all that could be acquired on the job.

Uh, what job?

Exactly.

Well, I could have hung around LA. I hadn't acquitted myself badly on my internship, so I could always try to promote some kind of academic position at the UCLA Neuropsychiatric Institute.

Nope, not for me.

Or, I could have stayed in LA and tried to "network" some kind of clinical work, or even offer to be a psych assistant in somebody's private practice.

Nope, an entire childhood in Los Angeles, plus one year's internship spent there was quite enough LA for one lifetime.

I could go back to Tennessee and try to. . .

Nope. 'Nuff said.

I wanted a job in the "real world," working with real people who needed real help, someplace where I actually wanted to live. I'd always lived where I had to live. Now finally was my chance to flip that script and choose where I wanted to be, where I wanted to put down roots.

Someplace that felt like me.

Gee, San Francisco—that was more like it. Oakland, maybe, or somewhere, anywhere, in Northern California.

But how?

I went to the Santa Monica public library (remember, we're talking mid-seventies here: no Internet) and checked out the phone books for all the major, and minor-major, cities up north, not just the Bay Area but everywhere: Santa Clara, Fort Bragg, San Jose, Monterey, Salinas, Santa Rosa, Eureka, Yreka—hell, Paprika, if necessary. I looked up every category I could think of: psychology, social service, psychotherapy, sanitariums, mental mealth.

I developed a form letter, and jettisoned a slew of them northward, to anyone or anyplace that could conceivably want a young, cheap, willing psychologist-in-waiting.

Whew. Waiting—that was the operative word.

Tick tock.

Finally, I got a response.
From Monterey.
About a job in Carmel.
My God, Carmel! Monte Carlo, without the gambling. Ibiza, but they speak English. Heaven, but with better beaches.
I called the number on Monday, talked to the guy on Tuesday and made a flight reservation for Wednesday.

We, the boss and I, sat at a red-leather booth in some swanky restaurant—swanky but low-key casual of course, since this was Carmel-by-the-Mofo-Sea. Was it the Hog's Breath Inn, owned by Clint Eastwood? I don't remember, but if I was supposed to be dazzled, I certainly was. Calamari, Dungeness crab cakes, perfect sourdough bread and blood orange sorbet floated by, chased by champagne and a couple of screwdrivers.
We lingered and made pleasant small talk till late afternoon, then we moved out to the patio to continue our conversation under the cypress trees, while watching the last sunbathers leaving the perfect white sand beach as the sun set over a storybook ocean.

At last it was time to rejoin real life, already in progress. My prospective boss leaned toward me and finally got down to it. "We need someone to organize and run a group home for adolescent girls. Does that sound like something you could do?"

I had no experience whatsoever with adolescent girls (other than the checkered dating life of my youth, which shall go mercifully undocumented). I had no idea in hell what a group home was. But I had a chance to work in Carmel for God's sake, and I wasn't going to muff it. "Well no, not really, but, uh, I'm a quick learner and, well,

I like women, and girls too—that is, I mean I respect them. That is—well, you know what I mean, I hope."

Ta da! There it was: a perfect meal, a beautiful setting, the chance of a lifetime, and all I had to offer was a garbled mess of verbiage that wouldn't have qualified me for a learner's permit, much less a psychology license. Oh God, what a mess I had made of this whole thing!

He smiled much more graciously than I deserved, and said, "Well, just the same, I have a feeling you can handle it." He raised his glass toward mine in a toast. "You'll start at a thousand a month."
Stunned, I clinked glasses with him and smiled. "That'll be fine." My mind had shut off the second I understood that he was offering me the job. He could have said, "You'll start by paying us a thousand a month," and I still would've clinked glasses with him. Heck, I had a job! In Carmel! And they were going to pay me! Did I already mention that it was in Carmel?

I called everyone I knew. "I got it! I'm moving to Carmel!"

Little did I know what awaited me.

*   *   *

I soon found out what group home means. Roughly, it was for girls (in this case) who had been placed for various reasons in foster care and where it hadn't worked out. So a group home was for kids who needed something more than individual foster care, but below the level of the California Youth Authority. Some came from the social welfare side, some from the juvenile justice system. Ages twelve to seventeen. Girls who were just getting into gang life. Girls who were pimped out by their mothers, or abused by their fathers, stepfathers or mothers' boyfriends. Girls whose parents had died, or were in jail. Girls who were "beyond parental control."

In short, girls whom somebody had decided needed to be placed (and just maybe, "rehabilitated"?) in a closely supervised, controlled environment.

By me.

Except it turned out that someone else was already running the group home. Not just someone: two people, two very large, very unfriendly people—at least, unfriendly to me. A large, unfriendly older man and his wife, who weren't very happy that I was hired to be the "hatchet man" for my boss.

The Joneses.
And sure enough, it turned out that I was hired to serve as a "buffer" between the boss and these two people. Much later I learned through the office rumor mill that the large, unfriendly "house-father" had pulled a gun on my boss at some point in the recent past.

Oops. So let's see, this thing was starting to sound like the plot of a bad Western: the mayor (my boss), a bombastic but dithering politico, was terrified that the Dalton Gang (the Joneses), the evil terrors of the West, who had killed women and children, who had strung up the town blacksmith just for looking at them, had come in and taken over Dodge City. And now, still wanting to look like he was in charge, the mayor scoured the countryside for a man who was so powerful, so confident, or so stupid and inexperienced (now you're getting warmer) that he would take on the Daltons in a fair fight and face down the bullies who had scared the wits out of the populace—in short, a town tamer.
Oh, and not only all that, but a guy who'd do it all for next to nothing.

And that stupid, town-taming, risk-taking, underpaid dope?

That would be me.

Gulp.

Boys and girls, that's what happens when you get a job out of the Yellow Pages at your local library.

But hey, it was in Carmel, right?

Well no, not exactly. The house was located in a neighboring town, in a semi-rural area—a very white, untroubled enclave. Where the citizens—notwithstanding that many of them were smart, nominal liberals—wanted to keep it that way. So I had more than one potential objector to my new wonder job, but more on that later.

The first thing I did after I got settled was to visit the house. Of course at that time nobody had told me yet about the house parents from hell, the gun, the buffer, or the hatchet man, so I figured it'd be the standard meet and greet: "Hey there, I'm the new guy, here to help you in any way I can. I'm new on the job, so let's all do anything we can for each other, okay?"

Nope—oooooh, nope. The couple had much more important things in mind, like establishing that they were the boss, period. I parked my car in the driveway of the red, ranch-style house. Yes, I had been given a key, but I figured it never hurts to show respect, right? I gathered myself. *Knock knock.*

No answer.
I knocked again, louder.

The door cracked open, revealing a burly, middle-aged man who looked like he ran a tough bar in a seedy neighborhood, where he kept a sawed-off shotgun under the bar and a nightstick close at hand. He looked me up and down and sneered, "So, you the guy?"

"Uh, yeah, I guess so. That is, I mean, yeah." I stuck out my hand, until it got lonely out there all by itself.

"Well, get in here then, and let's get this thing over with." He waved his head at a doughy woman who looked like she ran a tough bar in a seedy neighborhood, with a sawed-off shotgun under the bar and a nightstick close at hand, and muttered something to me. I think I caught the word, "wife," but knew better than to stick my hand out again. Like I say, I'm a fast learner.

"Glad to meet you. Say, uh, maybe you'd like to show me around a bit?"

They rolled their eyes at each other, like people who don't realize that the other person can see they're rolling their eyes at each other. Then they shuffled back through the living room to the place where a darkened hallway began. The woman stood there and fixed me with dead-shark eyes, then jerked her thumb toward the hallway. "It goes back."

I walked back; four bedrooms branched off the hallway. Nothing on the walls, no personality whatsoever in the decorations. Nothing indicating that living teenage girls resided here. Two bathrooms completed my solo tour. I took a deep breath and checked my insides; there was something creepy about the whole set-up. Like Norma Desmond's mansion in *Sunset Boulevard*, it felt heavy and dead. My chest felt like someone was sitting on it—someone who ran a tough bar in a seedy neighborhood, and kept a . . .

Actually, not just "dead," more than dead, more like... dangerous. Suddenly, I wanted out of there, right then.

"Well, it's got lots of room, right?" I smiled, trying to lighten the mood as I sidled my way toward the front door.

No response.

"So, where are the girls?"

Shark-eyes barked, "School, of course."

"Oh yeah, of course." The gotta-get-out-of-here feeling was getting stronger now. I kept edging toward the door, still covering my tracks with feeble small talk. "The girls all healthy? Any special problems I need to be aware of?" Crickets. "Guess I'll have to come back in the evening and meet the girls, eh? Maybe a nice dinner together, just to, you know, bond with them a little, since, you know, I'm gonna be working with 'em and all. . ."

I had almost made the front door.

Suddenly, the man stepped in my way, blocking the door. "We get Orville Redenbacher's."
I angled my head in confusion. "Uh, excuse me?"
They did that mutual eye-roll thing again, and then the woman took over. "He said, we get Orville Redenbacher's." She sighed heavily, impatiently. "Is that clear?"
"Oh, you mean, like, to eat? Like, you prefer Orville Redenbacher's to other brands of popcorn?"
Shark-eyes spoke again, spitting out, "Not prefer, *get.*"
I felt like Roy Scheider at the end of *Jaws*, facing those dead, menacing eyes as the ship goes down. But now, despite my fear, I was

also getting mad. Before I knew it, words started flying out of my mouth. "Look, I don't really care what brand of popcorn you eat. I'm not here as a damn dietician; I'm here to run this place. I have the responsibility for the whole . . ."

"Oh, we know why you're here, sonny," the man snorted with derision. "You're here because your boss ain't man enough to deal with us, so he sent a kid down here to be his little hatchet boy. But you ain't gonna come in and turn this place upside down, because it's our place: the girls listen to us, they obey us, they do what we say. And," he smirked with his power, "they go with us."
The second I finally made it to the porch, he slammed the door in my face.

Ah, so that's the way it was: their hole card was that they would take the girls with them if they didn't get everything they wanted, or maybe whether they did or not. As I got in my car and drove off, more and more things occurred to me—things that nobody had "officially" bothered to tell me about. Damn, they had probably already contacted the referral agencies and told them their version of the story, not only setting themselves up to take the girls and set up their own group home, but poisoning the well against me with the referral agencies, before I'd even talked to a single person.

Shit, what was I going to do about that?

It didn't take a PhD to see that Orville Redenbacher was going to be the least of my troubles.

*　　*　　*

Fortunately, it turned out that in order to fulfill the famous fifteen hundred hours of post-internship supervised work experience, my boss had arranged for me to be supervised by Richard, a young local psychologist, who had a thriving private practice in a nearby area. Hooray, at least I had a sane person to talk to about all this, who wasn't embroiled in (or compromised by) the politics of the Agency, which is what I took to calling the place where I worked. I didn't know then—and I still don't—how much my boss had told Richard about what was going on, but I do know he sometimes saw the girls from the group home in individual therapy, and we both had releases of information to share relevant information. It never occurred to me before now that maybe there was some kind of "arrangement" between him and my boss, but I do know he was kind and helpful to a raw beginner. God knows I needed help and support as I tried to figure out what to do with the SS Group Home, the "vessel" I had just inherited—a vessel that had sprung a leak before I even stepped aboard.

So after conferring with my boss (who never did really admit that he had withheld the backstory from me) and with Richard, I finally realized that all the things I had been afraid of had already happened and that the Joneses were on their way out, no matter what I did or said, after having destroyed the good name of the Agency with every referral agency in Northern California, before setting sail with their captive crew of girls.

I was left with a group home with no group, zero employees to run it and a reputation that had already been sabotaged with agency people I hadn't even met—the same ones I needed to impress to get more girls.

Oh well, at least now I could drown my sorrows in all the cheap popcorn I could eat, without anyone pulling a gun on me. Plus, I had the house all to myself, free to redecorate and spruce things up as I saw fit. So for the first couple of months, the PhD Executive Director (that's me) spent his days grouting the shower, sweeping the floors, replacing burned out bulbs, putting out the trash, pulling weeds and painting the walls a soft, "please like me, seventeen-year-old-girls" beige.

Finally, the place looked great. I was ready to head out and storm the referral world. You pick up girls—wait, that didn't sound right— that is, you locate and acquire potential group home residents mostly in county seats, because that's where the social services and probation folks hang out. Do you know that the county seat of San Benito County is Hollister? I didn't. Or that the county seat of Kings County is Hanford? I do now. Or for that matter, that in Monterey County it's Salinas? I hit the road on my "taking back the night" tour and tried to get meetings with the right people, talk to them pretty and try to see if they would give us a chance, after the Joneses had done their worst to paint us as monsters.

Of course, nobody would really talk about anything, and for that matter, there was no point in my bringing up the past; after all I was there as the new, well-scrubbed face of the future, the earnest lad who was going to set a new tone and create a safe space for their vulnerable charges.

Finally, after enough groveling, a few people were willing to give me a chance, to forget the past and let me show what I could do. And I really appreciated it. (Of course, treating them to Togo's sandwiches—from my personal funds, of course—may have had something to do with it.)

And at the same time, I had to get out there and recruit some new house parents, people who could relate to kids, were trustworthy and would work for basically minimum wage, plus room and board. And I had to coordinate these steps with bringing in the new girls, because after all, even at minimum wage, paying two people 24/7 adds up quickly, and I had to get the house on a paying basis as soon as possible to justify my own magnificent salary.

But here was my dilemma: when you have a house that's a "going concern," with say five girls already in residence and solid house parents on the job, and you bring in a new girl, you're bringing her into an already-established social network, with rules, habits, ways of behaving, menus and chores already in place. A household, in other words. But when you're throwing two (or more) new, likely inexperienced house parents into a house, and then dumping five or six new girls (if you're lucky enough to get that many) into the mix—girls who, I might add, are from dysfunctional families at best, and more likely abusive families, or no families, and who don't know each other, as well as having all the destabilizing characteristics of being teenage girls in the first place—and you're bringing them all into a new location, and a new subculture, in a neighborhood where they're going to be looked on with alarm and targeted at school as "the girls from, you know, that place," well you don't need to be an Einstein to connect the dots and see what I was up against.

But I always liked a challenge, or as I say now about my challenging therapy patients, a worthy opponent. I placed newspaper ads and began to interview potential house parents, in between running up and down Northern California (to county seats, remember?) to locate girls who might be suitable for this mixed-media installation piece I was creating on the fly.

The job applicants ran the gamut from out-and-out hippies (this was the seventies, remember) with lice in their hair and the reek of pot, to elders who thought playing parent to a few "young ladies" might be a pleasant way to spend their retirement years.
One young woman, dressed like a Navajo gypsy, read my palm

during the interview, then whispered to me that if I closed the door, she would show me some tantra "moves" that would open me up to a whole new world of sensuality.
I passed, probably sidestepping all kinds of problems.

And all the while my boss was pressuring me: "Let's go, go, go. Gotta make this thing pay!"

Then, quickly, one after the other, I got a commitment from a social services agency on a sweet girl with dead parents, then a girl from a coastal city who had been sold by her mother to her mother's male friends for unmentionable acts, and then a girl from a probation department up north who had just begun shoplifting with gang members, and was headed to the California Youth Authority (basically, jail for kids) if I didn't take her.

I took her. I took them all, ranging from thirteen to seventeen (and that's a big age spread, at that age).

Gee, I had done it: I had half a "census," ready to go!

The yard was weeded, the locks were changed, the kitchen was scrubbed and the proprietary soft beige paint was on the walls. The fridge was stocked, there were sheets on the beds, soap in the bathrooms and Tampax under the sinks. I even laid in a good supply of Orville Redenbacher's in the pantry (I prefer it, too!). Now all I had to do was have a few other minor items—such as house parents—in place, when those girls hit that ranch house.
I intensified my interviews, argued with my boss to offer slightly higher wages and, bingo, I had my first crew: two twenty-something women, both taking a break from schooling, and a nice young couple who seemed kind of lost but got along well with each other and seemed sincere enough.

We were in business!

I figured out a rotating duty schedule, worked with the new house parents to develop a list of household chores and duties for the girls, got the girls enrolled in the local schools (though we also had a private teacher available for those who needed it), installed a donated pool table in the garage and put a record player in the living room.

As the girls began to arrive, something else arrived too. It was something in me that was unexpected: a kind of fierce, protective drive, a drive to make this house what those girls deserved, a safe, trustworthy environment where they could try to make a new start and put their chaotic, traumatizing (and in some cases, horrifying) pasts behind them.

I mean, I knew this wasn't some upscale, swanky residential treatment center, a ritzy private sanitarium or The Menninger Clinic—after all, for minimum wage you don't get treatment personnel who are the cream of the crop, and for a thousand a month, you don't get an Executive Director who has years of experience and a top reputation. But I was sincerely determined to make this house a real home for these girls, a place where they could finish up their teenage years with some sense of self-worth and discover that there are some people in this world whom they could trust and rely on.

No, I wasn't stupid—I knew that you don't just throw a wide range of troubled kids together and make nice and have it all run smoothly. And you can't just put out someone's past like last week's garbage. But I was surprised at how strongly I wanted the best for them, wanted to do everything we possibly could with what we had. I might be making only a thousand a month, but I wanted to give them a hundred thousand a month. I had been putting in seventy-hour weeks, between all the house improvements, the traveling, the interviewing and the coordination with schools and local resources.

The truth is, I was giving an extended pajama party for a bunch of teenage girls who had no knowledge of each other. And the "hosts" would be a few adults who really didn't know each other either, or what to do with a house full of disparate kids in trouble. All we could really do, as the girls arrived, one by one, was welcome them and hope that somehow it would all gel into something resembling a family, or at least not devolve into an extended riot.

But this was what I had waded through all that training for, the classes and the seminars and the dissertation and all the rest: not for what it could teach me, but for the opportunity to put all my caring into action in the real world.

Now, finally, I was going to get that chance.

Part Two

The good news is, everyone pitched in together, and before long, we actually had a functioning group home for girls. Most of the girls attended the local high school, performed chores around the house, attended house meetings, had individual sessions with me once a week and slowly began to settle into at least some sense of belonging and family.

Of course there were problems all the time: "Maria claims to be some big expert on makeup, but she doesn't know shit!", "It really feels like everyone's against me—probably just jealous.", "I met this guy at school, and he wants to, you know...", "If someone's cheating at Monopoly but no one else sees it, should you tell?", "Someone ripped the crotch out of my best tights. It's obviously because they think I'm, you know. . ."

Not surprisingly, we had some early trouble with staff too, during those first months: some because they couldn't handle the, shall we say, "ups and downs" of life with the girls, some because they decided to go back to school and some because they just turned out to be wrong for the job. But eventually we got it all squared away, and I could go out to the county seats on "fishing" expeditions with my head held high. We were putting up a pretty good track record of not just being a holding pen like many of the homes, but actually starting to help some of our girls, teaching them life lessons and giving them a little pride in their own identities.

Of course, I was still pretty wet behind the ears and did some dumb things. The Agency had a "foundation" composed of civic leaders and local folks who were kind enough to take an interest in our activities. The foundation had a newsletter, and one day my boss told me to write a brief notice for the newsletter, including a request for donations for our "new and improved" group home, donations that would help us get a few things beyond the basics the county money afforded us. So I wrote up a nice little description of what we were doing, and ended it with something like, "Suggested minimum donation: five dollars."

Well, the boss hit the roof. "You can't ask these kinds of people (i.e., wealthy) to give money, and then tell them how much!"

Ouch, lesson learned. I guess I was so proud of our house that I figured five dollars was pretty paltry acknowledgment of what all of us had all put into it, but then I realized that "these kinds of people" are asked for money all the time and probably by enterprises far more worthy and grandiose than ours. So I learned something about humility, and also about asking people for money, including the fact that I never again wanted to be in the position of asking rich people for money.

Meanwhile, back at the ranch home, some things were happening that stressed me out, beyond the stress of the incredible work hours I was putting in. One night I got a call from one of the house parents: "There's been an, uh, incident here that I think you should know about."

"Can't you just tell me tomorrow?"

"No, I think you'd better get out here right now."

I hopped in my old Dodge van, the one that had the engine between the two front seats that just about asphyxiated me with gas fumes, and beat it out to the house. The girls were sitting on the living room floor, some looking guilty, and the others just plain scared. It seems that one of them had seen a movie on TV where a girl was "raped" with a broom handle by a bunch of other girls (gee thanks, producers of that movie!), and it inspired a couple of the tougher girls to reenact that scene with one of the girls, whom they had a grudge against.

Nobody was willing to talk, at least in front of the two tough girls. But I immediately separated them all and, by talking to them one at a time, got the true story from a couple of the other girls. Apparently it was more of a scare tactic ("If you don't do what we want, we're gonna hurt you, bad!") than an actual assault, and it got out of control and became kind of a Lord of the Flies thing, where the other girls became a "mob" and joined in on the taunting and threats.

In retrospect, I think it scared them too that they could act like that. We talked a lot, both then and later, about mobs and gangs, and we talked about having pride in your own standards, even under pressure from others. We also talked about letting the house parents or me know when you got wind of something going on that made you uncomfortable.

I strongly considered forcing the girls who started it to leave then and there for the safety of the others. But after I spoke to them individually, it was clear that they both came from families where force, or the threat of force, was how their parents "kept the kids in line," and I felt that they both deserved a second chance to learn other ways. Asking them to leave on this basis would most likely have meant California Youth Authority for both of them (they'd both had some previous gang involvement) and I finally decided to let them stay, on the condition that even a whiff of violence or threat of violence from them would lead to immediate expulsion.

So much for violence.

And that leads us to sex.

A few months later, I received another one of those "calls in the night." This time it was a different houseparent, who said, "There's something big, that you need to know about."

"Can it wait till tomorrow?"

"Yes, because it's over, for now, and it wouldn't happen in the daytime, anyway."

Hmm ... another lovely night of tossing and turning.

The next day I hopped in the van and raced down the freeway to the house.

The house parent who called me was just going off shift, and she could barely make eye contact with me.

"It's that bad?" I said, holding out my hands beseechingly.

"Well, let's say, for community relations, it is."

"Okay, shoot."

"Well, uh, Jane was, uh. . ."

"Jane was uh, what?"

"Well, I guess you'd say, uh, you know, turning tricks, out the back window."

My heart stopped. "With who?"

"Uh, with all comers, apparently."

Oh My God—now I knew what she meant by "community relations"! "When?"

"I guess, about a week ago. I just heard about it last night, from one of the girls."

Oh shit, wild tales of this thing had probably been circulating among the boys in the high school for a whole week!

Holy mackerel, and my boss had hit the roof about my suggesting a minimum donation!

What would he—and the foundation, and the community, and the referral agencies—say about this?

I knew that the girl in question saw Richard, the local therapist. Before going off half-cocked, I figured I'd better get in touch with him and put our heads together. Besides, I'm no hero, and there's safety in numbers! I set up an urgent appointment to see him about lunchtime that same day.

When I told him what it was about, he smiled, looking not too concerned (but then, he wasn't trying to run a group home in the middle of a conservative community!) and said, "Oh yeah, she just told me about it in today's session, and I was just about to call you. She was kind of bragging about it. She said, 'I had to walk funny for the next week!'"

Oh my God, redux. That's not exactly what one would call "remorse." To me, the signs and symptoms pointed to the possibility of some kind of history of sexual or physical abuse. But if that was the case, Jane had certainly never told me about it. She did have a tendency to dress provocatively, and she was a pretty girl—sometimes that can feel like a power to a girl who feels she has nothing else going for her.

In this case Jane did end up leaving, to go to individual foster care, as I remember.

This, and many other smaller incidents, were things I had to deal with on a regular basis. I wasn't willing to use "force, or the threat of force" to keep the girls in line, as many other group homes did. I wanted them to develop pride in themselves, to feel they were worthy of being cared about for being themselves and to at least begin to see that "power" is the ability, and courage, to be yourself, not something you obtain by getting the attention of boys, or posturing as something you're not.

Yes, I realize that that is a big goal, especially for teenage girls from difficult backgrounds. In therapy it often takes years to teach those things to grown women, who come from intact, even privileged backgrounds, had lots of advantages and went to fine schools.

But we tried hard, and I felt we made real progress with many of the girls.

Eventually, as much as I cared about the home and the girls, I had to move on. The stresses of running the house had taken a toll on me and besides, I always knew that my goal was to go into private practice. However, when I was hired, I had signed an agreement that I wouldn't go into practice in the local area.

I did move on, but I still thought about the girls a lot and missed them. They might be surprised to know that even all these years later, I still think about them almost every day. They are never far from my heart. They were my first "daughters."

One of the sweetest and most lingering memories I still cherish from my final days at the group home, after I had begun to think seriously about leaving, was during a drive I took with Barbara. She was one of the younger girls at the house, about fifteen. It kind of encapsulates for me what it's like working with young girls, both the joy and the craziness.

I was going on a grocery run, and Barbara had asked to go with me to help with the shopping. Kind of unusual, but then I thought she might have had something else in mind.

I was right.

About five minutes into our ride, she seemed to be working up her nerve to tell me something.

I helped her out. "Sweetie, just go ahead and spill it. I'll hold it in confidence, and I promise I won't judge you or lecture you."

That seemed to help. She sneaked a quick peek at me, then kind of gushed, "I think I'm in love."

"Okay. Who is it?"

"This guy in my English class. He's really cute."

"How well do you know him?"

"Well, he asked me to do his homework for him yesterday, so he must, you know, like me, right?" She looked over at me, her face kind of squinched up.

I tried to feel my way into the "right" answer, but finally just said, "Barbara, you know, love is a lot more than a guy being cute."

"Oh sure, I know that."

"Good, but the thing is, do you really want a guy who's going to ask you to do his work?"

She twined her hands together and sighed, "But he's really cute."

"Well, so are you, but that's not all that matters. You want a guy who's going to treat you well, and respect you, and . . ." I could see she thought I was beginning to lecture her, and she was probably right. I said, "Okay, then here's what I think: you're just starting your life—your romantic life, that is—and it takes time to get to know different boys, so you can compare the qualities of different kinds of people, and start to figure out what kind of boy works for you."

She nodded, "Yeah, I guess you're right."

"I know that sometimes when you're young, it feels like a particular guy is going to be your last chance, your only chance, when in reality, he's just your first chance. You'll meet lots of boys as you grow up, and I guarantee, when you get older and more experienced, sometimes you'll look back and say, 'Wow, how could I ever have cared about that guy?'"

She kind of shrugged, knowing I was probably right, but understandably reluctant to give up her dream of the moment.

We were quiet a while.

I'd had the car radio on real low that whole time, but just then, figuring our talk was over, I reached out and turned it up, and an old Motown song came on.

We both looked at each other and burst into laughter.

The song? "Shop Around."

What I didn't tell her was that it was that very moment when I realized the time had come for me to shop around, too. Like Barbara and the "really cute" boy, I now had enough confidence to see that the group home in "paradise" was only my first chance, not my last chance.

That night as I drove home, on impulse I decided to take a detour to old Cannery Row, the place where John Steinbeck had spent his younger years. As I walked the twilit streets and went down to the old pier, I thought about the love Steinbeck had for this small world and the haunts of his youth. But he moved on from his old haunts. He had bigger things to do in life, and a need to make his mark.
As I stood there looking at the rippling water, the light fading with the setting sun, I felt something stirring in me too. The constant crises and responsibilities of the last two years had certainly stressed me, but they had toughened me up, too. The scared kid was gone, and the man in me needed to make his mark.

There was a whole world waiting for me, and I was ready for it.

Apache Ways

My wife comes from a big Mexican-American family: ten brothers and sisters. The family believes it is part-Apache. *All right*, I thought, *that's cool with me*. Kind of a neat connection with the old West, with fierceness, stoicism and pride of place. And since her family can seem pretty angry and isn't much for words, it all kind of made sense, before.

But it never really meant that much to me—not until we lost my son. Because that's when it happened. Unlike us Anglos, who talk about the loss endlessly and "process" it, maybe in groups of people who wail and moan collectively, my wife just quietly went away, unannounced, to some kind of inward spiritual world, a place where no one else could enter.

And that's when I started to believe the myths about her family.

Picture picking up the flap of a teepee at nighttime and seeing an Apache woman alone, squatting by a fire in perfect stillness, the flickering flames casting ghostly shadows on her wide cheekbones, the wind swirling some of the sparks around her head, and her not noticing the sparks, or you, or the outer world at all. She just nods her head slowly in tune with some kind of inner music, an invisible barrier all around her, saying, "Go away. You don't understand now, and you never will. This is my way; the way it must be."

That woman was my wife, and that was my life for five years. I thought we were going to talk it out, that she would cry on my shoulder, that we would go to the gravesite every week and say special things, that I would hold her and comfort her and we would share the depths of our grief.

I was wrong.

I'm not saying that she neglected me, or didn't take care of her responsibilities, or that we didn't talk about important things together. Just that during that time, her deepest soul went somewhere private and inaccessible, known only to her.

Except at night, when muffled screams and strangled lamentations punctured her jagged, fitful sleep, leaving me powerless to make everything right again for her and her lost child.

And yes, it hurt to be shut out, to not be able to comfort her, to have her too distraught, too gone, to comfort me, to have her not need me. But I also learned something about respect and dignity, and about the power of silence. I started to see the Anglo ways a bit differently, with all the talking, the neighbors bringing food, the celebrations of life and the sharing of stories. Our culturally acceptable norms of dealing with profound loss can also be a way of covering up the experience of loss with busyness, and ritual, and false motions that try to tease us away from the core of the matter, which is what that Apache woman was doing in the teepee: staring straight into the heart of loss, of death, of reality, in its raw form. .

Because eventually, as time goes on, you realize that it's not about hugs and kisses, or casseroles, or weeping on your spouse's shoulder. It's about the fact that a part of your heart and soul is now gone, forever, and that you have to find a way to go on that takes you straight through that fact.

So, by being in her own world, she forced me to go into the heart of my own darkness, too, and face facts without any fancy trimmings. And by the time she did eventually come back to me, I had realized it wasn't a rejection of me at all, or an attempt to shut me out.

It was just her way.

I had to step back and respect her ways without my ego being involved. And after all, isn't that what love really is anyway?

And by the time she did come back, we were closer than ever and I had a much deeper respect, even reverence for her, because I now realize that, in staring into that fire alone, that lady had more guts than I ever could have imagined.

*   *   *

We can't make people be what we want them to be; we can only love them for who they are.

We can't make life be what we want it to be; we can only love it for what it is.

And now, I feel like I'm part-Apache too.

Emmaline

She was a whip-smart Jewish woman who was as "out" as out can be in our society. She had been diagnosed with borderline personality disorder (BPD). She was a social misfit, an ugly duckling, a psychological refugee. An intense, Eastern, big-city type, living on the laid-back West Coast.

Even her name was a contradiction to her nature: Emmaline, for God's sake—something you called your great-aunt, maybe—simple, sweet and old-fashioned.

So not her.

She was a communist by nature, but came from money. She was a Philadelphia girl, but grew up in semi-rural Wyoming. She could quote from Tolstoy and Proust, but loved hot dogs. She thought the kids she grew up with in Wyoming were idiots, "pimpleheads," but she loved horses. She would go on and on about GMOs, the evils of additives and how Big Agra was poisoning us all, and yet she smoked like a chimney. She was a dog-walker, living on the fringes of the fringes, but revered professional tennis and mostly, especially, adoringly, Roger Federer. To her, he personified devotion to craft, dedication beyond ego and, most of all, elegance in motion. To hear her deconstruct a Nadal-Federer match, blow by blow, with sparkling erudition, verve and élan, was to come to love tennis—a sport I cared nothing about—for at least an hour.

Emmaline was alone in the world. Her wealthy playboy father had died long before of alcoholism; her mother, out of touch in every possible way, had moved elsewhere, preoccupied with her own problems. Her brother and older sister were scattered to the winds, and she had long ago alienated her wealthy aunt, her only possible benefactress, by her outrageous and intemperate remarks.

How many times had I told her, "Emmaline, you can't just go around telling the truth all the time."?

She would just shake her head, cackle at me with her smoker's rasp and say, "Don't be such a coward."

So she had no family and no real friends. But that doesn't mean she didn't have emotional closeness in her life. The dogs she walked were her family, and I came to know most of them by name, breed and personality. I worried, right along with her, whether Jack was going to get along with Dandy, whether Sugarbush would be accepted by the new "pack," whether they were finally going to open that new dog park they had been promising for months. I fumed, outraged, right along with her, when Rollo was cut back to once a week by his owners, "up in the hills," who, though wealthy, were "pet cheapskates."

And worst of all were the park rangers in Tilden Park, that wonderful green open space in the hills above Berkeley. In Emmaline's world, those rangers were the "Dog Nazis" who picked on her, targeted her, and laid in ambush for her, for the sin of walking her dogs without leashes.

Leashes—that would be it, of course. Emmaline hated leashes, and restraints of any kind, on humans or dogs. She hated authorities too, whether they were "those dog haters" (park rangers) or "the striped skunks" (tennis line judges who ruled against Roger Federer), or "that witch" (her landlady) whom she claimed she could hear, "laughing up there in her room, late at night, hatching new schemes to cheat me and force me out." And Emmaline believed these things: she was the living incarnation of that old joke, "Just because you're paranoid, doesn't mean they aren't out to get you."

But that doesn't mean she had a high opinion of herself. She was not pretty by any stretch of the imagination, and she'd had very minimal sexual or romantic experience with men. And women? She said, "I'm not attractive to women, either, but it's no great loss; from what I can tell, most of 'em are afraid of their own shadow." She had no idea about "doing anything" about her appearance, nothing remotely approaching a sense of style, or interest in same. At one point she started coming in with a colorful bandana around her hair, and for a moment I thought she was at least trying to show some flair. But it turned out it was just a way to cover up her hair so she "didn't have to fiddle with it at all anymore."

For all her failings though, Emmaline was very sophisticated and, to her credit, mostly self-taught. For most patients with borderline personality disorder whom I have treated, at some point I sit down with them and say, "Now don't panic, but I think this will help explain why your life is so chaotic: you have a condition called borderline personality disorder. Here is a book that lists the symptoms. Please take a look at it and let's go over them together, and see if it doesn't ring a bell."

But with Emmaline, she had done her own research, years before. In fact, she had not only acquainted herself with the work of the famous psychiatrist Dr. James Masterson, one of the preeminent theorists of BPD, she had sought him out and worked with him personally. She had great praise for his deep understanding and caring, and always said, "He had amazing eyes."

She was always in financial trouble, and one of the reasons was the fact that she had terrible difficulty asking her dog-walking clients for the money that was due her, even though she treated their dogs like royalty and took a personal interest in each and every one of them. But it was hard, so hard, for her to ask for anything. She finally confessed to me that she had been stashing the checks they gave her in one of those round metal candy tins.
Why?

Because she was mortally afraid of banks and terrified that she would get in trouble if she brought in a big bunch of checks to deposit, because she didn't declare any of her income. I tried to point out that she had earned the money and that she didn't make enough for the IRS to bother with her anyway. I finally got her to bring in the big round can, and I would group together small stacks of them from Wells Fargo, for example, so she could go to Wells Fargo and cash them. I also encouraged her to ask her clients to pay her in cash, but, again, that was asking too much, and they might fire her if she "demanded" that. Besides, beyond a certain point, she became afraid to even talk to them about the fees, because it might draw attention to the fact that she hadn't deposited their previous checks.

Do you begin to see what it's like having BPD?

But wait, there's one other important thing about being an outsider, being marginalized, being a pariah, being a borderline. Yes, you may distort reality and misread human cues, but at the same time, since you don't really have a stake in society, you also don't have a stake in the convenient distortions that so many of us share:

"Anyone can make it (especially in America) if they try hard."
"The good and the bad eventually even out."
"Good things happen to those who are deserving."

For a borderline, the ultimate outsider, these things are laughable, even ludicrous. What you learn is:

"No matter what I do, I'll always be seen as a freak... Just when you think you're getting somewhere, something happens to pull the rug out from under you... People who say they care, only care when it coincides with what's good for them... Society is basically one big clique, so don't kid yourself, because you'll never really be a part of it."

Emmaline used to say that she wasn't surprised that young people followed Charles Manson: "Most of what he said about society was true. The parents *had* misled and alienated the young with their hypocritical beliefs in a system that was dying. Madison Avenue, and Pennsylvania Avenue, were trying to brainwash us into falling into line so capitalists could continue to reap billions from business as usual. Yes, Manson was a sociopath who eventually misused it all for his own personal benefit and power, but that doesn't mean that much of what he said wasn't valid."

She was brilliant. She could have been anything, but for her, to "be somebody" in society's terms extracted too great a price—in freedom, in independence, in truthfulness. Yes, it's a given that her emotional problems derailed her life, but it's also true that she had the courage to speak out in situations where remaining silent would have been smarter and more self-serving.

It's not hard to see why she ended up reveling in the company of dogs. For her, dogs weren't phonies. They didn't make fun of you, they didn't try to con you, they didn't try to be something they weren't or expect you to be something you weren't.

She would say, "Dogs are what people should be. If you treat them well, if you respect them, then they love you, period. Isn't that what life should be all about?"

Patients like Emmaline force you to question your assumptions as a therapist. They test your humanity and challenge your beliefs about treatment outcomes. After all, there's a difference between "normalizing" someone in society's terms (or the Diagnostic and Statistical Manual's) and helping them find their own kind of normal. The latter is infinitely harder to accomplish, but infinitely more valuable. Emmaline made me walk that fine line and, in the end, pushed me hard to find my own kind of normal, as a therapist, and as a person. Her love for "her" dogs—way beyond the call of duty—taught me a lot about how to care for my patients. Hearing her do a breakdown on the social dynamics of a pack of dogs, and what that meant as far as handling them, was a rare and precious gift. She even made me read Masterson on borderlines, and finally learn something about my craft.

You don't forget someone like that.

*   *   *

One day, Emmaline came in, and between bouts of smoker's cough, muttered something out of the side of her mouth. I couldn't understand a word of it, and I asked her to repeat it. She pulled the blanket I keep in the office up over her face, and forced the words out: "I have stage four lung cancer."

She said it like she was afraid it would bother me. Of course, it did bother me, but not in that way.

"How do you know?" I asked.

"Oh, I went in for tests a few months ago."

"And you're only telling me now?"

"Sorry, I didn't mean to upset you."

Oh my God. What do you say to that?

"I'm going in the hospital on Friday."

"Is there anything I can do?"

"Come and see me, if you can fit it into your schedule." She pulled the blanket over her head. "You're my only somebody."

I choked out the words. "Of course."

And, of course, I did go and see her in the hospital. And of course it went fast: stage four is no joke.

I told her it was an honor to know her.

The last thing she rasped was, "I feel sorry for my dogs."

I did too.

*　　　*　　　*

Here's a little secret I want you to know: even now, with many years gone by since that last talk in the hospital, every time I open this one particular drawer in my office, there's that big, round tin container, stuffed with well-earned but undeposited dog-walking checks, always sitting there.

I can't bring myself to throw it out, but I do have an idea.

Maybe one of these days I'll take it up to Tilden Park, tear up all the checks and scatter Emmaline's *ashes* on the trails.

And if later that day, some of the Dog Nazis come by and wonder who littered the park, I'm betting that if they listen closely, they'll hear a disembodied smoker's cackle coming from somewhere beyond the trees.

Little Things

It's almost Christmas, and depending on your faith, your hope and your charity, some big things are about to happen: seeing family and friends, decorating the tree, giving and getting presents, making and eating special foods. Are you having turkey, a ham, fancy stuffing, mashed potatoes, Grandma's famous tricked-out yams? Or Bubbe's famous latkes, kreplach, strudel? In our household, I make matzo brei in schmaltz every year on Christmas morning (one year it was even fried in bacon grease; fortunately, Jahweh didn't seem to mind), and if that isn't the American melting pot for you, well, I don't know what is.

All of these "big things" are the traditions that we wait for, look forward to and even rely on to make the end of the year a special time for pausing to celebrate family, loved ones, the joy of giving and the fun of receiving. For some of us, Jesus even manages to squeeze in there somewhere between the rum balls and the mince pie.

As a sentimentalist and a traditionalist, I love those old, familiar ways that we revisit together again and again, down through the years.

But I love surprises, too. The little things that weren't planned but seem to happen because, for the holidays, we've gotten out of our regular ruts and made way for them. Today, the last Sunday before Christmas, brought a few little things that I particularly enjoyed:

Figuring out the chords to "Georgia on my Mind" with my young son's twelve-year-old friend Krister, on my old player piano, the one that doesn't play on its own anymore, since Angus, my Scottie, peed on the electric cord and it dissolved. Krister has been around forever, almost like a brother to my son, and almost like another son to us. There have been lots of ups and down, ins and outs in our relationship with him over the years, but I'm glad he's back in the fold. It was especially fun to figure out that E major seventh on the second "Georgia" in the lyrics! (That's when played in the key of C; by the way, I play everything in C.) And then, when we nailed that whole Edim-to-Dm7 change, whoa, that's what I'm talkin' about! And to see Krister pick it up and start playing it on his own, with a big smile, well, that's what I mean by "little things." Maybe it wasn't Hoagy Carmichael, but it was damn fine.

And afterwards, he and I worked together to string the lights on the tree, and when we plugged them all in for the grand unveiling, well, there went another big "little thing."

And then later, we went to see the movie *Wild*, and it was sort of percolating along, just okay, when, out of the blue, there was an unexpected scene near the end where a little kid sang *"Red River Valley"*—wow! Before that, the buttered popcorn was the best thing about the movie; after that, well, that kid kind of sprinkled salt and butter over the whole rest of my afternoon.

After the show, we were walking down Piedmont Avenue, still glowing about the kid in the movie, when a little kid in real life, walking down the street with his mom, suddenly dropped down on all fours, started crawling and yelled with glee, "Me baby!" Wow, talk about a blast from the past! It took me back to walks with our twins, when they used to put their arms up and cry, "Hold you!"

And twenty years before that, when Mhat would do the same thing and cry, "Carry!"

Those little things—they really get to you. Unplanned, unexpected, unwrapped gifts from the universe that sneak in under your habits and your defenses, and put a smile on your face, or tears in your eyes, or just a warm glow in your heart.

One of the fun things about being a therapist is that I get to hear about other peoples' little things, too. Recently, a woman about my age, whom I have seen off and on for a long time, told me a story about her father's last days. While he had a warm heart, he could also be, quite frankly, a grinch. My patient and her sister had been taking care of their aging dad in the last days of his life. One day my patient came over to her sister's house, where Dad was in residence, in sort of a home-based hospice. Dad hobbled to the kitchen, where they all sat together playing cards and dominoes, as they always had. As she and her sister had always done, one of them started singing a show tune, and then the other sister joined in.

And as always, their father rolled his eyes in dismay, shaking his head in an, oh-boy-here-they-go-again gesture.

But a little while later, my patient looked up from her dominoes in surprise: Dad was singing too!

He died the next day.

See what I mean? Little things—they mean so much.

Another patient, a young woman who's simply an amazing person, was having difficulty with insomnia, over a long period of time. Finally, I suggested something that I use to help me sleep—a CD of falling rain, that also has some other sounds of nature periodically as it goes along, including a memorable hoot owl about an hour into it.

She said she'd give it a try, so I made a copy of it for her, and we spoke no more about it.

A few weeks later, I asked her if she'd ever used it.

She nodded, "Yes, it helps, sometimes."

I was pleased and figured that was that.

But then she looked up at me and added, kind of shyly, "Do you ever make it to the bird?"

Well, maybe you had to be there but, to me, it was about the most adorable thing ever.

Still, we don't need to wait for these little things to happen, do we? If we pay close attention to our moments and have an open heart, we might notice them all the time, kind of like how, when you're looking for red Volkswagens, you start noticing them all over the place. Sure, some might call it "mindfulness," but hell, you can save yourself two hundred bucks for a weekend seminar and not even have to listen to some boring dharma talk by just shutting up and taking a good look at the world around you.

How about we just start with the miracle of sight, being able to read this writing like you're doing right now? The eye is a crazy-fantastic instrument, and it comes standard on almost all models!

Or how about noticing the humor in everyday life, like something I overheard at a Chinese restaurant:

A diner asked the waiter, "Do you have long beans on the menu?"

The waiter said, "No, but we do have green beans."

The diner was pensive for a moment, and then he nodded approvingly and said, "Well, *they're* pretty long."

Or take something you're interested in, like gardening, the weather (a patient of mine checks the weather forecast every day, for Paris!), politics, books or architecture, and make a point of noticing one little thing about it every day.

Take baseball, which I happen to love. One of my favorite little things in baseball is a story I read about the 1961 season. For those of you who aren't baseball freaks, that was the season that Roger Maris and Mickey Mantle, of the Yankees, were chasing Babe Ruth's single-season record of sixty home runs. Well, for much of the season, they were both neck and neck, keeping up with the pace Ruth had set back in 1927. As the season went on, and they kept hitting homers at a record pace, the whole country sat up and took notice. I'm telling you, people who barely knew a baseball from a football actually knew who Roger Maris was, and how many home runs he had on any given day. I mean, people in *foreign countries* were checking the totals every day!

Finally Maris started pulling ahead of Mantle, who went down with a leg injury, and soon it was just Roger Maris against history, with big headlines every single day on the sports pages:

"Maris Hits Another One: 56!"

"Maris Fails—Stuck On 57!"

But here's the thing: Roger Maris was a very private, edgy guy, who had never had this kind of attention paid to him—heck, *no one* ever had. Every day, hordes of media types crowded around him, in the clubhouse, in his apartment, at his restaurant table, hounding him for details, pressing for answers to impossible questions—nasty, probing questions. Remember, this was before social media, before *People magazine*, before the cult of celebrity meltdowns. Baseball players had never been subjected to this kind of scrutiny before, and here was this introverted, laconic guy from South Dakota being analyzed to death, prodded to the point where his hair started falling out.

Every day the same relentless questions came, over and over:

"How'd you feel out there today, Rog?"
"Do you really think you're better than Babe Ruth?"
"What was wrong with you today, Rog?"
"What makes you think you can beat the record, when the greatest players of all time never could?"

Finally, it was coming down to the end of the season. The Yankees were playing a series in Detroit. Maris had 57 home runs—only three to tie the record, four to beat it. The place was in an uproar every time he came to bat, every pitcher saving his best "stuff" for this young punk who thought he was better than Babe Ruth.

Maris stepped up to the plate. The pitcher prepared to throw the ball, and forty thousand people held their breath.

Suddenly, Roger stepped out of the batter's box, and looked up at the sky.

What was he doing? He was taking a "mindfulness" moment to look up at a flock of geese, flying in formation, high over the stadium.

Here was this young country boy, under the fiercest media pressure of all time, and he had the presence of mind to step out and take the time to watch a flock of geese.

Now, that's my idea of a beautiful "little thing"!

Yes, Roger Maris did go on to break Babe Ruth's record; though when he did it, the Commissioner of Baseball decreed that he hadn't "really" beaten the Babe's record, since that year, the season had been expanded from 154 games to 161. Oh, and by the by, it turns out the Commish, a former sportswriter, had once been Babe Ruth's ghostwriter!

But they couldn't take away from Roger Maris that one, small, beautiful moment that he had taken for himself, and that's why it's my favorite little memory of that famous season.

So, you can take seminars, pay gurus, spend weeks at a time in silent retreats, or chant your mantra, but eventually, it all comes down to taking the time, every day, to look up at a flock of geese, or notice a little kid who wants his mom to carry him, or join your daughters in singing show tunes, or listen to my rain CD.

So come on, people, if you pay close attention and don't miss the moment, maybe we can *all* make it to the bird!

What We Came Here For

May I have the courage today
To live the life that I would love,
To postpone my dream no longer
But do at last what I came here for
And waste my heart on fear no more.

—"A Morning Offering," by John O'Donohue

You have been given the gift of life, and if you're lucky, quite a few decades to do your thing.

All right, what is your thing? Checking your Facebook page five hundred times a day? Acting like everything is okay when it isn't? Fitting in, so nobody gets upset? Keeping so busy that you never have to be with yourself? Doing just enough to keep out of trouble? Keeping your eyes down and endlessly repeating what you did yesterday?

What if you looked at yourself in the mirror every morning and said, "Well, for cryin' out loud, here I am again. It get to live another whole day. For all I know, it may be my last. What am I going to do with it? What could I do that I would look back on tomorrow and say, 'Kid, you took that precious day and did a pretty good job with it.'"

No, I don't mean being a "do-gooder," although that may be one thing you could do with it. I'm talking about living from the inside out, really manifesting who you actually are, right out in the open. What is it to be you? I'm talking about coming up with an active answer to the complaint, "I never get a chance to really do what I want to do. I never get a chance to be who I really am."

Sure, maybe you're a jeweler and all you ever really wanted to be was a newspaper reporter. Maybe you're working in a day-care center and you're really fascinated by numbers. Or maybe you're like most people and you don't know "who you are." It doesn't stop you from feeling that you never get to be who you are, though, does it? You still have that vague unease that you're not really being you, even if you have no idea what that would look like. It still feels frustrating and unsatisfying, doesn't it?
I can hear you saying, "Hey, we can't all save the world, dude." True, but fortunately, that has nothing to do with what I'm talking about. I'm talking about incremental steps toward letting the cat (you!) out of the bag. Small steps for tiny feet.

It might start with this exercise:
I always wanted to _____ (fill in the blank).
I wish just once I could _____.
The people I really admire are _____.

I can hear the classic comeback:

"You can wish in one hand and spit in the other, and see which one fills up first."

Yes, I get it: just wishing alone does nothing. But wishing can lead to more than "nothing." Most new things start with an idea, a wish, a concept, a drive, a desire, a "vain" hope. And then, by allowing those things to rattle around a bit in our heads and hearts, they lead to a wish, dream, concept, drive, desire and hope that is more realistic, that is, in fact, a first step. One that is a revised version of the original dream.

The hokey saying, "Dreams plus effort equal success," is not so crazy after all, because the primary thing holding us back from reaching some version of our dreams is that we give up before we start. This happens because at the start we can't envision the modified version we might discover along the way (or we aren't willing to admit to ourselves that we "settled" for a very downgraded version of our dreams).

If you talk to people about their lives for a living, as I have done for decades, you begin to hear things, like the fact that at the beginning, most people had never heard of what they ended up doing for a living. And, if they had, they might have rejected it because it was not what they had dreamed of.

It takes emotional work to process a dream. Let's say you start out wanting to be a famous performer. Of course, you know the odds against you are astronomical. You may feel you're talented, but not that talented, so you give up, accepting "reality."

But what would happen if you continued with your dream?

As one example, this was the sequence of events for a woman I worked with—we'll call her Josephine—who dreamed of being a performer:

1) You take singing and guitar lessons. You do pretty well, but nobody ever suggests you should go on *American Idol*.
2) Nevertheless, you do develop your singing and playing ability and your performance chops, to the point where you are able to perform at local open mikes. You get some pretty good responses,

but again, no one says, "I've never heard anyone as good as you, Josie," either.

3) Hanging out at the clubs, you get to know more and more people in the music scene, and also land a few paid gigs at local spots. It is gratifying, and some people really like what you do. You meet an agent who is in the audience at a local club you're working, and she's a really cool person. She doesn't offer you anything, but you talk a lot together, and it's pretty interesting. Maybe this thing could actually work.

4) You get a better gig, but it's on weekends, out of town. You are hostessing at a nice restaurant where you live, and on weekends you can make pretty good money, even though hostessing is a million miles away from what you really want to do. But you can't afford to quit your job just to pursue one gig out of town. What do you do?

5) For some reason, you call the agent you met at that club. You end up talking to her for two hours. She talks to you like a Dutch uncle (aunt?) and says, kindly, "Josie dear, you're an amazing person, but to tell you the truth, I don't feel you have what it takes to make it as a performer." She's nice about it but it hurts, bad. But on the other hand, there's something about her that you trust, so you can't just dismiss what she's saying. She does say, "You should call me sometime when you're feeling better. We should talk." (Whatever that means.)

6) You cry—a lot.

7) You cry more—a lot. (Hopefully you have good friends. They help—a little.)

8) When you get off work late one Saturday night, you suddenly remember that the agent said to call her sometime when you're feeling better. You check: hmm, you're feeling better, marginally.

9) You call her, hoping against hope that she has reconsidered her death sentence of you, and wants to work with you on your performance career.

10) She doesn't want to work with you on your performance career—but, she does want to talk to you about something else. She's a top agent in town, and has noticed that you are good with people and know a lot of folks locally around the music business by now. She is trying to expand her business and, maybe, could use someone like you. Of course, you would have to "start at the bottom," but she feels you might have it in you to grow into a significant role in talent representation one day. You're flattered, sort of, but inside you're still really wounded that she didn't want to talk to you about you-know-what. But you tell her you really appreciate her time and comments, and you'll have to think about it and get back to her.

11) You sulk alone. You sulk with friends.

12) Hmm, you sigh—a lot—but it kind of makes sense, what she said: you are a good judge of others' talent, you are good with people and you have always liked helping people pursue their dreams, even if you can't pursue yours.

13) You cry.

14) Sigh. You call her, and say you're willing to talk more about it. Sulk.

15) You do talk more about it. It's starting to sound like a possibility. Your friends say, "I can totally see you doing it; helping people like that."

16) More sighing. After all, if you accept this, it means throwing away your "real" dreams, right?

17) Secretly, you're getting kind of excited about this whole thing: "Wow, I could work for a talent agency. I'd still get to be around performers, watching them, helping them, and I always thought I had a good eye for talent."

18) Last-ditch sighing, last-ditch crying. First-ditch excitement. All mixed up together.

19) You make a decision: you're going to do it. It's not as much as you're making hostessing, but it's in the field you love, and the po-

tential in that field is a bit greater than in the profession of guiding drunk people to their tables.

20) You have a new dream: being a talent agent. "Gee, now that I'm a 'professional,' I have to get some real working-woman clothes. This might be fun!"

Okay, I can hear you saying, "Oh sure, he came up with an example where it all worked out, but what percentage of the time does that happen? My uncle Arnie wanted to be an opera singer, and now he's a broken-down bum on Skid Row. Dreams, schmeams."

Folks, this is the way it really happens. Not always of course. Not every person finds work that's a perfect fit. But I have helped many, many people "evolve" their dreams. And note, in the example above, Josephine did not literally achieve her original dream. But pursuing it did lead her to people and circumstances that made it possible to develop other dreams that were achievable. She had no thought whatsoever, at first, that being a talent agent was a possible (or desirable) dream for herself. And if I had been prescient (or stupid) enough at the beginning to say, "Josephine, you should be a talent agent," she would have been hurt and angry, and rightfully so.

Does this mean . . .

Buy my new book, *Twenty Steps to a New Dream*, now with detailed instructions on how sulking can lower your insulin level and burn carbs!

No, of course not. Each person has a unique path to follow. You cannot know beforehand what someone's path will be, you cannot know beforehand what it will lead to and it would be arrogant and disrespectful to try to. But you can know beforehand what basically needs to happen. Following a dream, with a lot of support, will often lead to something meaningful and authentic, even if the path takes unexpected turns and involves a lot of sighing, crying and rejection. Sure, it might hurt sometimes, but sighing and crying are not end points; they are only emotional way stations. If you are willing sometimes to sit with the sighing and crying, and have someone who believes in you (a therapist, in the case of those I have worked with), you will move beyond sadness and disappointment, to a new formulation of yourself and your possibilities. All the emotional processing you have gone through will bring a maturity that will serve you in good stead in your "new" dreams, a maturity you would never have earned if you had instantly achieved your dreams (see Woods, Tiger) or if you had stayed home and never pursued them at all.

With a dream, anything might happen, but without a dream, you don't have a chance.

So, the next time you stand there in the morning and look in the mirror, ask that sleepy guy or gal you see before you, what he or she can do to make sure the day isn't wasted.
Yes, I know, you read all kinds of "inspirational" things, and sometimes they confuse you even more, even if they're well-intended. It's been said, "A dream is just a dream, but a goal is a dream with a plan and a deadline."

Well, I'm not sure about the goals and the deadlines, but I do know this: a dream paired with some courage and some help? Now that's a plan!

Where does *your* plan start today, sleepyhead?

Note to Self

Evan Langston was not morbidly obese. He wasn't even regular obese. Yes, he was "heavy," but his weight, per se, wasn't really the problem.

Obsessive eating was.

Ice cream, candy, cake and, in a pinch, cake batter, straight out of the bowl, with a big spoon— behavior that, in any Overeaters Anonymous meeting anywhere would be ordinary, mundane, tame, run-of-the mill and S.O.P.

But to Evan Langston, it felt frighteningly out of control.

To you "normies" out there, you folks who eat pretty much what you want, when you want it, and stop when you're full, you think the problem is the weight itself. You look at overweight people and say to yourself, "Dude, get it together. Don't you have any pride, any self-respect? Just say no! Oh, and you might want to get a little exercise, while you're at it!"

And yes, the weight itself is a problem, but to a true compulsive eater, getting through a day is like a car ride down a steep, tortuous mountain road. You never know when the brakes are going to go out—you only know that they will, repeatedly and unpredictably.

Plus, you have to drive on that road every single day of your life.

You see, the thing is, with an alcoholic, a drug addict, a cigarette smoker or a compulsive gambler, when they "swear off," they can get a sponsor, work the steps and then just stay away from the drugs, the booze, the gambling or the cigarettes, from then on.

Hard, but not impossible.

But an overeater? He or she still *has* to eat, every day; has to be around food, every day; has to watch other people eat, every day. Has to see food being prepared, eaten, enjoyed, savored, talked about and displayed, on TV, on billboards, in restaurants, in grocery stores, at home.

Every day.

So, as opposed to other kinds of addictions, it's impossible to "just stay away" from food.

And that's the first reason it's incredibly hard to stop.

But there's more: unlike other addictions, it's also incredibly easy to get access to food.

You don't have to deal with criminals, or worry about getting pulled over, or breathalyzed, because food is legal. You don't have to spend a fortune, or steal to get the money, because food is cheap. You don't have to ask others for anything, because overeating can be a solo operation, in fact preferably solo, because like most addictive behavior, it is secret and feels shameful.

So food is easy, it's cheap, it's legal, it's everywhere and you can do it alone.

We've all seen movies where the plot hinges on whether the hero can really trust the shady, unpredictable character or not. The suspense, the wondering, can carry us, quite enjoyably, through a whole movie, as we sit there idly munching our popcorn.

Fun, right?

But what if that shady, unpredictable character you had to trust was yourself?

Oh, and what if that popcorn, the one with the guilty butter, was the whole point of going to the movies? And the candy, the ice cream, the bon bons, the licorice whips, the whole snack bar?

A compulsive eater once told me, "Look, you have to understand that, basically, I'm a bowling ball, and the whole world is the pins! I can't avoid my addiction, because I'm rolling right through it, all day, every day."

*   *   *

And that brings us to Evan Langston, the journalist. Well, on second thought, let's just start with Evan Langston—the "journalist" part came later.

It was my first case of the week: Monday, 10:00 a.m. As you can see from that start time, I am not a morning person. I sleep through sunrises if I possibly can. I don't "do" coffee, latte, mocha or any other drink that involves heat and special preparation. And for God's sake please don't wave eggs, bacon, pancakes, cereal or any other edibles in my face before noon, unless you want to wear it.

As I sat in my office and wiped the night-owlery out of my eyes, trying to adjust to the manic California sunshine, I remembered that first brief exchange with Mr. Langston on the phone.

Langston: Can you help with food?

Me: Well, I'm not a caterer or anything. I'm more in the clean-up end of things.

Langston: Yes, that's what I need: clean-up, because I'm a mess. I have a real compulsive eating problem.

Me: Oh, like, "Stop me, before I kill again?"

Langston: Something like that.

Me: Sure, let's set up a time.

I held out my hand to a tallish, rather portly gentleman in the waiting room. He was about forty-five or so, well-dressed, with expensive penny loafers.

I nodded. "Nice shoes."

"Thank you."

I led him back to the inner sanctum. "Welcome, Mr. Langston. Have a seat, anywhere that feels comfortable."

"Thanks, but nowhere feels comfortable right now."

I took out my pad and my green Pilot. "And why is that?"

"Because there's something living inside me that I hate."

I nodded. "Are you referring to the compulsive eating monster you mentioned on the phone?"

He nodded back. "That's the one." His piercing green eyes were leveled at me, unblinking, but his trembling mouth gave him away.

I liked this guy right away. He didn't duck or weave or hem or haw; he looked right at me and spoke his truth. I could see he wasn't a coward, but this thing scared the hell out of him and he admitted it, straight up. He looked like a man who came in to confess, to make a new beginning, a man who was past pride, ego or image.

My kind of guy.

I wanted to help him.

But you can't skip past the stages of building a relationship just because you like someone. You have to start with the foundation.

I held my pen at the ready and said, "Please, tell me something about yourself." Sure, it's a stupid question, too open-ended and non-directive to make much sense, but when you've been asking people that same question for forty years, what someone does with it tells you a lot.

Evan sighed, as his mind sifted through a thousand possible responses. Finally, he just said, "To tell you something about me, I would have to tell you something about . . ." His eyes drifted to the ceiling.

"Your father?" It was just a hunch, but a rock-solid one.

He licked his lips and blinked. "Yeah, that's right. My mythical, overwhelming, there-but-not-there father."

"How so?" I angled my head.

He sighed hard, and then waited for two seconds ... four ... ten. When he ran his hands over his face, I knew it was the second-act curtain. He said, "Why does the future always begin with the past?"

I began, "Because . . ."

He held up his hands. "Nope, that was rhetorical. I know why: because of the boy inside the man, and the man inside that boy."

"And that man is . . .?"

"Doctor Ernest Bloch Langston, my esteemed sire, and lord and master of all he surveyed," his eyes narrowed, "including me."

My immediate association? The "something" inside of him, the something he hated, that he had mentioned not ten minutes before, in a different context. But, of course, I didn't say anything—most of a therapist's job is not saying anything. This is not a job for show-offs.

I scribbled a few notes, then raised my pen. "He sounds delightful. Please go on."

"Have you ever loved, adored and been desperate to please someone, but hated them at the same time?"

I smiled. "I believe it's been known to happen, on occasion."

"Well, this is one of those occasions. You know, over and over, I
keep thinking I'm free of him, but then . . ."

"He pulls you back in?"

"He turns me inside out." Evan buried his head in his hands. "And
I am so sick of it." He brought his head up and looked me in the
eye again in that level way. "Tell me, why do I keep going back to a
poisoned well?"

"Because the boy in you thinks it's the only well in town. But we can
change that."

"How?"

"By working together, just like we're doing right now. It'll take time,
but we're going to reclaim that sweet, sincere boy, and put you back
in touch with him."

"How much time?"

"As little as possible, but as much as he needs."

Evan chuckled. "Inscrutable?"

"I'm not trying to be."

He held his hands up. "I know, I'm just ... impatient, especially with
myself, always have been." He flashed a wry smile. "One of his primary traits, too."

"Who, Dad?"

"Yeah."

"And that's exactly why we need to take our time—because that boy
wasn't given enough of it."

His head went down again as he shook it back and forth "How ironic. Now, because Dad was impatient, it's going to take us till eternity
freezes over to get me better."

"It won't be eternity, I promise."

"Don't promise things you can't deliver."

"Why, because you're impossible, incurable, unworthy and a hopeless loser?"

"Is it that obvious?"

"I was just repeating what you believe: I don't believe any of that crap."

"Careful. You're going up against the master."

"I haven't been afraid of ghosts for a long time."

"You never met this one."

*   *   *

Over the course of those first few sessions, Evan filled me in on the "master" more thoroughly. Daddy Langston was a physician and surgeon who built an empire in "Doc in the Box" medical care centers in underserved suburban areas across the country. When Evan was nine, the family moved from San Francisco to a mansion on the water in Tiburon, with priceless art on the walls and a new trophy mistress every six months. That is, after Mommy was tossed out with a tidy financial settlement that included her agreeing to be "diagnosed" as a mentally unstable alcoholic (and therefore an unfit parent), and a sub-rosa agreement that she must stay away from Evan and his younger sister, Berta, except for rare visits, "supervised" by Daddy's thugs. These became irrelevant after Mommy drifted to Europe and lived up to her billing, dying of cirrhosis in Vienna when Evan was nineteen.

Game, set and match: the Master.

"Jeez, what a bloodless bastard—oops, did I say that?"

Evan smiled. "Join the crowd; it's nothing countless others haven't said, including me." Then he looked right at me again. "But like I said before, why does someone keep going back to a poisoned well?"

"Someone?"

"Okay then: me."

"Because when you're dying of thirst, even a mirage looks good."

"Don't you mean hunger?"

"Yes—in fact, that gives me an idea." I stood up and walked across the office, as I often do. "We need to get you off the gold standard."

He cocked his head. "Excuse me?"

"What I mean is, we need to change the source of what you're seeking."

"I'm still confused."

"Okay, so tell me, what does it feel like just before you go on a binge?"

He frowned in frustration.

I prompted him. "Come on, dig deep. Breathe. Be patient with yourself, for once."

"Okay, okay. Just give me a minute."

"All the time you want."

He closed his eyes and went inward. "Well ... empty, I guess."

"You guess?"

"Yes: empty."

"Okay, where?"

His right hand went up and down, doing a slow body scan, until it stopped just below his rib cage. "Here, I guess." He breathed again, slowly, twice. "It's like ... like I want something, need something, to ... to fill the hole."

I was ready. "Okay then, it needs something. So let's *give* it something."

He opened his eyes. "What? Dad's love, on a stick?"

"No, let's give it something we have access to."

"A hot dog on a stick?"

"How about *your* love?"

He laughed out loud. "My love? That's just a rumor; you know that."

I nodded, slowly. "Maybe now it is, but by the time we get done growing it, it'll be more than a rumor. Imagine being off the impossible gold standard of Dad's love—imagine being able to give yourself what you need!"

He shook his head again, slowly. "You are one serious weirdo, doctor." Then a tiny smile began to appear. "But, wow, imagine if I could love myself like that."

"And don't forget, I'm here for you, too, as a back-up plan."

"Supplemental health insurance? Okay, okay, maybe this thing isn't so crazy after all. But how do we compete with ice cream?"

"Wow, did I hear a 'we'?"

"Down boy, your caring is still just a rumor, too."

"I grow on people."

He smiled. "All right, Yoda, so what's the plan?"

*   *   *

Over the next few sessions, we worked out a plan. No, this was not a "master plan," because despite the books you may read by people who want to reduce psychology and therapy to a series of techniques, or sell you their formulas for self-improvement, working with people on this level is mostly a seat-of-the-pants enterprise: informed by experience and intuition of course, but still a far cry from prescribed steps or actual science.

First off, Evan was to "slow it down" when he got the urge to eat ice cream: go inside, breathe into the desire and "ask" it what it wants. Of course, the first answer would be, "I already told you, stupid: ice cream!"

But he was to stay with it, go deeper into the desire, into the hole and see if he could get an answer, any answer, rational or not.

And then, he was to "respond" to any wishes and needs he could sense, as a caring friend would. I suggested writing down his responses, as it would help him gather his thoughts and serve as a record of his efforts, for himself and for me, too.

We ended that last "prep" session like this:

Evan: But I'm not a writer!
Me: This isn't about writing; it's about caring—for yourself, for once.
Evan: Now, that would be a novelty.
Me: It's going to be more of a diary, Evan, a diary of your return to life.
Evan: (Crying) I don't know what to say to that.
Me: There's nothing to say, except, "Good luck! And I'll be with you."
Evan: Okay then, into the unknown!"
We shook hands.
It felt like shaking hands with H.G. Wells' protagonist before he embarks on his first voyage in *The Time Machine*.

*   *   *

That week went by uneventfully, though I did find myself checking my email a bit more than usual. Our session wasn't until Thursday evening, and not having heard from Evan, I assumed that nothing had happened. Maybe he, like many, if not most, patients, when given an "assignment," wouldn't even make an attempt to carry out the plan.

Finally, eight o'clock came, and my signal light came on.

I felt like saying, "Welcome, traveler, what news?" but then I sometimes have a tendency toward the dramatic.
Evan took his seat and settled himself in carefully. Hmm, was he exhibiting patience? Hush.
"Well, that was a bust."
Uh oh. "What do you mean, 'bust'?"
"I did exactly what you suggested. I wanted to eat ice cream, and . . ."
I held out my hands. "And?"

"And ... nothing."

He looked crestfallen, maybe broken.

I nodded slowly. "Okay, so go over it carefully, step by step, for me."

"Well, Friday evening, I was sitting there, watching TV, when it hit me."

"Go on."

"I wanted ice cream."

"So noted."

"I tried to breathe into it, like you said, but . . ."

I leaned forward, fascinated. "Yes, but. . .?"

He sighed, his shoulders slumping. "But nothing: I ate a whole pint of Ben and Jerry's phish food."

I put up a Hail Mary. "Well, at least it wasn't a quart."

"Please, don't try to pump this up artificially."

"So noted."

I regrouped. "Okay, so once again, tell me exactly what happened when you tried to breathe into the feeling."

Evan shifted in his chair. "Like I told you: nothing."

"C'mon, you can do better than that. Try!"

"Okay then, I wanted the ice cream."

"Got it."

"I tried to feel where I wanted the ice cream, and what it felt like."

"Good."

"Uh, you don't have to say something every time, okay?"

(To my credit, I didn't say, "Good.")

"It felt like ... well, it just felt like ice cream."

I took that in for a moment. "Well, I guess that's not surprising: all these years, when you've felt that ice cream feeling, you've just eaten ice cream. The ice cream feeling doesn't know any better."

He narrowed his eyes. "Are you being weird again?"

"I don't think so. What I mean is, no one ever asked it anything before. How can we blame it when it just goes straight to ice cream?"

"You may have a point there."

I had an idea. "Do you feel like ice cream now?"

Evan checked his insides, then nodded. "As a matter of fact, yes." He paused a moment, then went on. "I think it's because of the ... the ... uh, frustration, you know, of talking about all this, and about how it all didn't work out."

I was beaming. "Thank you."

"For what?"

"Excuse me, I'm not talking to you."

"Uh, who else is there?"

"Him, the ice cream boy. He was willing to give us the word 'frustration,' and I really appreciate it."

Evan squinted at me. "Are you trying to pump things up again?"

"Well maybe I was before, but this time I mean it."

"You really think this is something?"

"Yep. Frustration, and failure: that's what I think is down there in the hole."

He squinted again, puzzling it out. "And that's why I'm so impatient with myself?"

"Yes, because he doesn't think there's anything beyond frustration and failure."

"Except ice cream?"

"Except ice cream."

I could see tears welling up in Evan's eyes. I went on. "And I think there's a lot more, beyond frustration: hope, help, trying ..."

He was shaking his head again. "I hope you know I'm going to go out and get ice cream as soon as this session is over."

I shook my head back at him. "It doesn't matter anymore. All the ice cream in the world can't wash away the start we made together, just now. Sure, ice cream might win a few rounds, but the fight isn't over, and we're more stubborn than they are."

He was upset, twisting in his seat. "How do you do that?"

"Do what?"

"Turn absolute failure into . . ."

"Ice cream?"

"Yeah. Isn't that illegal, and, you know, phony, like turning lead into gold or something?"

"I'm licensed."

He looked skeptical.

"Now go get your ice cream; you've earned it."

"Really?"

"Really."

A half hour later I got an email: "I only ate half of it. Threw the rest in the trash, where it belongs. I have just begun to fight."

This time, the tears were in *my* eyes.

*   *   *

Once again I heard nothing all week, despite, once again, checking way too often for emails with the keyword "phish food."

Thursday night came, and my signal light glowed green.

Evan sat down, same as always. No sign of anything.

I began. "So, how did it go?"

He returned me a tight smile. "I went one for two."

"What does that mean?"

"I had two really big urges for ice cream; I lost one and won one, kind of."

"Take me through it."

He closed his eyes. "Okay, Sunday night I felt that empty, desperate feeling again . . ."

"The one under your rib cage?"

"Don't interrupt."

(I was silently thrilled at his spunk.)

"Okay, like I was saying, Sunday night I felt that same feeling again. I tried to sit with it, breathe into it, all the stuff we talked about." His green eyes opened, maybe checking to see if I was paying attention, then flickered closed again. "For a second, it seemed like I was winning..."

"It's not about winning or losing..."

"I asked you to be quiet—is that so hard?"

"Got it."

He closed his eyes again, burrowing back into the moment of the ice cream urge. "Okay, for a second there, I tried to talk to myself, and something shifted, or at least I think something shifted, but then," he clapped his hands together, "whammo."

I sat there for a full minute, afraid to open my mouth.

His eyes flipped open. "Don't you want to know what whammo means?"

"Uh, you already have me in the penalty box for talking out of turn, so I'm a bit reluctant..."

"Dude, that was completely different!"

"Okay then, what does whammo mean?"

He sighed. "Isn't it obvious?"

"Ice cream?"

He didn't even bother to respond, just sat there staring straight ahead, the picture of dejection.

"So, go on."

That broke the spell. Evan lifted his head up and pressed his lips together. "Sorry, I guess I got lost there for a minute." He sat up a little straighter in the chair. "Uh, yeah, so the next time was Wednesday night."

"You mean yesterday?"

"Didn't we talk about dumb interruptions already?"

Damn! "Got it."

"So, repeating once again," he shot me a withering look, "it was Wednesday night, and a really big one hit. I felt so empty and desperate, that . . ." He reached into an inside pocket of his jacket and pulled out a piece of paper. "Here, this is what I wrote to the hole; I printed it out for you."

I unfolded it and took a quick look. "Do you want me to read it now?"

"Why do you think I gave it to you?"

"Out loud?"

Now I had a withering sigh to go along with the withering look and the withering tone. Suddenly I had a better idea what Daddy must have been like.

I put on my reading glasses and began:

"I'm sorry you were hurt. I know that you're trying to tell me something, and that you feel like nobody's listening. Well, I'm listening, or at least now, finally, I am. I'm sorry it took me a lifetime to get the message. I guess I haven't been a very good dad to you, which is really sad, especially after you already had the world's worst dad to begin with, but I'm going to be better from here on out. I just want you to know that I love you, or I'm trying to love you. I don't know what else to say."

I looked up. Evan's eyes were wet, but then so were mine. "Wow, good job."

He shrugged. "I still ate, but only a few spoonfuls."

I shrugged back. "Like I said before, when I was so rudely interrupting, it's not about winning or losing: it's about staying with it, being persistent—kinda like love."

"I have to admit, when I was writing it, it felt like gibberish, a joke, like tossing seeds into a hurricane, but now, hearing you read it . . ."

"It sounds almost like a person?"

"Almost like a good dad."

I smiled. "Who knew, you had a good dad within you all along?"

Evan shook his head. "I don't know; let's not get ahead of ourselves. Remember, I still ate some ice cream."

I checked the clock. "It's about the war, not the battle. We have to stop for now, but we're not going to stop in the long run."

He smiled. "Is that speech from the licensed alchemist's playbook?"

"If I answered that, I'd have to kill you."

$$* \qquad * \qquad *$$

The next few weeks went by with some wins, some losses (okay, I admit it: there are wins and losses), but Evan stayed with it, and his "love notes" to the boy in the hole seemed to become deeper, richer and more sincere, establishing a real connection between his caring self and the painful lack that lurked down below.

We talked a lot about his father's game-playing, shallowness and power-grabbing and even, for the first time, about the pain of his mother's willingness to take that big payout and walk away from her children, knowing that she was leaving them with the truly unfit parent.

Evan kept addressing the ice cream hole, sometimes forwarding me what he had written, sometimes bringing in printouts and sometimes just keeping it to himself. He still struggled with the ice cream at times, but mostly it had become more of a special treat than an out-of-control demon.

Finally, one night at the end of a session, he handed me another printout. It was short. He said, "This time, it's not what I wrote."

"What do you mean?"

He pointed to his stomach. "It's from him. He finally answered me."

I opened up the paper and read:

"Dear Evan,

I know you're there. I'm glad you know that ice cream never solved anything, because I've known it for a long time. I finally have a real dad, who is willing to fight for me. I am not alone. We are a team. Thank you."

It was beyond moving—it was spiritual.

I handed the paper back to Evan, and I saw him lift his pen and quickly cross out something, and then add something else and hand it right back to me. "Here, you should have this."

Startled, I took the paper and looked down.

At the top, he had changed it to read, "Dear Gregg."

What's beyond spiritual?

The Goner

Part One: Whistling Through the Grass

8/29/2014—This is the day my son Brett would have been eighteen—knocking on the door of manhood.

So today, I want to talk about things that have to do with Brett, the "goner." Why do I use that term? Because of a long-ago patient of mine. We'll circle back to Brett and that patient later on, but first, a little background.

A long time ago, I did a summer internship at a Veterans Administration Hospital in Asheville, North Carolina. I have only fond memories of Asheville, though some of them are leavened, and I suspect, improved, by the passage of time. Like what? Well, like the fact that in the little clapboard cottage (well, shack, actually) where we were staying, out on Old County Home Road, if you turned on the lights at night the walls teemed with hundreds of big, fat cockroaches. And they didn't just sit there and look at you when the lights went on—they all scrambled madly for the closest available darkness, making the walls a riot of squirming bugs.

And they invaded the kitchen too. If we didn't put our silverware in sealed bags, our food, everything—well, it was "game on." Oh, and it didn't stop at roaches, either. Big, bullying raccoons owned the night, and they weren't subtle or scared, not a whit. They would bang around in the darkness of the night kitchen, searching angrily and with total ownership for whatever goodies that you had, in their opinion, procured for them and them alone.

For years, my wife would laugh about how, that first night, hearing the coons scuffling around aggressively, I jumped out of bed and said, "What the hell? There's a goddam bear in the kitchen!"

But she wasn't laughing when, the next morning, as she went to put a tablespoon full of cereal in her mouth, a roach suddenly shot out from the underside of the spoon and made a mad dash for her Cheerios!

Asheville is famous for a few things. The author Thomas Wolfe was born there, and his book, *Look Homeward, Angel*, is set in the Asheville area. The Vanderbilt estate, Biltmore, is a tourist mecca. They even had a minor league baseball team, the Asheville Tourists. In the old days, the first tuberculosis sanitarium in the United States was established there, and it was widely believed that Asheville's "salubrious" climate was ideal for healing all manner of ailments. After the Civil War, the government began to establish what were then called old soldiers' homes, to take care of the medical, and later psychiatric, needs of veterans. One of these became the Oteen VA Hospital (now the Charles George VA Medical Center), which was my "placement" that summer. The hospital has lovely, large grounds and high-ceilinged buildings that give some of the feel of the old, gracious South.

I first realized that the place had a work ethic and a pace all its own on my first day on the job. I was gung-ho, hoping to impress my superiors with my dedication to my job, my willingness to learn and my potential. As we gathered at lunchtime in the office of the Chief of Psychology, I expected maybe an informal in-service training session, or at the least a grilling on what I had done with myself all morning.

Instead, the Chief and his colleague, a friendly, older guy who had been there forever, looked at each other and said, "Okay, we're all here. Ready."

I looked from one to the other. "Ready for what?"

The Chief smiled indulgently at my ignorance, picked up his hat and said, "Botanical rounds, of course."

And with that, we all trooped out to take a long, leisurely stroll through the extensive, green grounds of the hospital, which included, as I remember, picking blades of grass and attempting to whistle through them—one of the manly arts of a Southern gentleman. They could name most of the flowers, trees and birds of the grounds, and aside from an occasional bit of juicy gossip about the staff, no business whatsoever was discussed on these daily perambulations.

So it turned out to be a kind of in-service after all, just not about work. There was a courtliness and gentility about this custom and these men that I never found anywhere else I ever worked. And though I didn't get the fast-lane, sophisticated educational apprenticeship about being a working psychologist that I had hoped for, I ultimately ingested something far more valuable by hanging out with these guys: namely, that while work matters, so does *life*. Don't forget who you are, don't forget the natural world, don't forget your family and don't forget to have some fun every day.

In effect, they were telling me, "Sure, you may think we're just backwater old-timers. But remember this, boy; you may become a big-city success someday, but you're still just an ordinary Joe, along with the rest of us. So learn to enjoy it, and you'll be ahead of the game." And man, were they right. I never did learn to whistle through a blade of grass, but I did learn from them a couple other critical manly arts: humility and the capacity for a light touch.

*　　*　　*

And then there were the patients. For some reason, I seem to remember that most of the guys I dealt with were Korean War vets— forgotten men from a forgotten war.

Two memories of patients called Sonny and Victor stand out especially, because they involved lessons taught to a young, insecure kid who had doubts about the value of spending that summer in Asheville.

The first one, Sonny, was a small, beady-eyed, unprepossessing guy in his mid-forties. He was diagnosed with paranoid schizophrenia, and he had a wild look in his eye, along with a Southern accent like dark molasses. I was assigned to interview him and provide a progress report. You understand, everyone was supposed to be making progress, thanks to the powers of our treatment plan. The "plan," along with medication, meant group therapy, where we talk-ed about life issues, daily problems and how cute the nurses were. I'm not knocking it—if I was a paranoid schizophrenic veteran in 1972, that's what I would have wanted, too. It definitely beat sitting in a bare, one-room apartment and nursing your delusions with Camels and Southern Comfort all day.

I was assigned to meet with this guy and assess his progress, of which there was, to be honest, virtually none. Well, maybe the fact that he wasn't out stabbing people or causing the police any trouble. But for Sonny, progress mostly meant keeping his inner demons at bay, rather than getting "better" in the sense that a layman would think of it. In truth, he was an odd duck who unfortunately got caught up in an odd war, and it had "affected" him. I remember his mental disability was rated as 80 percent service-connected, which meant that somebody, at some point, had determined that whatever happened in Korea had significantly degraded whatever pre-service mental stability he'd ever had.

I wouldn't know, because he wouldn't talk about the war or his ex-periences in Korea, though I asked. All I knew was that American men had gone in there to help unite North and South Korea, but that whatever tragedies he saw there had only separated Sonny's own north and south, mind from body. So I just let it go at that. It's not like in the movies, where you help a guy recover lost memories of how a sadistic platoon sergeant sent him out on night patrol for kicks, knowing the area was infested by North Koreans, and then he sobs into a pillow and screams, "I hate him! I hate him!" for an hour, and is then miraculously cured.

Nope, Sonny was "gone" for good, and nobody ever really knew what caused it. My guess is that he was simply a very odd guy who was probably barely making it in civilian life, and never should have been subjected to whatever things he went through in war. Such trauma and stress would probably have made even a normal man a bit odd for the rest of his life, but pushed this fragile guy around the bend for good.

I didn't look forward to my assignment: the guy not only had that molasses accent that suggested "ignorance" to me, but a major mouth on him, too. Plus, he had a chip on his shoulder about every-thing and everybody in general. He had earned his paranoid wings honestly: when he wasn't being crazy, he could verbally slash and carve with the best of 'em, and sometimes the staff almost hoped he was in his private delusions so that he wouldn't spray his verbal machine-gun fire around and disrupt the staff and patients with his accusations. He was crazy enough to harbor wild suspicions about everybody, but just un-crazy enough that his suspicions had the ring of truth and could really hurt.

I thought I would try and put him at ease with some small talk, es-tablishing rapport. After he had taken his seat, I noticed him look-ing at a poster on the wall—of a castle. I nodded toward it. "Pretty amazing place."

His eyes shifted from the poster to me, and back. "Oh yeah?"

I nodded. "Yeah. It's in Austria."

He smiled. "You mean, that place near Germany?"

Wow, this was going better than I expected. He was "responsive."

Actually, I had been to the castle, but I didn't want to flaunt that in front of him—not now, when we were doing so well. I played it low-key. "Yeah. I guess Hitler stole their country for a while there, but they got it back after World War II."

He nodded.

Why stop now, when I was doing so well? "I hear Walt Disney used it as the model for the castle in one of his cartoons."

He pointed. "You mean, that castle?"

I nodded, enthusiastically.

He pounced. "You mean, Neuschwanstein?"

Oops.

I scrambled to regain lost ground. "So, you were stationed in Germany?"

"Nope, never seen the place. I think it's pretty common knowledge that Ludwig II built that castle as a refuge for himself. Like me, he didn't 'specially like people." Spoken with no accent—could have been elocuted by an Oxford don.

Double oops.

Of course, you know what I was thinking at that point, but he even anticipated that.

He smiled at me, knowingly, his accent back full strength. "Yeah, yeah, if ah'm so smart, what the hail am ah doin' heah? Well, what the hail else could ah do? They don't make no jobs for crazies, and gals don't cotton to 'em much, neither, an' that's a pure fact." He paused. "Ah on'y tail you this cuz ah lah'k ya." He paused, then sort of muttered, "Y'all done good with Bobby."

I racked my brain and finally made the connection. "Bobby" must have referred to an African-American patient the staff called Robert—who insisted on being called Robert, in fact. Some of the staff had been trying to transfer him to another unit because he was annoying and provocative to staff and other patients. I dimly remembered a heated discussion at the nurses' desk weeks earlier, where I and others had pointed out that Robert's "problems" were precisely why he was here in the first place, and that to transfer him because of them ran counter to the whole purpose of our being there. Apparently, Sonny had overheard the conversation, or someone else had, and passed it down the grapevine.

But two things really struck me: one, that a confirmed Southern redneck had appreciated my standing up for a black man, and two, the realization that the white patients had apparently called him Bobby all along. It took me a long time, but because of this incident and others, I realized that Southerners then didn't just hate black people, pure and simple, as I'd thought. White Southerners saw black people almost as children—hence the automatic use of the diminutive (even affectionate) "Bobby," a name that Robert probably accepted as normal from them. And, at least at that time, they felt in a sense protective of blacks, as they would toward children. From their point of view, the real problems only arose when blacks didn't know their "place," and therefore forfeited their status as protected children. Yes, I know it's called paternalism, and it's ugly and nobody could condone it and it had to change. But I learned that it wasn't as simple as pure hate, either. As someone once said, stereotypes work best from a distance. Once you get up close and personal, it's a little more complex.

I think Sonny had used up all his energy making his point with me. Soon after his victory over my own paternalism, he lapsed back into his psychotic delusions, and though he nodded to me vaguely whenever he saw me, we never really connected again.

But I'll never forget that exchange, and will always honor even the momentary glimpse I was afforded, into the mind of what could have been an extraordinary man.

Part Two: Blowing Out the Speakers

The summer weeks drifted lazily by in Asheville: group therapy, botanical rounds, the cockroach and raccoon wars, semi-adopting a
neighbor's puppy named Shane and doing individual therapy sessions. Hopes were borne out with some patients, dashed with others. Our days there included teaching my wife how to drive a stick
shift in the Blue Ridge Mountains, claiming my gifts, accepting my
limitations, crossing back and forth through Beaucatcher Tunnel,
work and home, heat and humidity, summer rain, lessons, lessons,
under the hot Southern sun . . .

A new patient arrived: Victor. A Vietnam vet. His diagnosis: Depression. I don't know why, but I gravitated to him. Make no mistake, all patients in a facility like that are not treated the same. Not
that all don't get the benefit of everything the program has to offer,
but sometimes a staff member will take a special liking to, or a special interest in a particular one, and spend "more time than you're
getting paid for," as a supervisor once put it, in the patient's care and
treatment. Such was the case with Victor.

He was a big, likable guy, a heavyset white Mississippian with a
deep, resonant voice that you noticed right away. Paul Robeson
came to mind, and William Warfield or maybe Billy Eckstine. But
for obvious reasons, I wouldn't have made any of those particular
comparisons to Victor's face.
I scheduled some individual sessions with him, and we talked of all
kinds of things: the wife he still loved (she had left him for another
man while he was in 'Nam), his lonely childhood (an only child of a
drunken mother and a father who was on the road all the time), his
own drunkenness and addiction to pills (he had kicked both years
before, "on his own") and, most devastating of all, his loss of the

guys he called "the only family I've ever known"—the platoon that was annihilated by the Viet Cong.

All except him.

Victor was the first person I ever heard say, "I wish I had died instead of them," and really mean it. He explained, "The dead get to rest. I have to face hell for the rest of my life, because aloneness, and life without the Goners, is hell."

That's what he called them: "the Goners."

I thought about that, and thought I could understand it, a little. I had never suffered a significant loss of a person in my life, but I could see what he meant about the dead "getting the best of the deal," in that their struggles were over, while the living had to go on and face life without their loved and lost ones.

But what about that peculiar phrase, the Goners? For some reason, I felt I needed to file that question away for later.

In the meantime, I tried to talk to him about the things he *did* have to live for.
What about other women?

He would shake his head sadly, and say, "For me, Mandy was the beginning and the end."

Subject closed.

New friends?

"What's the point? You let people matter, then you just lose them, and it's worse than never having them in the first place."

Subject closed.

Work?

"I'm an electrician. I do my job. I go home. What else is there to say?"

Another one bites the dust.

Finally, I mentioned his voice.

"You've got quite a voice. Ever done any singing?"

That got a small smile. "Singing? Sure, when I was a kid, in church. I was a soprano. Then, my voice changed."

"It sure did."

He really smiled, for the first time ever. "Now I'm a bass, like Daddy." He grinned, proudly.

Hmmm, were we finally onto something? "Daddy?"

"Yeah, you know, my father."

I smiled. "Yes, I know, Vic. It's just that I never heard you talk about anyone before—anyone other than Mandy, or the Goners—with any feeling. I guess your dad meant a lot to you."

He pursed his lips in thought. "He meant everything to me." He paused, his eyes moving as he searched his past. "He used to sing."

"To you?"

"He sang all the time: in church, everywhere." He paused, his eyes lighting up, head nodding proudly. "He used to blow out speakers, you know."

I angled my head. "What do you mean?"

"Sure, a really powerful, deep bass can do that, you know."

"No, I had no idea."

He was quiet a moment. "But he also sang, special, to me."

"How do you mean, 'special'?"

"At night, in my room."

"Like, bedtime songs, lullabies?"

"Not lullabies. Just anything: popular songs, hymns, gospel—you know, church."

I smiled. "Yeah, I know gospel has something to do with church." I paused, considering. "Would you sing for me?"

He did a double-take. "What, right here?"

"Yes, right here."

He looked at the closed door. "Is that *okay*?"

I did my best Bogart. "If they come to arrest us, I'll take the rap, see?"

He looked down, clearing his throat. "Well, I don't really sing anymore. It's kinda like, when Daddy died . . ."

"The songs went with him?"

"Um hmm."

"So, you don't really feel entitled to do it on your own?"

"I don't know about that. I, uh, just haven't done it."

"Would you do it for me? I'd be honored."

He looked around again, like we were up to something illicit. "What do you want to hear?"

I shrugged. "I don't know, maybe some of that hymn and gospel stuff you were talking about?"

"Like, what hymns?"

"I have no idea, I'm just a Jewish kid from California."

That earned a rumbling laugh. He looked down and cleared his throat again. "Okay, then."

He began, timidly,

"Shall we gather at the river,
Where bright angel feet have trod,
With its crystal tide forever,
Flowing by the throne of God?"

Now, he really gave it his all, his voice molten gold:

"Yes, we'll gather at the river,
The beautiful, the beautiful river,

Yes, we'll gather at the river,
That flows by the throne of God."

He looked at me. I nodded, "Keep going." He continued through the verses, belting it out, body swaying, his eyes closed, and ended with,

"Soon we'll reach the shining river,
Soon our pilgrimage will cease;
Soon our happy hearts will quiver,
With the melody of peace.
Yes, we'll gather at the river,
The beautiful, the beautiful river,
Yes, we'll gather at the river,
That flows by the throne of God."

My lord, I almost converted, right there on the spot!

There was a knock at the door.

Victor flinched.

I said, "Yes? Come on in."

The door opened and two nurses poked their heads through a crack in the door shyly, one head on top of the other. "Everything all right in here?"

I nodded. "Everything is great in here." I looked at Victor, then back at the nurses, asking them, "What did you think?"

The one on the bottom had her hand clapped over her mouth. They both had tears in their eyes. The one on top said, "It was just ... just so beautiful."

Victor looked alive for the first time since I had known him. Something had happened. It didn't matter what, or why, or how, only that it happened. A spark of life had been struck. Now it was my job to keep that spark alive.

I continued to meet with him, and though he was still depressed, it seemed he had turned a corner and stepped out onto the street of life. There was only one thing I still wanted to know, and I waited until our last meeting to ask him. Maybe he'd be willing to tell me now.

"I know you don't like to talk about the war, but could I just ask you one thing?"

He drew in a breath, hesitating. He still didn't want to go "there," but he said, "Okay, what is it?"

I had earned my one question. "Why do you call your platoon the Goners?"

He smiled. "Oh, is that all? That one's easy." His eyes did that moving-back-and-forth thing again, searching the blackboard of time. "When I was a kid, and my daddy came home, which wasn't often because his job kept him on the road, he used to play soldier with me all the time. And whenever I would 'kill' him, he would clutch his hand to his heart, spin around, say, 'I'm a goner', then fall down.

"So, every time he had to leave home again, it became a regular thing that I'd say to him, 'Guess you're a goner, huh?' And he'd say, 'Yep, I'm a goner, boy.' Somehow, it made it easier.

"So, when the guys were all killed, I just took to calling them the Goners—like they were up there with Daddy, somehow." He looked at me, but not really at me. "I guess it makes it all easier."

I nodded and stuck out my hand. "Thank you, I appreciate it. I think I understand now."

Little did I know that thirty years later I would appropriate his father, and the platoon, to make it easier for myself when Brett died.

Oh, but before I get back to Brett, there's just one more thing about Asheville, and it's in the nature of an amends, I guess. While we lived in Asheville, the older, nice guy whom I mentioned as the Chief's cohort earlier, was wonderful to us. He had us over to his lovely house for dinner, did everything possible to make me feel welcome, talked with me patiently about my doubts and questions at work and even laughed at my dumb jokes sometimes.

And yet, there was something sad about him, something very human. Maybe he was a self-questioner, a self-doubter, like me? I don't know. I didn't know, then, that "old guys" were human, too, could need companionship, too, could be lonely, could doubt themselves. I just know that on my last day at work, on my way out I glibly said to him, "I'll be in touch."

He immediately replied, "No you won't."

Not like an accusation, or anything of the sort—just straightforwardly, like a statement of hard-won truth. It took me momentarily off guard. People aren't usually that direct or that honest. I think I shrugged it off at the time and continued my merry way down the hall.

So, for the record, I just want to say that he was right. I was a boy in a hurry—to get my PhD, to grow up, to get paid, to earn respect, to make it. I so wish that the Botanical Rounds, your generosity toward me, and the South itself, had taught me to slow down and let my heart put down roots in life, sometimes.

I know it now, but I didn't, then.

And I'm sorry because I'm the one who missed out on the privilege of a continued relationship with you. I'm the loser. And now that I'm an old guy, I know that age has nothing to do with it; I think you recognized in me a fellow traveler, and wanted to know me longer than my three-month "hitch" in Asheville. Maybe at the time I couldn't imagine an older guy actually wanting to know me, or finding genuine companionship with me. I didn't think I had that much to offer.

But now that I'm older than you were then, I see that, when a soul connects with another soul, things like age, race, gender or background don't matter much at all. Sure, maybe those superficial similarities make it easier, but if the actual connection isn't there, those things don't make up for it. The connection is the precious part, and I let a true connection fall by the wayside when I failed to follow up on our friendship.

Maybe someone reading this now will learn and realize that truth and think twice about letting a special connection lapse.

That's all I can offer you now, wherever you are, but I *am* offering it, with all my heart.

Part Three: Mission Accomplished

And now we come back to the part about Brett, and death. Part of me says that people don't want to hear this stuff. It's too personal, too hard, too self-indulgent.

Well, maybe that's true, but I always think about what the great baseball player Joe DiMaggio said when someone asked him why he went all out every day: *"There is always some kid who may be seeing me for the first time. I owe him my best."*

I feel I owe anyone out there who may have lost a child my best. Oh, and anyone who hasn't lost a child, but might. And anyone who has lost anyone, but may be trying to make sense of loss, of death or even just looking for a reason for going on.

And what does "my best" mean? It's kind of like in AA: it doesn't mean advice, or rules, or Ten Commandments. It means being willing to share my experience, in the hopes that some small part of it may help someone else, because we're all in the same boat.

I'm just saying, "I've been there—and survived. Here is my story. I hope you can use some of it." Don't panic—I'm not going to go into gruesome detail, or really much detail at all. There will be no stories about tossing and turning all night, or wandering down Broadway dead drunk.

It's just a story that could happen to anyone, but it happened to me, and now I'm sharing some of it so that when something happens to you, you'll know you have company.

I know I could have used some, then.

What does it "look like" to lose a child?

Well, to me it looked like this:

My wife had wanted to take the boys (six-year-old fraternal twins) to a relative's birthday party in Modesto. When your wife is Mexican-American with ten brothers and sisters, there are a lot of birthday parties. Me—I had no intention of driving to anyone's party anywhere. It was a beautiful fall day, and for me, that meant the baseball playoffs were on. Neither of the kids really wanted to go to the party—I don't think—but Nick was more insistent about wanting to stay home with me than Brett. Not that Nick cared about baseball—no such luck with any of my kids. But he knew I would probably take him to the park to fool around together.

And as for Brett, well that was the whole thing about him: Brett was a good boy. And by that I don't mean a goody-goody. No, not that, by any stretch of the imagination. I mean that he was a good person. He could see that Mom needed at least one recruit for this gig, and he would never let her down. Besides, he could have a good time *anywhere*, as long as there were people and action.

So they left. And Nick and I did go to the park and fool around together. In fact, we had a great time. Finally, it was time to go back home. As we pulled into the driveway, I saw two people standing there. Two people who shouldn't have been there: one of my wife's older aunts, whom I had seen maybe one time before, and a cop.

Shit.

The cop said I needed to pick up my mother-in-law and get to Memorial Hospital in Modesto. Right now. And Nick needed to stay with the aunt. There had been an auto accident.

No details, just that.

Crap.

Now I *am* going to skip a bunch of the details, because they don't affect what I want to say to you and because the details aren't the issue—what it *feels* like is the issue. If you want to know details, you can contact me anytime and I'll talk your head off, but now we're getting to the important stuff, like why I titled this part "*Mission Accomplished.*"

I can't speak here for most people who have lost a child, because everyone has a different personality. I suppose some people would have gotten into rage or blaming (there was a lawsuit involved, later, against Ford Motor Company), or hatred, or utter despair.

Maybe some people would have said, "Well, we can always have another child."

Maybe some people would have considered revenge against the "other driver"—the one who caused the accident.

I know I did.

Also, I wasn't there when it happened. So what my wife had to deal with—the guilt, the helplessness, the mental images—was far beyond anything that was on my plate. I hear that many marriages break up in these circumstances. "They" say women need to talk, and that men don't talk, and that that brings relationships down. I don't know about that. I'm a talker, and I talk to people all day about heavy issues, so the talking/not talking thing wasn't in play for me.

All I can speak to is *my* experience, and somehow, I suspect that the way I thought about my loss is specific to men. As you'll soon see, that's why I prefaced this whole thing with my experiences at the Veterans' Hospital. In the film *Saving Private Ryan*, Tom Hanks plays an Army captain in World War II who is in charge of a company of men tasked with locating a particular paratrooper, just after D Day. At one point in their mission, they are "crashing" for the night in a bombed-out church. It is the first time they have had a chance to stop and gather themselves, to talk and be human beings for a few minutes.

At one point, Hanks and his trusted friend, Sergeant Horvath, are talking about a man in their company who was killed some time before. At first, they're laughing at the memory of some of the crazy things this kid did. Then, Captain Miller (Hanks) intones the name of yet another man who was killed, the same day they are talking. The mood suddenly shifts, downward, as he continues, with terrible pain and irony: "You see, when you end up killing one of your men, you see, you tell yourself it happened so you could save the lives of two, or three, or ten others—maybe a hundred ... Do you know how many men I've lost under my command?"

Sergeant Horvath asks, "How many?"

Miller say, "Ninety-four... But that means I've saved the lives of ten times that many, doesn't it? Maybe even twenty, right? Twenty times as many?" He paused, his face showing the devastation. "And that's how simple it is. That's how you rationalize making the choice, between the mission and the men."

It is obvious from the dialogue, and throughout the film, that while Captain Miller wants to help win the war (he's in the Rangers, an elite unit), his primary emotional investment in this whole thing is all about protecting his men. He carries with him, every day, every night, the exact number of men he has "killed."

And that's exactly how I felt: through my ineptness, I had lost one of my men. It happened on *my* watch. I was a failure. I had failed Brett as a parent, as a guardian, as a protector.
He wasn't supposed to know about *life*.
I *was*.
No, I wasn't crazy with it: I knew that having allowed him to go to a birthday party in Modesto wasn't "negligent," not in any real sense, but I still felt like I had been negligent, asleep at the switch.

Maybe I should have gone.

Maybe I should have been driving.

Maybe I shouldn't have let him go.

Maybe ... Maybe ... Maybe . . .

In this kind of situation, you realize the crazy, happenstance quality of life. Anything—anything at **all**, that would have changed the scenario by even half a second—would have prevented the disaster.

If only this, if only that . . .

And *this* makes you realize the crazy odds against something like this happening.

And *that* makes you wonder: *Why? Why was my boy chosen for this insane spin of the Russian roulette wheel?*

And *that* brings you back to your own "responsibility." Am I being punished (by God) for something I did? Something I didn't do?

Maybe if I had been a better person ... But if I *have* been a bad person, why was it taken out on *him*? Because "they" knew how much I loved him, so that I would have to live with the unbearable pain of losing him, of being responsible for losing him, for the rest of my life?

You go through all these things. It doesn't matter if they make sense; you go through them anyway.

You look at your wife sleeping at night—twitching, moaning, crying, whimpering out loud, jerking around, and you blame yourself, somehow: *It happened on my watch.*

You look at your wife during the day, half crazed with loss, pain, despair, and you blame yourself, somehow: *It happened on my watch.*

You look at your other son. Yesterday, he had a twin, a best friend, a soul mate, an "other half." Today, nothing. And you blame yourself, somehow: *It happened on my watch.*

I found myself starting to think about Victor again. Now I understood: it wasn't that he'd lost his platoon, his "family." It was that *he* had lost his platoon, his family. He must have thought, *Why am I alive, and they aren't? What could I have done differently? If anyone should have died, it should have been me!*

I thought that a million times about Brett: *Why not me? Please take me! Make time go back, and take me, dammit!*

There were things I couldn't listen to anymore. One of my favorite songs was "Moon River." I've written before about the songs that got me through the hard times of junior high and high school. One of them was "Moon River." I don't know why; something about the lyrics was evocative in a way that really registered with me. But now, no way. Why, you ask? Listen to these lyrics:

*"Two drifters, off to see the world—
There's such a lot of world to see . . ."*

To me, that was always Nicky and Brett. Now, those words were just a hole burned all the way through my heart.

There were many others. You realize, suddenly and unwelcomely, that the lyrics to almost any love song can "apply" to your child— your lost child. You see him everywhere: cloud formations, shadows, children walking down the street, alive.

Now I understood Victor's pain. And I started thinking of Brett as one of the Goners. He was the platoon member that I, as his commanding officer, had lost to enemy action. And, crazily, it helped. It felt like I had a kinship with Victor, with all the vets I had worked with—men who had lost something irreplaceable, whether it was their buddies or parts of their normal selves and lives.

And it felt like Brett had company, honored company: the Goners.

And it felt like *I* had company, too: the vets I had worked with. When you're in war, you change. Then, you have to come back, but you're still "changed." What do you do? You walk the streets feeling like a freak. You're not part of normal life anymore, but then the "normal" people are not part of *your* life anymore either, or your memories.

That's how it feels walking around when you've lost a child. Like nobody understands your pain; they haven't "been there." Oh, they *think* they understand, but they don't—they *can't.* They want to be nice, to help, but your pain scares them.

My wife told me a story about an encounter with a relative who asked her, "So, how are you doing?"

My wife said, "Okay."

The woman frowned solicitously and said, "Just *okay*?"

My God, at that point, "okay" was a fucking miracle! I remember talking to a colleague I saw on the street one day, a few months after "it" happened.

He said, hopefully, "So, is it getting any better?"

I said, "I've read it takes about ten years to really get better."

He flinched, visibly, and then walked off as if I had electrocuted him with a hot wire.

Guess what: It takes about ten years to really get better. Sorry, folks, but that's my experience. That doesn't mean every single day is unbearable, until a sudden bolt of lightning strikes you ten years later, and you're fine. No, it means you're "working on it" actively, all the time, for about ten years. Then, you seem to reach some kind of crazy truce with reality, most of the time.

Still hard nights?

Hell yes.

Still depressing sometimes?

Darn right.

Still feel like a failure, a loser sometimes?

Absolutely, just not all the time, and not as intensely.

And, if you're lucky, you eventually find your own personal ways to honor the lost and keep their spirit alive. You find that, in a way, you can "memorialize" them by incorporating their best qualities into your everyday life, so that their life wasn't lived in vain. In the case of Brett, a sense of aliveness, pure joy in the moment, was his hallmark. I'm definitely not noted for any of those things. But dammit, I try; I try *harder* now that he's gone and can't do it for himself, and for others. And sometimes I succeed, for example in helping my patients appreciate and even revel in the "moment." And in those moments I feel that I have carried out the sacred obligation I owe to Brett.

And for some reason, military things seem to come to mind when I think of Brett. Maybe because honor, duty, valor, courage, loyalty and fidelity were his strongest suits. He wasn't afraid of anything or anyone, especially when in the service of someone else. One day, we were going to be riding the Skunk Train, a small old-time railroad in Northern California that we really loved. While waiting for the train, the boys and I were passing the time at a sort of restaurant and store near the station. One of those kids' rides was there, the kind where you put in a quarter and "ride" the horse, or car, or whatever. Except in this case it was a locomotive.

This much older kid was riding it over and over, kind of giving Nicky and Brett the gloat and flaunting the heck out of his hegemony over the locomotive. Nicky was getting agitated and starting to lose it.

I was just about to say something when Brett got in the kid's face, jammed his hands on his hips and said, "Get down, kid. You're through for the day."

The kid meekly got off and slunk away. Then Brett waved Nicky onto the train—not proudly, just like "mission accomplished." He went through his whole life like a soldier on a mission—a mission to have fun, and to make sure everyone *else* had fun, too, and was treated fairly. There was a seriousness about him, a strong claiming of place, that was striking and unusual.

Once, when he was about five, and I came to pick him up after school, I noticed him playing "soccer" with some other kids on the playground. They weren't really playing by any rules, they were too young and most of them were just paying attention sporadically and mostly goofing off.

But Brett was determined and focused on the game and on his moves.

Later, I said to him, "Wow, we should get you on a soccer team."

He turned to me, eyes shining. "Dad, I'm *already* on a soccer team."

You know, on second thought, looking back on the kind of person he was, even at age five, maybe I *did* kind of accomplish my mission after all.

*   *   *

Eventually we all lose our beloved comrades and fellow warriors, but we go on with the mission, loving, losing, dreaming, succeeding, failing, being knocked to our knees and getting up, again and again.

We are all veterans.

Alone

We are all alone. You are alone, and so am I. Nobody else can live your life for you, or know exactly how you feel or what is most important to you, or share precisely what goes on in your inner world. Nobody else can take that responsibility off your shoulders, take the risks for you, take the blame for you or face the outcome of your decisions. You live in a world with others, but as an entity, a being, you are alone. As the old hymn goes,
"You got to walk that lonesome valley;
You got to walk it by yourself;
Nobody here can walk it for you,
You got to walk it by yourself".

It's almost cruel, isn't it, stated that starkly? And human beings will do almost anything to soften, shift or deny that stark reality. Some classic coping favorites are drugs, alcohol and sex. There are others, more sophisticated perhaps, that are used either unconsciously or for higher purposes. What we call "psychological problems" are in large part clever, unconscious ways for people to deny being all alone.

Let's say that, as a child, you have parents who are unable to love, or cruel, or neglectful, or emotionally disabled, leaving you, for all intents and purposes, alone.

What does your mind do?

It comes up with a new paradigm: I am bad, or I am unlovable. If I was just good enough, smart enough, nice enough, pretty enough, strong enough, they would love me. Now, the perceived locus of control is in *you*, not the parent. True, you may never be "good enough" to be loved, but that's because of *you*, not them. And that's an enormous relief, in a certain sad way. And in the meantime the fantasy, or potential, of bonding and connection is preserved, kept under wraps, "in hopes of better days," as the psychiatrist Donald Winnicott once said so eloquently.

Religion sometimes provides another, seemingly higher level, method of assuaging the pain and fear of being all alone.

Jesus is with me, always.

Comforting, isn't it? God is everywhere, and I am part of God. What a relief! Again, this is not to trivialize genuine spiritual beliefs, but you can see the distinct possibility that these beliefs can be used or misused, to make our condition more bearable, whether or not Jesus is actually on the job.

Even Buddhism can be misused to mask our existential fears:

There is no self—self is just an illusion.

In this system, there is no "I" in the first place, to be alone. "I" am just a part of universal awareness, one with the universe, and division and separateness are just distortions of reality. Again, all spiritual systems are noble pursuits, but even noble pursuits can be misused. I have had therapy patients who are avid meditators come in for help and, when I tried to explain that their emotional problems were the result of a poor or distorted sense of self, tell me confidently, "Oh no, that is irrelevant, since there actually is no self."

Well, believe it or not, even Buddhists need a sense of self (in the "mundane" psychological sense) to function well in the world!

But perhaps there is another clue in everything that I've said above—a sense of belonging, a sense of being in the same boat with others. Religion provides this, spiritual traditions provide this and sex—even addictive sex—at least implies an "other." Even drug and alcohol addicts often derive a sense of identity in their usage. I have often thought that one of the major reasons why AA and NA work is that they force addicts into a functional emotional relationship with others, requiring transparency and disclosure and the emotional give and take of humanity, rather than the "one-person system" of drugs and alcohol ("I don't need anybody else in order to feel better; I've got my drugs to keep me warm."). Saying, right out loud, "I am an addict, and I need you," is not just breaking the denial of the addiction itself, but just as importantly, the denial of the *need for others* that is implicit in the addictive lifestyle of using substances, rather than people, to feel better.

Today I remembered a passage from a book by Melody Beattie, who has written extensively on co-dependency. But this book (*The Lessons of Love*) is about her dealing with the loss of her son, and her daughter's struggles with addiction. At one point, her daughter returns home from a recovery program. Her daughter's friends, who call themselves the "Get Along Gang," have gathered to welcome her home. Melody is appreciative of the way the friends support each other. Her daughter explains: "We each go through different things...We know the other person doesn't understand, because they haven't been through exactly that same thing. But we listen, and we tell each other we don't exactly understand. But we care. That's what makes us a Get Along Gang. We help each other get along."

What a beautiful and sophisticated way of expressing what we can do about being "all alone." There is no denial here, no distortion, no pie in the sky, no tricks, no cheating: just the straight skinny on the human condition and how to live with it. And I hope in my therapy practice that this experience is what I am offering people.

As Jimmy, an ex-patient I saw as a teenager, once said to me many years later, "Thanks for giving me a safe place to face the truth."

You're welcome, Jimmy, and thank you for the privilege of letting me be a part of your facing the truth, because we are all afraid; we are all in the same boat. We are all that crazy creation, the animal that not only is subject to life and death, aloneness and loss, but has to know it, too!

Yes, we are all alone.

But we can be alone, together.

Down By the L&N

It's funny how things come back to you. Unbidden, nagging little tag ends of memory, that come a-knocking on your life in the middle of the night.

Recently, I had a midnight visit from a memory of the L&N, the Louisville and Nashville, a railroad that ran down from Louisville to New Orleans. They called it the Old Reliable, but by the time I got to Knoxville in 1971, it was being swallowed by "consolidation," its passenger service discontinued. However, it was still a freight carrier, and a survivor, having come through the Civil War and everything else, intact and thriving.

There was always something about the romance of railroads that called to me, and something about the South, too: a sepia nostalgia, a valuing of past glories, a certain taking of time with things.

Perhaps I'm just filling in the blanks now in retrospect, but something strong drew me down to the L&N tracks that night, so long ago, me and my guitar. I was learning to finger-pick, and one of the first songs you practiced on was "Freight Train," at least in those days.

So I grabbed my steel-string Gibson and wandered my way down to where I had heard the train whistling for so many nights as I sat pondering life in my little room at the boarding house. I guess I've always been a ponderer—and a wanderer, too—for one reason or another.

There was a big moon that night, fat as a watermelon, lighting my path down through neighborhoods that became scrabbier and meaner as I went. Railroad tracks are usually not in the luxe part of town.

By the time I heard that ding-ding-ding and saw the red light swinging back and forth at the crossing grade up ahead of me, it was mostly tar paper shacks and shabby lean-tos that were as seamy and worn as the faces of the old folks who sat rocking on their front porches, looking at me with flat expressions: *What's a white boy wit a guitar doin' down here this damn time a night?*

I was wondering pretty much the same thing myself when I first heard the train coming and saw the bench. It was nothing much, just an old wooden plank thrown across a couple of big rocks. But it was a welcome place to sit while I watched the passing parade and worked on my picking a while.

I took a seat and bent down to open my guitar case.

"What you got there, boy?"

I looked up in panic. That guitar had cost me $325 in Nashville, which made it the most valuable thing I owned—a major splurge—and it meant everything to me. No one was going to get it from me, even if I had to…

"Relax, kid, I ain't gonna do nothin' to ya." A tall, stately looking old black man took a seat to my right and nodded down at the guitar. "She's a beauty though, sure is."

Off to my left I could hear the train bearing down on us now, maybe two hundred yards away, not slow, but not fast either.

I clutched my Gibson tighter and nodded politely. "Yeah, it means a lot to me."

He chuckled to himself and smiled. "Yes, I can see that, son."

I felt embarrassed.

Suddenly the old man shot to his feet, all his attention focused on the train. As the locomotive approached, he thrust his right arm straight out and held it there. I saw someone high up in the train's cab smile down at us, and then point to him in recognition. "Hey yo, Willie!"

The old man beamed back at him, and then continued to stand there as boxcars, flat cars, tankers and hoppers all rolled by, as if he were inspecting the whole operation. Finally the caboose crossed, and the old man stuck his arm out again, while a brakeman leaned out toward him. "Willie, mah man!"

Now I was even more embarrassed. Willie was apparently "somebody." What did that mean I thought he was before? Nobody?

"It's all right, fella: White people afraid o' black folk, and black people afraid o' white folk." He nodded to himself, then added, "Always was, always will be." He pointed up at the sky. "Especially on a full moon." Before I could answer, he threw in, "Porter, thirty years with the L&N."

Oops, was that his name, or his occupation?

He licked his lips. "Thirty years is a long time." Then he offered his hand. "Name of Willie Lee Abbott. You?"

I shook his hand. "Gregg Bernstein. I'm a student up at UT, but you probably guessed that."

He smiled. "Either that or a traveling true-bee-door."

I cringed, grinning. "Hardly."

He nodded at the guitar again. "What you workin' on?"

"Fingerpicking. I've almost got 'Freight Train' worked out."

"Let's hear it."

"Listen, I'm just a beginner, really. I don't know..."

"Let's hear it." He didn't need words; his tone said, "Cut the crap and play."

I got my fingers ready and concentrated, then let fly. It was slow, but not half bad.

Willie Lee nodded his appreciation, then just said, "Blues?"

"Uh, well I know the chord progression, but..."

He reached out five long, guitar player's fingers to me. I handed over my prize, but it was okay; he sure knew what to do with it.

"Did you ever go down on the Mobile and K C Line?
Did you ever go down on the Mobile and K C Line?
I just wanna ask you did you ever see that gal of mine?"

I'd never heard anyone really sing the blues like that, right up close. It gave me goosebumps, being in the presence of a kind of greatness.

"I rode the Central, and I hustled the L and N..."
He gave me a wink.
"I rode the Central, and I hustled the L and N,
And the Alabama women, they live like section men."

He finished the song and handed me back my guitar, which, to be truthful, now felt like his guitar. It wasn't just his playing, but some quality in his voice that made it magical. I remember an old movie where someone said, "The colored people, they know what trouble is," and corny or not, there's truth in it. And that made me think twice about the way he'd waved at the passing train men. There was something wistful about it. Did I dare ask? I figured I'd work up to it subtly.

"So, how do you know all those guys from the train?"

"Hah! They got rid of me. Thirty years, and they got rid of me."

"But why?"

"Boss trouble."

"What do you mean, boss trouble?"

"I caught him taking money didn't belong to him, so..."

"So, he had to get rid of you?"

"Yeah, that's how it works. See, shit flow downhill, boy."

"But that's not—"

"Hah, fair's nothin' in life, son. See you remember it: nothin'."

I didn't know what to say.

"But I got my pension, so I'll be all right, all right." He motioned toward the Gibson. "Besides, we still got music." He reached down and picked up a brown paper bag from beside him, that I hadn't noticed before. He lifted it to the sky. "We still got the moon, and we still got," he patted the bag, "joy juice." He took a big drink, then passed it over to me.

I took a polite swallow, and passed it back.

After a few more slugs Willie seemed to fade away into another realm. He started to mutter to himself, about himself. "Willie Lee gonna" this, and "Willie Lee not gonna" that.

I admit I had the thought that his drinking might've had more to do with his getting fired than he was acknowledging to himself.
But I would never know.
Kind of like how I always used to wonder about the lives of the people on the passing train—who they were, where they were going, what was going to happen to them.
I always wanted to know. I think I was mentally studying the arc of a life, trying to learn by watching: how to avoid the pitfalls, how to bypass the traps, how to avoid being fired after thirty years, how to avoid ... what? Unfairness?

The moon was going down by now, the wind was whipping the branches around and the shadows were starting to look spooky. I needed to get going if I didn't want to get caught in neighborhoods where "unfairness" might happen to me. I still clutched my guitar tightly, still would have fought like crazy to save it, but now it felt more like a precious artifact on loan to me from sometime before me and on its way to sometime after me. I was just its caretaker for the time being. It had been blooded now; it had a history now, and a...what's that fancy word?

Provenance.

It was then and there that I decided to call that guitar Willie, and it's been Willie ever since. I never did get a heck of a lot better on the guitar, but I did get to where I could fingerpick a bit, enough to accompany myself through grad school, which is what I really needed. And somehow, I always felt elevated by being the owner of a guitar that someone once played so beautifully.

*   *   *

I was wide awake and stirred up after the visitation by Willie Lee had gotten all those old wheels turning again. Who knew that a lifetime later, the L&N would be running its freight all the way to the West Coast and right through this old heart of mine? I went out to the kitchen and snuck one of those peanut butter cookies my wife had made for her book club. It hit the spot.

I thought I was ready for bed now, but I found my feet detouring to the closet where I keep that old Gibson I've had all these years. I opened the case, lifted it out of the crushed red velvet and clutched it to my chest for a long time, inhaling the musty redolence of fugitive dreams and vagabond hopes.

When I'd had enough togetherness, I eased it back into its case very gently and whispered, "Hey yo, Willie—thanks for the provenance."

Fighting with the Air

Part One

What is life? It is a feather, it is the seed of the grass, blown hither and thither, sometimes multiplying itself and dying in the act, sometimes carried away into the heavens. But if the seed be good and heavy, it may perchance travel a little way on the road it wills. It is well to try and journey one's road and to fight with the air.

—*King Solomon's Mines*, by H. Rider Haggard

If you've survived past, oh maybe age two, you've probably noticed that life can be a bit frustrating. You want what you want, but Whoever's In Charge doesn't seem to have been in class the day you announced it. And you don't want what you don't want, but good old WIC doles it out to you anyway with glee, the way an army mess sergeant slops ice cream on top of your mashed potatoes and your chipped beef: service with a smile.

For most of us, life involves, psychologically speaking, participating in moving the ball a couple yards closer to the goal line. We want it to be memorable, we want it to be grand, we want it to matter, but then, "It is what it is," as some sadist once said, unfortunately with great wisdom.

We want to stand upright and beat our chest and say, "Look world, what I did! I moved mountains! I made the deserts bloom with flowers! I made the land give up its riches! I made things different and better for all mankind! I wrestled the gods and all the elements to the ground, and made them cry uncle!"

But what did we really do? Maybe we got on the seven fifteen to Manhattan five days a week for thirty-five years, and ended up with enough to get by, and maybe a little more. Maybe we raised a decent child or two. Maybe we served meals to annoying customers for decades, and always made our best effort to be pleasant. Maybe we ran a company, or a corporation, and did our best to abide by the golden rule, or at least not completely desert all the principles we started out with.

And for some of us, maybe it's just that we didn't rob any banks, or kill anyone, cheat our neighbors, or steal to support a heroin habit—and maybe in our case that represented a herculean effort.

We are all given the gift of life, but how much choice, really, do we have about not squandering that gift? My job is to see to it that the people I work with don't squander that gift. Over the course of a career, generations of people come in to work with you, each one wondering, *Why am I not doing the things I thought I could do?*

Psychotherapy is a very weird enterprise, because it involves telling people who come in saying, "What's wrong with me anyway?" some seemingly contradictory things:

1) There is definitely something *wrong* with you.
2) There is nothing wrong with you, or rather, with the person you really are.
3) And then, as they're sitting there totally confused, you say, "Follow me!"

So it's not surprising that a long-ago patient of mine ended up saying

to me, "Dude, make up your mind! Am I fucked up, or am I just fine?" And of course, in typical inscrutable therapist riddle-speak, I responded, "Well, it depends on whom you're calling 'I.'"
In hindsight, it's amazing he didn't throw the couch at me.

But the thing is, even though we are all given the gift of life, we are not all given the gift of self. Because a functional sense of self depends on a great many things, having to do with the kind of emotional atmosphere our parental figures (if any) created, how our innate nature jibes with those of our parents, and our innate nature itself. In an old movie, the villain is trying to involve the hero, a private eye, in his evil scheme, of which the eye wants no part. The villain says to the private eye, "Can you listen?" He responds, "I can hear." And that's the difference between merely being alive and being a self.
We are all alive, but are we really living?

When I was a kid, there was an insistent meme in books, movies and TV that said, "The human brain is capable of great things, but unfortunately, most of us are using only 10 percent of our brain's capacity." Somehow, for my generation, that seeped in and we all spent our youths wondering where that pesky other 90 percent— the part that was keeping us from our rendezvous with the Nobel Prize—was hiding.
I'm not sure anyone really believes that stuff anymore. But the irony is that the meme was partly right, except that what many of us are "missing" is actually a large portion of our potential emotional capacity, and that deficit is keeping us from "being all we can be."
As you're growing up, older people, often with the best of intentions, put their hand on your shoulder and say, "Son, you can be whatever you want; it's just a matter of sticking with it." Or they cite Woody Allen's famous comment, "Ninety percent of success is showing up."

Well, if "you" aren't there, it doesn't matter if your body shows up or not; "you" are not there!!

But enough of words and theory—let's talk about a real person and what all this meant for her.

Liza was nineteen and a student at Berkeley the first time I saw her in the waiting room. She had a slight Latin cast to her face, with full lips, dark eyes and a kind of quiet, girl-next-door beauty.

As I recall, the session went something like this:

Me: So, what brings you to therapy?

Liza: (Looking around the office suspiciously) I really have no idea.

Me: Well, is there a particular problem, or unhappiness, or crisis you're dealing with?

Liza: Uh, no.

Me: Well, let me put it this way: since you'll be paying me money, what will I be doing to earn all this money?

Liza: (Squirming in her seat) Maybe I should leave now.

Me: Wouldn't that kind of defeat the purpose of your having come here today?

Liza: (Squirming around even more, casting eyes around the office) Do you have, like, a blanket or something?

Me: Uh, sure. Are you cold?

Liza: No, it would just make this whole thing easier.

Me: Okay, hang on a minute. (I went over to the corner where I keep these things) Would a quilt be okay?

Liza: As long as it's big enough to, you know... (She motioned to cover her head).

Me: Ah, I see: you want to be incognito? (I handed her the blue quilt).

Liza: (Covering her head with the quilt) Yes. You see, I don't want to be . . .

Pause
Me: Here?
Liza: Anywhere.
Me: Hmm, you don't want to be anywhere, or you *aren't* anywhere?
Liza: (Little voice) How'd you guess?

I found out a little more in that first session. Her father was a noted Ivy League English professor and her mother a brilliant, disorganized, zany artist. Her father would catch Liza reading Zane Grey, or
Mad Magazine, and say, "So, what kind of illiterature are you reading
now?" But at first, not much of that information mattered. What did
matter was Liza making my office safe for herself, tentatively planting
her flag, making the decision that it could be more than a place of
self-protection, maybe a place of self-disclosure, and eventually even
a place of self-expression. Before a mama bear can have her cub, she
has to find a den that will be secure and trustworthy for the long
winter months.
Peering from beneath the blue quilt, she peeked out at the book-
shelves, the lamps and the artwork on the walls. She took in the pile
of fresh Kleenex boxes, the Native American throw on the leather
couch, and, maybe most of all, the ridiculously tall stacks of books
that towered precipitously on my desk.

Toward the end, as I continued my feeble attempts to liberate little
bits of "history" from her, she said, "Why all the books?"
It was the only thing she had initiated during the whole session.
I smiled, maybe a bit self-consciously. "Because I love them."
"But why are they all here?"
"Well, I guess, because *I'm* all here."
And with that, she nodded, pointed to the clock, threw off the quilt,
stood up, walked over to me and very ceremoniously shook my hand,
saying, "Okay, you'll do."

As she opened the door to leave and started down the hall, I needed to say at least something about all the things we hadn't discussed— the fee, the schedule, the "deal"—but when I said, "Wait, we haven't . . ." she waved her hand behind her and tossed back, "You're in charge of all that."

I felt like a petty clerk or a myopic bookkeeper, bothering a fairy princess with piddling details.

* * *

The next day, I called to offer her another session the following Wednesday evening. All she said was, "Fine," and then the line went dead.

I had a hard day that Wednesday, working with several clients in a row that were intractable, or maybe "non-compliant," as the psychiatrists say. What does this mean? For a psychotherapist who works like I do, it means they don't let you in, they won't sit still to let themselves in, and they bat away any connection you try to make. These are the people who come in for "tips," "techniques" or "ten steps to a new you." They have no interest in (or capacity for) mining the therapy relationship itself for understanding their issues, or using it for a safe place to practice the fine art of relating to a human being, or finding out about themselves.

Usually they're not "resistant," but they just don't get it: when I say, "Right here, right now, we have a front-row seat to observe how you relate to other people," they say, "Uh, so what's the take-home on that?" Or when I say, "It feels like you're pushing me away," they say, "I'm sorry if it hurts your feelings, but I was focusing on my lessons." Then when I say, "No, it wasn't hurting my feelings; I was just giving you some feedback about the process of trying to connect with you," they say, "Okay, so I'm glad it wasn't hurting your feelings, but if it didn't, then why did you say it? And now, can we get back to our lessons?"

That's what I mean about having a hard day.

But I digress. All day, I was looking forward to the meeting with Liza. Something about that combination of empty sense of self, right alongside the unconscious haughtiness—now that intrigued me.

As soon as I appeared at the waiting room to get her, Liza swept down the hallway and into the office, went right over to pick up the blue quilt and threw it over her head, like a queen donning an ermine cape.

She sat down in the big chair, then said, "All right, where were we?"
I didn't respond.
"Speak," she said (to the Lord Chamberlain?).
"I'd rather hear what's going on for you," I said.
She was quiet for a few moments, and then, just when I thought she was going to issue another imperial directive, she whispered, "If I knew what was going on for me, I would answer."
I waited.
Silence.
Then I said, "Well then, tell me what it feels like to not be able to answer."
"Do I have to?"
"Well, it is what we're here for."
She sighed audibly, then said, "Okay then: a fool, an idiot, a loser, a failure, an imposter." There was a long pause. "Or, as my father would say, 'Love's labor's lost.'"
That brought me up short. "What's that supposed to mean?"
Again, she was silent for a while, then after another heavy sigh, she

said, "It means that all the love he poured into me had come to nothing. He used to say it to me whenever he was disappointed in me ... or disgusted with me."

"Sounds like quite a guy," I tried to stop there, but couldn't, "in his own mind."

Instantly the edge of the quilt flipped up and she glared at me. "How dare you!"

I held my breath, letting the endless seconds creep by.

Then, suddenly she added, "You're right, but how dare you?"

Now that it made sense, I said, "I'm sorry."

"Don't pity me."

"Caring isn't pity."

"And pity isn't caring. You don't even know me."

I was defiant. "Well at least I *want* to."

The blanket went back up over her head. "Which is more than he ever wanted."

I shut up—it was her show now.

From under the blanket, "What does it matter anyway? It's all over now."

"If it was all over, we wouldn't be here talking."

"We're only talking because I'm paying you."

"And you're only paying me because I know what I'm doing."

"Says you."

"Give me a chance to prove it."

"I'm not stopping you."

I laughed. "We would've made a good vaudeville team."

"Who's the straight man?"

"Hey, for this kind of money, you get to be the comic."

Liza was quiet for a long time. "Today I don't feel so funny."

I was feeling generous enough to feed her another straight line.

"What was that again about being a loser and a failure, and . . ."

"And an imposter: don't forget imposter."

I glanced at the clock. I had fifteen minutes to tie a bow on the session. "You know, it's a funny thing about feeling like an imposter: it's predicated on the belief that you're supposed to be something, or someone, other than who you are."

I thought I heard a muffled sniffle. "Well, who *wouldn't* want to be something other than who I am?"

"I like who you are."

"Well then, maybe you're the one who needs the therapy."

"See, I knew you could be the comic."

"Maybe I just needed the right straight man."

"Well, you've got one now."

I let her think about that for the last few minutes.

Then, like the previous session, she peeked at the clock and said, "Time's up." She shot to her feet, removed the quilt, folded it very carefully and placed it on the couch.

I said, "I can do that, you know. I even know how to tell when the time's up."

She pulled her purse strap up over her shoulder. "Not yet, you don't." Then, without once looking at me, she strode out of the room.

Whew. Time for debriefing and deconstruction, if not defibrillation. What did I know so far? For one thing, that her way of processing her father's arrogance was to feel terrible about herself, and then adopt his manner unconsciously, so that the arrogance "leaked out" without her knowledge, producing this interesting mélange of low self-esteem while also (unknowingly) coming across like a queen bee. And I knew that, eventually, we would have to meld the two into something more complex, more integrated, more survivable.

You might also wonder why I encouraged those "vaudeville act" rapid-fire back-and-forth exchanges we had a couple of times. Well for one thing, it's a lot easier for someone with little sense of self to react to a "foil" than to just be themselves, on cue, as many therapists ask them to do. By providing her with a friendly antagonist of sorts, I energized her to spit out her feelings without so much calculation and carefulizing. I also learned some things I might not have known, such as how fiercely protective she was of her father. If I had just said, "What do you feel about your father?" she would likely have given me a measured, "mature" answer, whereas when I feinted at attacking him a bit, she leapt to his defense immediately, then was able to think it over and back away from that position a bit and reveal some of her "underside" feelings.

This type of good-natured sparring also gives the patient a safe way to experience that it is all right to disagree with me, so that later, when we may really need to "get into it" in earnest, we will have already established that give-and-take is survivable by all hands.

I also knew that she needed control—the blanket over the head told me that, and so did her taking charge of the clock and folding the blanket up herself. What do I mean? Well, the clock routine told me she didn't want to be "kicked out" of the sessions by me, or cut off either (i.e., "*I'll* do the cutting off!"). And the blanket-folding told me she didn't want to rely on me, or be beholden to me for anything. That's why, as you may have noticed, I kept referring to my fee: it was a central topic in her therapy, as she clearly wanted to keep it on a "fee for services" basis, therefore denying the whole issue of my actually caring about her. Whereas I wanted to use the fee to say, "You're paying me for my expertise: let me do my job," which translates into the phrase I literally said to her, "Give me a chance."

So at this point, in my mind, it was like most therapies, a case of the irresistible force (my skill, I hoped) versus the immovable object (her defenses) and something had to give.

Little did I know that what would "give" would be my delusion that I knew anything at all of what was about to happen.

*   *   *

The following Wednesday, Liza arrived with a purple duffel bag in tow, which I assumed was maybe her workout clothes, so I paid it no mind. In the office, she immediately hustled over and tossed the blue quilt over her head, with the duffel bag clutched tightly to her chest. I noted that there was purpose in her movements now, like a shortstop taking his position, knees bent, looking in at the batter, rocking slightly back and forth, all business.

Did this mean she was done with the preliminaries, ready to rock 'n' roll? I had no idea, but I could feel that game tension in my chest and stomach, and I knew, intuitively, that I had to be on my game, because she was going to be on hers. I felt watched, stalked and tracked, by the mind and the eyes under that quilt.

I waited a moment for her to start, and then a few more, but she was silent. I could have waited longer, but somehow, it felt like she could use some help, maybe an icebreaker. I figured we'd start with something safe, neutral, like the opening break of a pool game.

"Were you at the gym?"

"Shhh!"

I wasn't sure where to go with that; I've never been shushed by a patient before, or at least not when I was trying to make small talk. Again, I waited a long time in silence, and believe me, in therapy, twenty minutes is a *looooooong* time. Then I thought I'd give it a try once more, just to see what would happen.

I took a breath. "So . . ."

"*Shhh!*"

Hmm, okay. I checked inside, and I didn't get vibes of anger, which I normally can sniff out like a bloodhound. No, it felt more like that old movie, *Man Hunt*, where one man hunts another: in the film, they called it a "sporting stalk." Nope, she wasn't angry. If anything, the feeling was more that she was getting herself ready.

For what?

I had no idea.

But I knew it mattered.

I waited another eternity of fifteen minutes, and was just about to address the silence itself, when I saw some shuffling going on under the blanket. Then, to my amazement, a hand puppet of a little brown bear popped out from under the right side of the blanket.

"I don't believe in gyms," it said in an adorable, squeaky voice.

I was startled for a moment, then said, "Well, I only asked because you look like you're in pretty good shape."

"You're only saying that to be nice: I'm *supposed* to be fat, this time of year."

I shrugged. "I'm sorry, I meant to say that you look like you're in good shape, for a bear at this time of year."

"Hmph, well that's better, then."

Suddenly, a spotted giraffe puppet popped out from the left side of the blanket and faced the little bear. "Are you going to let him get away with that? He's obviously just covering up for insulting you, Millicent," she said in a voice like a giraffe with a raspy throat.

The bear swiveled to face her antagonist. "I believe in 'live and let live,' Gladys." Then, nodding with finality, she added, "And so should you!"

"Don't tell me what to do, or who to be!" Gladys answered, as outraged as a little giraffe could be.

Then Liza's voice said, "Be quiet, the both of you; it's my session!" And just like that, Millicent and Glady both disappeared beneath the blue blanket.

Meanwhile, yours truly, while delighted, was also scrambling to regroup. Suddenly it was family therapy! Well, therapy is nothing if not trying to make the best of a fluid situation, so after a while I said, "Are you guys okay in there?"

Gladys' unmistakable rasp said, "We're not guys!"

"Gee, I'm sorry once again. I meant are you people okay in there?"

"We're not people! Geez, Louise!"

I shook my head in dismay. "My goodness, I can't seem to get anything right today. All I meant is, how's the disagreement going?"

Liza's voice said, "How many times do I have to say it? It's my session!"

I felt like a fool, "in character," while at the same time getting a kick out of Liza's creativity and verve. I said, "Okay then, Liza, what would you like to talk about today?"

"Well, it's about time."

"You mean you want to talk about time, or that it's about time I let you say something?"

"That smart-talk won't get you anywhere, mister."

"I'm sorry; I was just trying to be exact and careful."

"Well, being exact and careful hasn't gotten *me* anywhere, I can tell you that."

I nodded, "Thanks for the tip."

"Neither has being sorry."

I said, "You don't have to be exact and careful in here."

"That remains to be seen."

I waited quietly as two or three minutes ticked by. We were almost at the end of the session. Maybe she had done everything she could do for one day.

Then I tried another tack. "Do you have any other friends?"

"Yes."

"Can I see them?"

"Him."

"Can I see him?"

"No."

"Why?"

"Too shy."

"Touché?"

"You heard me. And remember what I said about the smart talk."

"Okay, got it."

Gladys: We out of time?

Me: Well, yes.

Gladys: Well, yes, or just yes?

Me: Just yes.

Gladys: Try to be more exact and careful.

Me: But Liza just told me—

Gladys: Don't listen to her!

Me: Sorry, but she's the boss in here.

There was silence. Then after more shuffling under the quilt, Liza shot to her feet, folded the quilt carefully, placed it on the couch, turned to the door and left, without making eye contact.

Touché, indeed!

The game was afoot.

*   *   *

That night I lay in bed awake for a long time, trying to feel my way into "Liza and friends". Notice I didn't say I lay awake thinking, because thinking, or figuring, is a fool's errand when it comes to therapy. Puzzling out a therapy session is more like analyzing a piece of literature or art. First, you experience it whole, letting it wash over you, and then you breathe and see what bubbles up from below, whether it makes sense or not. Therapy is not about making sense; it's about creating a safe space, and then watching what happens in the patient (point) and in yourself (counterpoint).When I work with therapists about one of their sessions, or patients, I'd a thousand times rather hear, "You know, I had the craziest thought," than, "I think I figured it out." First comes the "crazy thought," then, working backwards, comes whatever understanding, or apprehension, might be possible (subject to constant revision and processing).

So here is what I felt, lying there in the dark. First, that she was a "worthy opponent," and for a therapist, there is no better experience. Yes, you could say she took control of the session, but she did so in the service of giving me her all, of letting me in on her identity, of opening herself wide to the moment. And that's all you can ask of a therapy patient—that's everything. And the irony is, the more vulnerability the patient gives you, the more you will fight to be worthy of that trust. For me at least, it's like the emotional equivalent of the conservation of matter: vulnerability begets protectiveness, in equal measure—what the famous psychologist Carl Rogers called "prizing." Liza, in spite of being short-changed in life (I didn't know the details yet, but I "knew" it was true) had not short-changed me in the session. She had brought creativity, vision, humor and soul to the table. What more could I ask? She had absolutely no way of knowing how I was going to react to the puppets—her friends—and to her boldness and her challenges. But she was willing to "walk the plank" anyway, on pure faith.

What a remarkable woman.

I only hoped that I had the goods, and the guts, to return her gifts.

Part Two

Liza canceled the next two sessions: she had "big tests" at Cal, and who was I to say that her therapy was more important? On the other hand, I also had no way, really, of knowing whether she was using the tests as a hedge against continuing what we had begun, or not. On an emotional level, I knew her to be an honorable person, and normally someone who intends to whiff on their therapy or hold me at arm's length wouldn't bring special puppets to their sessions and put that kind of freshness into the endeavor. But people do fall into emotional valleys and "forget" that they're worth bothering with, especially when they have only just begun the journey. Sometimes it's easier to say, "Skip it," (i.e., "skip *me*"), than it is to face what they know is going to be a grueling trek into unknown lands, with a guide who has not been fully vetted under fire, at least by them.

But my fears were unfounded, because sure enough Liza agreed to meet the next week.

Oh yes, one more thing had evolved from my musings about Liza: I knew that she was a "revealer." By that I mean there are patients who discover things and flesh out who they are as the mark of their progress, and then there are other patients who reveal things as the mark of their progress. Liza was a major revealer. I knew that we would get as far as she would let me in to her secrets. I knew that there were things locked inside, that, if handled correctly, would free her from her emotional bonds. My job was to navigate her minefield without setting off any fatal explosions.

The next session was late on a Friday, a day I usually don't work. But since it was the only day Liza was able to make it, and since I was anxious to keep the momentum (or what I thought was momentum) going, I was glad to work with her schedule.

Would there be puppets? The blanket? I tried not to anticipate anything at all. I just cleared my mind and waited, ready for anything.

When I came out to the waiting room, there she sat, wearing a beautiful white lace mantilla over her head, looking every bit like a Spanish princess. Her hands were folded in her lap just so.

No eye contact—none.

And below that were faded jeans and ballet slippers.

No duffel bag.

She looked like she was ready for confession. I hoped it was true.

I didn't say a word, just led the way back to my office.

She took her chair, not once looking at the quilt I had laid out on the couch.

Maybe today, the mantilla was enough.

Again, there was silence, her large brown eyes focused straight ahead, lost in some inner world.

Sure, I could have thought, *For God's sake, can't she even make some effort to get this thing moving?* But as a therapist you can't afford to think that way. You take what you're given and assume it's not only the best the person can do, but the exact right thing for them to do, if only you can do your part and respond to it correctly.

So what was she telling me? The mantilla and the staring straight ahead felt to me like a religious or spiritual space, that I needed to honor and respect. I needed to put myself in that place and then "get" what I would want to hear from a therapist.

I said, "Somehow, this feels sacred."

I detected a slight nod.

Then I got a flash. "Is it an anniversary?"

Tears filled her eyes, and began flowing freely down her smooth, white cheeks.

I was feeling brave. "Of something horrible?"

Her eyes cut to the quilt—panic.

Oops, I needed to put the brakes on. "Okay, let's just breathe and sit with this. I won't ask any more questions. Enough is enough."

A tiny sigh told me I had done the right thing.

I breathed too, feeling like an idiot. She wanted me to know, but dammit, she didn't want me to take over! I got excited when I "got" the anniversary idea, and just went with it. Well, I hadn't destroyed the session... yet. Patience, patience, patience.

Another fifteen minutes went by—like I say, a long time in therapy. But I couldn't rush her, especially now, after I had gushed on her parade like that. The minutes dragged by and I think I began to drift off, mentally.

"March fourteenth." A flat monotone.

That brought me back in a hurry. It was today's date: the "anniversary."

Of?

I looked at her eyes. They weren't looking at me, but they were talking to me.

Something bad.

Something very bad.

Liza stood up. "I'm going to leave, now." The words were clear, distinct, definite.

No eye contact.

I didn't move. I didn't breathe. I didn't dare.

Then she floated over to me and touched the top of my head, like when you're knighted.

I would've bowed, or curtsied, but I was sitting down.

She turned and walked away.

*　　*　　*

Okay, so what was the debrief this time? First, as I said before, I always assume the person has given me all they have, and that the "thrust," the momentum, is a lot more important than the details. And yes, of course, I had some ideas about what "it" (i.e., the Mac-Guffin) could be: a rape, a loss, a molestation, a betrayal, a horrifying family skeleton, a whatever. It mattered, but specifically defining

it wasn't the all-in-all of this case—maintaining Liza's trust and confidence was, that and helping her deal with the aftereffects of "it."

The eerie, spectral, quasi-spiritual feeling of this whole thing told
me that Liza saw it in those terms. In order to meet her where she
was (because, good luck getting a patient to meet you where you
are!), I was going to have to be willing to go to that place, or at least
learn the language of that place.

For that matter, with every therapy patient you have to learn to
speak ghost, or at least conversational ghost.

For Liza, March the fourteenth was ground zero for her ghost.

I was willing to go wherever she needed me to go.

I hoped she was willing to take me.

*   *   *

It was term break, and Liza took off for a two-week skiing vacation
at Tahoe with a few other students. Strange—she had never talked
about friends, or anyone really, so I had no idea who these people
were, or what place they had in her life, or heart. Not one mention
of a boyfriend (or girlfriend), or a flirtation, or a crush, had ever
crossed her lips, at least in my presence. I vaguely felt that she wasn't
"available" for any of that, that she had a previous engagement with
"it," and that until we untied that knot, she would not have avail-
ability for anything other than school and the occasional outing. In
many other circumstances, I would have worried about her commitment to what we were doing; after all, three sessions do not a
commitment make, but somehow with Liza I always felt that she
knew the only real answer was in our work.

Then again, many others in her place would have been impatient,
desperate to "get to it already," to jump in and resolve this problem.
But queens aren't impatient or desperate; they have a certain kind of
unhurried grace and timing about things, an odd, unusual self-con-

fidence that they will do their part. I felt that her only question was whether I would be able to do mine.

As I said, Liza was a revealer. If she told me, she would tell me in her own sweet time and, even more important, when she thought I could handle it. There were evil spirits in the offing, and like the priest in *The Exorcist*, I needed to be big enough, and sure enough of myself, to face up to them.

Fortunately, like an innocent defendant who doesn't have to remember any lies, it was good to have the truth on my side.

Between one thing and another, it was May before we met again. But that was not the next time we were in communication. When she was away on the skiing vacation, I received a note on her personal stationery, sent to my office address. It simply read: "Beware!"

My reaction? It just confirmed what I had thought all along, that Liza was living with ghosts and spirits, and that she believed (and was afraid) that as we pressed forward in her therapy, they were going to be angry and vengeful. I didn't respond, and I was sure she didn't expect me to. She just wanted to warn me, and maybe test my mettle. She wanted me to know what I was in for and prepare myself for it. And no, I didn't think she was going to spew foul curses at me, or that her head was going to spin around, but I knew she had inner demons that would be highly displeased if and when she told her secrets. And that when that happened, she would need me to stand my ground.

It might be surprising to laymen that many, many "normal" people live with spirits, ghosts and demons inside. But that doesn't mean they're crazy, or psychotic. Many of these phenomena come from early childhood experiences and defenses, when it's pretty normal to have "voices" that talk to you, or even threaten you. You might say that in certain ways, every family is a cult, with certain ways of being and relating that are prescribed, and certain other ways that are proscribed. The life of a young child is rife with experiences of, "You're gonna be in so much trouble!" and "You're gonna get it!" So the idea that, if you spill the beans about the family secrets, or talk to an "outsider" about what really went on late at night, "they" are going to get you, is not so weird.

Yes, most people outgrow these phenomena by adolescence. But if the conditions for growth aren't there, there is no "outgrowing." Even a genetically healthy plant can't grow if it isn't exposed to sunlight, water and nutrients.

Horror movies are so popular because they give us a chance to revisit these scary old places from a safe distance; but the reason we respond to them is that we recognize these demons and know way down deep that these things—monsters under the bed, being sucked down the bathtub drain or ghosts in the hallway—once terrified us.

Part Three

It was the middle of May. The days were getting longer and uniformly California-beautiful: "Stepford weather," I grumped to myself, missing my rain like I did every year. Liza had agreed to come in late that Wednesday evening after a lecture on Rembrandt for her Art History class. I wondered whether this was going to be the day she finally let down her guard and told me her secrets. Because after all, you don't tell someone "Beware" for nothing. But I tried not to anticipate, just be ready to go with whatever she did, remembering the therapists' mantra: whatever they give you is the best they can do, if only you know what to do with it.

I cleared my mind; an airplane can't land on a cluttered runway.

In the waiting room, Liza had yet another look: black beret, round tortoiseshell glasses, black-and-white striped Breton top and a long, black narrow skirt with black tights and ankle-height black boots. Hmm, I had a strange presentiment that black might be of significance today.

Oh yes, and she had a duffel bag, too—a different one.

It was black.

I ushered her into the office, and she very determinedly went over and picked up the folded quilt. But when she went to the chair and sat down, she clutched the quilt to her chest, as she had done with the duffel bag before.

No eye contact.

I was idly contemplating how the whole head-covering thing worked. Since she had the beret today, did that mean she didn't have to put the quilt over her . . .?

"That's when it first happened."

I froze. "Uh, did I miss something?"

"Apparently." Dramatic sigh of impatience, eye-rolling, but no eye contact.

My wheels spun. "Uh, let's see, oh ... oh, you mean the anniversary?"

"Duh."

"Sorry, I think I'm up to speed now."

"Don't let it happen again."

Uh oh. I was on probation.

She spoke each word distinctly. "That was the first time he . . ."

Now she did throw the quilt over her head, then reached down to pick up the duffel bag.

Silence.

More silence.

From under the quilt, "Don't you even want to know what happened?"

"Uh, yes, of course, I just didn't want to . . ."

"I mean, if you don't want to hear it, or can't handle it, we can just let it go."

Prickly, that would be the word. And imperious. But then after all, when someone is about to hand you the Hope Diamond, they don't need to be polite, too.

I nodded encouragement. "Please, go on. I care, and I'm interested."

A scolding, scathing silence. Did I forget something?

On a guess, I added, "Oh, and yes, I can handle it."

Another regal sigh. "It's about time."

I saw her shuffling things around in the duffel bag under the blanket. Then a small hand puppet of a fierce, fuzzy gorilla came out. "Take him."

"You mean me?"

"I don't see anyone else around here. Take him!"

I reached over and took the puppet, realizing that this was probably the "him" she had mentioned in the last session, that she wasn't ready to show me, then.

"Well, put him on!"

Shoot, why was I always ten seconds behind her? I scolded myself as I fitted "him" onto my right hand and waited.

Suddenly, a pink puppet of a small girl in a frilly, print dress popped out from her right side. "Hit!"

I froze, again. "I'm not sure . . ."

"Hit!"

This was way beyond any diagnostic manuals or treatment codes that I knew about. I still hesitated, unsure.

"Hit! Or we're leaving!"

Tentatively, I walked over to the little girl and tapped her lightly on the shoulder.

"Do you recognize the English word, 'hit'? Is there anything unclear about it? Now hit!"

I tapped the puppet again, slightly harder.

"Harder! More! Harder! More! Harder! More!"

Okay, I was either going to do this thing or not. There was no halfway. I raised the little gorilla and actually struck the little girl.

"Again! Again! Again!"

I "hit" her again, and again, and again, not really hard, but definitely more than a tap.

The little girl started crying, then yelled, "Get away from me!"

I immediately retreated back to my chair, thinking, "Oh shit, what have I done now?"

Then the Gladys puppet came out from Liza's left side. The little girl puppet "ran" over to her and said, "Mommy, look what Daddy did to me!"

Gladys (as Mommy) did nothing, said nothing.

"He hurt me!" The little girl puppet "pointed" to her head and shoulders.

Gladys said, "Honey, there are certain things you have to do."

"But I don't want to do this!"

Gladys went on, in a tired voice, "I'm sick of being the only one who takes all of his anger. The least you could do is handle some of the spillover. Now you pitch in and do your part!"

I gasped inwardly, horrified beyond measure, but this needed to be Liza's emotional space, not mine. I wanted to "do" something, if only to say, "Oh my God, I'm so sorry!" but this was not the time.

The little girl puppet, clearly crushed, trudged back in defeat to her place on Liza's right side and sighed heavily, "Okay, then."

It was the saddest thing I'd ever heard. I realized that tears were coming down my cheeks. I wiped my eyes and glanced at the clock. Technically, we had another twenty minutes, but . . .

"Okay everyone, that's a wrap!" It was Liza's voice, from under the quilt. By now, I knew what was coming next. She shot to her feet, folded the blanket, placed it on the couch, gathered her things and left, without a glance.

I actually canceled my next patient—the first time I'd ever done that in my whole career, because of a previous session. It wasn't just that I was sad, or even outraged, although of course I was those things; I was drained, empty, scoured out. Nothing more to give. I don't know, maybe battle-fatigued soldiers feel this way, pushed beyond human endurance.

But then it hit me, as I sat there in my chair, staring at the wall: *I'm feeling her feelings.* The way she said, "That's a wrap!" the way she shot out of there, almost chirpy, manic, clipped. It was all she could do to tell me about her nightmare—that in itself was a complete step. When things are that horrifying you have to cut them up into bite-sized pieces. First came "telling" on Daddy and Mommy. She couldn't risk facing what I did with the information, much less dealing with her own feelings about the drama she had enacted for me, that had to be presented as a drama in order to distance it from the white-hot hell it would have been to re-experience it first-hand. That helped. I now had a context for what I was feeling, and a deeper appreciation of why, and how, a young child couldn't afford to go to these depths of hell, especially with not only no help from parents, but an actual *demand* from parents to be a repeated victim of physical abuse like that.

I had no idea what Liza's next step would be. I had a pretty good feeling that I had passed her test again, but abused people are unpredictable: sometimes once they spill the beans they run away from you, because in their mind you become a wild card, a loose cannon, who now has this radioactive information, that can no longer be controlled. In other cases, they may run from you because they can't face you anymore, now that you know how "bad" they are.

My guts told me that Liza probably wouldn't flat-out run, but that we may need to throttle back the intensity for a while, so that we could regroup a bit and reassure her that she was still in charge of the control rods. I needed to let her lead the way and set the tone in our next sessions.

Of course, there are no sure bets when it comes to human behavior: I have had patients say, "You don't even care," if I didn't bring up the secret in the next session, and others say, "I just knew you were going to rub it in," when I did!

But then, I had an idea that I thought might just work.

*   *   *

These were the days before email, so I actually wrote out an "invitation" to Liza for the next session.
It went something like this:

> "We respectfully request the pleasure of your company next
> Wednesday at five o'clock, at my office. Please bring the gang.
> Signed,
> Dr. Bernstein, Flopsy, Puffie and Puffine"

Yes, it was a risk, a big risk. Would she see it as disrespectful to the "tone" of what had just happened? Or dismissive of the gravity of what she had let me see? My intuition told me no, that she would appreciate my joining in the spirit of "play therapy" that she had set and being willing to join her in her own mode. Play and curiosity were foundation personality characteristics for her.

But I could be wrong, and if I was, it would be a big goof. But then I was encouraging her to take chances, so why shouldn't I?

I dropped it in the mailbox and crossed my fingers.

I would have my answer on Wednesday.

*   *   *

All day Wednesday I was sweating it. Would she show, and if so, would she appreciate my admittedly unusual initiative, or would she resent me for taking over what had been her show? You will never find "mail your patient an invitation to share stuffed animals" in a book on sure-fire approaches to adult psychotherapy.

Ah well, it was done now—que sera sera.

I finished up with my four o'clock person and carefully set out my "office staff": Flopsy (a fluffy, brown stuffed bunny, with floppy ears), Puffie (a black-and-white stuffed puffin, male) and Puffine (a stuffed puffin, female), on the couch, on top of the blue quilt.

My signal light lit up, and I said to my assembled staff, "Okay guys, pray."

I had another surprise when I went out the waiting room. Liza was dressed like a duplicate of the little girl puppet: a pretty, summery, print-pattern dress, beaded t-strap sandals and even a barrette in her hair. Emotionally, it felt like the exact opposite of all the black of the previous week. I hoped it meant something about reclaiming her girlhood.

I know she saw the stuffed animals sitting on the couch, because she never missed anything. And I know she knew I had put them on the quilt, because normally the first thing she did was go get the quilt. But she just took a seat primly on the chair, unzipped her purple duffel and then placed Gladys, Millicent and the little girl on her lap.

Then she formally turned her head to the couch. "Don't we get introduced?" She looked directly at me, for the first time ever.

"Uh, yes, of course: from left to right, Flopsy, Puffie and Puffine, meet Ms. Liza, Gladys, Millicent, and, uh . . ."

"Priscilla."

"And Priscilla."

Well, I needn't have worried about "taking over." Liza went over to the couch, took out a miniature tea set and "served tea" to the whole gang. By the time the session was over, they had "played" elementary school classroom, working in a dress shop, post office and, best of all, a lengthy "therapy session" for Priscilla, who had apparently forgotten to feed her puppy (Puffine), and gotten in trouble with Mommy (Gladys). Liza acted as mediator between Priscilla and Mommy, and believe me, "Mommy" took some major heat from Millicent and Flopsy (acting as the jury) for her harshness toward Priscilla.

After that, we used play therapy a lot in our sessions (the little gorilla, George, was even allowed back occasionally, when we needed a heavy in the drama) and over the months, Liza brought in several more dolls and stuffed animals for "cameos," as she called them, in her productions. We even had some sessions when Mommy (Gladys) read to all of us from children's books, everyone's favorite being *Goodnight Moon*.

We never again talked about "it," but was clear that once Liza had gotten it all out into the open, it was like a fever had broken, and she was released from the thrall in which that secret had held her for so many lost, lonely years.

She switched her major from history to theater arts, and by the time she started her junior year, she was writing and directing plays. Eventually, she decided to suspend communication with her parents, who still insisted that what had happened was appropriate, and that Liza was "crazy" and disloyal for saying otherwise.

It wasn't necessarily a permanent decision, but for the present, it felt to her like the right thing to do.

She began to date, and made some good friends, and one day we decided, together, that she didn't need to come in anymore.

*   *   *

I didn't hear from Liza again for close to two years. Then, one evening in late May, after a long day of seeing patients, I had already turned out all the lights and locked up, when I found a small package addressed to me on the front porch of the building. So I unlocked my office again and stepped inside to open it. I almost flicked on the lights, but then I noticed that there was a full moon, so I went over by the window where it was bright and started tearing off the brown paper. Inside was a fancy-wrapped box, and inside of that sat Priscilla, holding an "invitation." I opened the envelope, and this is what I read by the light of the full moon:

"We respectfully request the pleasure of your company at my graduation from the University of California, at Berkeley, on June __.
Feel free to bring the gang. You will be making a cameo as
'The Parents.'
Signed,
Liza, Priscilla, Gladys, Millicent and George
(PS: Priscilla is my gift of appreciation to you; now that I don't need an alter ago anymore, she wants to come live and work in your office!)"

*   *   *

It just doesn't get any better than that.

I stood at the window for a while, looking up at the sky, so grateful to be doing what I love, not only with Liza, but with all the wonderful people I've known in this office.

Then I gathered up my things and was about ready to close the door, when I turned back and saw the couch, bathed in creamy moonglow.

Goodnight moon.

Goodnight couch.

Goodnight clock.

Goodnight chair.

Goodnight patients, everywhere.